XSEL'S PROGRESS:
THE CONTINUING
JOURNEY OF AN
EXPERT SYSTEM

John Wiley
INFORMATION SYSTEMS SERIES

Editors

Richard Boland
University of Illinois at Urbana-Champaign

Rudy Hirschheim
University of Houston

XSEL'S PROGRESS: THE CONTINUING JOURNEY OF AN EXPERT SYSTEM

Enid Mumford
Manchester Business School

AND

W. Bruce MacDonald
Digital Equipment Corporation

John Wiley
INFORMATION SYSTEMS SERIES

JOHN WILEY & SONS
Chichester · New York · Brisbane · Toronto · Singapore

Library of Congress Cataloging in Publication Data:

Mumford, Enid.
    XSEL's progress: the continuing journey of an expert system / by
Enid Mumford and W. Bruce MacDonald.
      p. cm.—(John Wiley information systems series)
    Bibliography: p.
    Includes index.
    ISBN 0 471 92322 2
    1. Management information systems.   2. Expert systems (Computer
science) I. MacDonald, W. Bruce. II. Title. III. Series.
T58.6.M86   1989
658.4'03—dc20   88-27013
                                                          CIP

British Library Cataloguing in Publication Data:

Mumford, Enid
    XSEL's Progress.
    1. Business firms.   Applications of expert
systems
    I. Title   II. MacDonald, Bruce
    658'. 05633

    ISBN 0 471 92322 2

Typeset by Associated Publishing Services Ltd, Petersfield, Hants
Printed in Great Britain by Bath Press, Bath, Avon

To Jan and Jim

Contents

Series Foreword

In order for all types of organizations to succeed, they need to be able to process data and use information effectively. This has become especially true in today's rapidly changing environment. In conducting their day-to-day operations, organizations use information for functions such as planning, controlling, organizing, and decision making. Information, therefore, is unquestionably a critical resource in the operation of all organizations. Any means, mechanical or otherwise, which can help organizations process and manage information presents an opportunity they can ill afford to ignore.

The arrival of the computer and its use in data processing has been one of the most important organizational innovations in the past thirty years. The advent of computer-based data processing and information systems has led to organizations being able to cope with the vast quantities of information which they need to process and manage to survive. The field which has emerged to study this development is *information systems* (IS). It is a combination of two primary fields: computer science and management, with a host of supporting disciplines, e.g. psychology, sociology, statistics, political science, economics, philosophy, and mathematics. IS is concerned not only with the development of new information technologies but also with questions such as: how they can best be applied, how they should be managed, and what their wider implications are.

Partly because of the dynamic world in which we live (and the concomitant need to process more information), and partly because of the dramatic recent developments in information technology, e.g. personal computers, fourth-generation languages, relational databases, knowledge-based systems, and office automation, the relevance and importance of the field of information systems, and office automation, the relevance and importance of the field of information systems has become apparent. End users, who previously had little potential of becoming seriously involved and knowledgeable in information technology and systems, are now much more aware of and interested in the new technology. Individuals working in today's and tomorrow's organizations will be expected to have some understanding of and the ability to use the rapidly developing information technologies and systems. The dramatic increase in the availability and use of information technology, however, raises fundamental questions on the guiding of technological innovation, measuring organizational and managerial productivity, augmenting human intelligence, ensuring data integrity, and establishing strategic advantage. The expanded use of information systems also raises major challenges to the traditional forms of administration and authority, the right to privacy, the nature and form of work, and the limits of calculative rationality in modern organizations and society.

The Wiley Series on Information Systems has emerged to address these questions and challenges. It hopes to stimulate thought and discussion on the key role information systems play in the functioning of organizations and society, and how their role is likely to change in the future. This historical or evolutionary theme of the Series is important because considerable insight can be gained by attempting to understand the past. The Series will attempt to integrate both description—what has been done—with prescription—how best to develop and implement information systems.

The descriptive and historical aspect is considered vital because information systems of the past have not necessarily met with the success that was envisaged. Numerous writers postulate that a high proportion of systems are failures in one sense or another. Given their high cost of development and their importance to the day-to-day running of organizations, this situation must surely be unacceptable. Research into IS failure has concluded that the primary cause of failure is the lack of consideration given to the social and behavioural dimensions of IS. Far too much emphasis has been placed on their technical side. The result has been something of a shift in emphasis from a strictly technical conception of IS to one where it is recognized that information systems have behavioural consequences. But even this misses the mark. A growing number of researchers suggest that information systems are more appropriately conceived as social systems which rely, to a greater and greater extent, on new technology for their operation. It is this social orientation which is lacking in much of what is written about IS. The present volume, *XSEL's Progress: The Continuing Journey of an Expert System*, exemplifies the social orientation that is of special interest to the series. In it, Enid Mumford and Bruce MacDonald recount the development of XSEL as an heroic adventure of people and technology. They tell the story in a way that both describes and confirms the importance of participative design strategies in even the most advanced technological systems.

The Series seeks to provide a forum for the serious discussion of IS. Although the primary perspective is a more social and behavioural one, alternative perspectives will also be included. This is based on the belief that no one perspective can be totally complete; added insight is possible through the adoption of multiple views. Relevant areas to be addressed in the Series include (but are not limited to): the theoretical development of information systems, their practical application, the foundations and evolution of information systems, and IS innovation. Subjects such as systems design, systems analysis methodologies, information systems planning and management, office automation, project management, decision support systems, end-user computing, and information systems and society are key concerns of the Series.

Rudy Hirschheim
Richard Boland

Acknowledgements

There are many people, too numerous to mention, whom the authors would like to thank for their help and encouragement in the process of building XSEL. A few to whom they would like to give special thanks are Dennis O'Conner, Ken Gilbert, Margaret Meehan, Tom Cooper, Donna Corbet, Melissa Gallo, Ray Wood, Chuck Pickle, Jim De La Houssaye, Cliff Lee, John Moorhead, Alex Barenblitt, Dennis Thalman, Campbell Ramsay, all of Digital Equipment Corporation who have helped XSEL on its pilgrimage with their time, energy, money, and, most of all, their understanding and support.

THE PILGRIM'S PROGRESS
wherein is discovered, the manner
of his setting out, his dangerous journey;
and safe arrival at the desired country.

Frontispiece to *Pilgrim's Progress* by John Bunyan, 1678

Introduction

This book has been written to assist managers who are designing and introducing new technology into their companies. It tells the story of XSEL, one of the Digital Equipment Corporation's first and most successful expert systems. XSEL, and XCON its predecessor, were created to overcome problems which the company had experienced for many years in correctly assembling all the multitude of different components which make up a particular piece of hardware. The task of specifying these components and their relationship is called 'configuring'.

Digital's systems and options had been growing in number over the years and this meant that the configuration process had to handle an increasingly large body of rules. The correct application of these rules became more and more difficult for both the production and the sales functions. This gave rise to what was called the 'configuration problem'. It was to deal with this that first XCON and then XSEL were developed and put into operation.

Although XCON and XSEL were Digital's earliest attempt to use the techniques of artificial intelligence, once implemented they were acknowledged to be the first successful large-scale expert systems in the business world. The authors believe that Digital's experience and approach can be of great value to those who are building and introducing expert systems today.

This book highlights the social processes associated with the building and implementation of XSEL. It describes the human dramas, problems and successes that occurred as the system grew and moved towards viability and use. The management of these human relationships proved to be as crucial to the successful development and acceptance of XSEL as the control of technical factors. This book will try to show that the route to successful innovation requires equal care to be given to both people and technology.

Designing a major expert system cannot be like a Cook's tour with everything planned and tested beforehand. It will be more like the journey described by John Bunyan in *Pilgrim's Progress* with many difficult and dangerous obstacles to be overcome before the promised land is reached. Nevertheless the journey will be exciting and the rewards of success considerable. Digital has built many expert systems since XSEL. But XSEL led the way and reinforced the company's belief that user involvement in systems design leads to systems which are acceptable and accepted.

There have been many descriptions of the technical design of XSEL. This book focuses on the management problems that had to be tackled and overcome before the system was successfully installed in the sales offices of the United States and Europe. There were many obstacles to surmount along the route to the implementation of XSEL. At times it seemed that the system might not survive the journey. The objective of writing this book is to give those interested in the management of change an understanding of the typical processes and problems that they should expect to experience when embarking on a large pioneering system—particularly a system that will affect an important business activity in a critical company function.

It will also show that although there may be risks and costs, the rewards of success will be considerable and well worth the effort.

Part 1
DESIGN, PARTICIPATION AND CULTURE

Honest. It happens to us as it happeneth to wayfaring men, sometimes our way is clean, sometimes foul; sometimes up-hill, sometimes down-hill. The wind is not always on our backs, nor is everyone a friend that we meet with in the way.

John Bunyan

Chapter 1

DESIGNING SYSTEMS—RETROSPECT AND REALITY

HISTORICAL INFLUENCES

Systems analysis, the term until recently most commonly applied to systems incorporating computers, emerged as a result of wartime knowledge and experience that was later taken over by business and industry. In the Second World War its forerunner was known as 'operations analysis' and took the form of a systematic approach to assist decision makers to deal with complex problems. Operations analysis required a careful definition of the objectives that were to be realized; an identification and comparison of the alternative means by which these objectives could be achieved and the costs and benefits of each alternative; a selection of the strategy most likely to achieve the desired results—given resource constraints, and an assessment of the success of the chosen strategy.

Operations analysis was pioneered by the Rand Corporation which was working on weapon development for the US Air Force (Ways, 1967). The approach proved so successful that in 1961 Defense Secretary Robert S. McNamara introduced it throughout the Defense Department and into all the armed services. The American Government also recognized the value of a systematic approach to complex decision taking. In 1965 President Johnson directed that a similar approach—called PPBS (Planned Programming Budgeting Systems)—should be introduced into all Federal Government Departments.

US industry's interest in operations analysis was awakened in the 1950s through a growing concern about the difficulty of taking decisions in complex environments. Large companies began using approaches similar to that developed by Rand which they called 'systems analysis'. They saw these as a way of substituting a rational weighing of alternatives and consequences for the hunches and rule-of-thumb methods they had previously used. The Ford Motor Company was one of these firms. Its President, Arjay Miller, described systems analysis as a excellent means for handling the problems of business and as a way of distributing responsibility for decision taking to larger groups of people (Ways, 1967).

Systems analysis, defined very broadly as a means for solving complex business problems, attracted increasing attention and generated much interest and enthusiasm. This interest was not confined to government and industry. Daniel Bell who, in 1967, was Chairman of a commission forecasting what would happen by the year 2000, saw the approach as a means for addressing some of the larger problems of society, widening choice and producing improved social policy. It would enable society to choose its own path in the light of its own values. Max Ways, an enthusiastic supporter of the approach, wrote in the journal *Fortune* in January, 1967.

> 'What matters to us is how we formulate our goals and how well we pursue them; that in worldly progress, as in another, the destination is inseparably bound up with the way.'

Systems analysis then started off in its early form as a novel, comprehensive, way of handling complex problems operating in conditions of uncertainty. It was seen by the early practitioners as providing a sense of direction and a means for intelligent, effective choice that would take account of important societal values. It was to be flexible, democratic and evolving—a contrast to the use of coercive or authoritarian power as a means for getting things done.

But new ideas change, are rethought and become operationalized in different forms and this was true of systems analysis. Rand, and the engineers and mathematicians that were influenced by its thinking, sought to make systems analysis more precise and mathematical. They called their work 'operational research' and other new names such as heuristics, decision theory and systems design appeared in the literature. An important group, influenced by ideas in Europe as well as the US, set about trying to develop a general theory of systems—a language with which systems could be described. They sought to identify a set of properties and functions common to all systems which could be mathematically modelled. These seekers after a general systems theory did not usually include the awkward variable—people and their behaviour—in their models. This may be the reason that an acceptable general systems theory has still not been found.

Another group, also influenced by the thinking of European scientists, defined systems which included people as 'open' and 'living', (Sommerhoff, 1969). They used these terms to describe systems which interacted with their environments, and believed that successful systems analysis required an understanding and characterization of the system environment. An influential group that looked at systems in this way was based at the Tavistock Institute in London after the Second World War. Their work led to the development of sociotechnical theory—an approach which takes account of human needs and technical requirements when systems are being designed and tries to optimize both of these (Emery and Trist, 1960).

While the debate between the 'general systems' and 'open systems' theorists was taking place computers were moving into industry at an increasingly rapid rate and methods were required to assist their successful introduction. It was clear that a computer could not just be dropped into the middle of a firm or department and the 'on' button pressed. Nothing at all would happen. Careful thought must be given to what the computer could and should be used for and to the reorganization of the business activities which its introduction would affect. A simple practical form of systems analysis was therefore an urgent necessity for this new technology.

WHAT IS 'SYSTEMS ANALYSIS' TODAY?

The term 'systems analysis' has always seemed narrow for the range of activities associated with it. Analysis implies the breaking down of things into small parts whereas introducing technical systems requires the creation of new structures once the original problem has been understood and defined. Systems design seems a more appropriate description for today's activities than systems analysis and we shall use this term from now on.

There are many definitions of design. It has been described as 'devising artefacts to attain goals' and as 'simulating what we want to do (or make) before we do (or make) it (Simon, 1981; Booker, 1964). Statements of this kind are not very helpful. They tell us something of what design is aiming to achieve but little about the important and necessary processes that have to be set up and managed before the end result is achieved.

These processes are complex when computer-based systems are being designed to solve business problems. They involve the use of tools, techniques, ideas, information and knowledge. Design also requires creativity for in the computer world there is usually no 'one best way' of achieving the goals that have been set for a system. It is greatly influenced by the philosophies and values of the individuals and groups involved in the design task and these have at their disposal a confusing array of methods, methodologies and concepts. All can help the designer gain some control over a mass of variables but because the use of one rather than another may influence the nature of the goals that are achieved, they need to be selected with care.

A method is a way of doing things and can incorporate a number of tools to assist the analaysis of a business problem or the development of a solution. The word methodology really means the study of methods but in practice designers often use it to describe a collection of methods. An example of a method in favour today is prototyping—in which a model of the system is built and tested before the final system is implemented.

Most designers work with a set of principles derived from experience and good practice which guide their approach. They may strive for simplicity—the simplest design that meets the problem specification; or for flexibility—a system that can be easily altered to meet new problems and needs (Leech and Turner,

1985). Systems designers also frequently have a multiplicity of objectives they are striving to achieve. As well as creating a system that successfully addresses a business problem they may also aim to produce one that has certain characteristics—one that is reliable, maintainable, efficient, secure and user-centred, for example.

A feature of computer systems that makes the design task particularly complex is the fact that design takes place in two completely different areas. There is both 'external' design and 'internal' design (Freeman, 1983). External design is concerned with specifying and analysing the business problem that the system is directed at solving, and at building a new task and procedures structure which incorporates computer functions. Internal design is specifying the structure of the software that will enable the machine to provide certain kinds of information. This structure may be constrained by the limitations of a particular machine. Both external and internal design should be user driven and today it is increasingly accepted that getting the business problem right should be the dominant factor. In the past, when computer technology was more primitive, the emphasis was often on the assembly of software and little attention might be given to a careful identification of the business problem or to the efficiency and job satisfaction needs of the user.

Today the definition of the systems design task is much broader. Because human, organizational and technical factors all have to be taken account of, it increasingly requires the coordinated effort of a multidisciplinary design team. This team will have to be carefully and sympathetically managed if its creativity is to be stimulated and maintained. Tight controls and bureaucracy will almost certainly be counter-productive and an environment which provides challenge, work freedom and opportunities for initiative is the one most likely to produce high quality design.

Designing systems for institutions and their employees is a heavy responsibility. Because technology can have such a dramatic effect on the human condition we need to think very carefully about how we use it and what we use it for. Schumacher in his famous book *Small is Beautiful* has written

> 'Technology tends to develop its own laws and principles, and these are very different from those of human nature or living nature in general. . . . The primary task of technology is to lighten the burden of work man has to carry in order to stay alive and develop his potential.' (Schumacher, 1974)

There is increasing concern that technology shall be introduced and used in a humanistic way with beneficiaries rather than victims. Systems designers have a major part to play in ensuring that technology is designed to have a positive and liberating impact on those who use it.

WHAT DOES SYSTEMS DESIGN INVOLVE?

Understanding Complexity

We have described systems design as a set of processes directed at the achievement of what should be clear business goals. Essentially these processes are concerned with 'change' and 'changing'. A part of the firm has to be shifted from its present organization and methods of working to a new structure. When systems design includes accommodating new technology then this will exert an influence on the kind of restructuring that takes place. In order to create new systems, designers need a clear vision of what they are changing. They need to understand the nature of the firm—its beliefs, perceptions, customs and business practice.

In the past many designers introducing new computer systems have given themselves restricted definitions of the firm and its activities. They have seen its primary task as the processing of information and their role as providing better information. This is certainly an important objective but it can be argued that today's sophisticated technical systems have a considerable organizational impact on the functions in which they are located. Today's designers need to recognize that they are concerned with organizational as well as technical design.

A broad definition of the systems design task requires a comprehensive description of the firm and its activities. A useful model is to regard the firm as a complex set of goals, activities and tasks taking place over time and carried out by people who are in designated roles and have required relationships with each other. Many of these tasks and roles are hierarchical in that what happens at a higher level determines what takes place lower down.

An added difficulty today is that many firms are operating in very turbulent business environments. To survive they need to be adaptive and flexible in their policies and in their organizational and technical structures. Building this flexibility into new systems is another challenge for the systems designer.

Effective organization requires planning, monitoring, evaluation, communication and control. As firms become increasingly complex these are all activities which the systems designer must understand and be able to cater for. This means that computer-based systems must become increasingly complex. But complex systems are not easy to use and the systems designer is presented with the dilemma that, ideally, this complexity must be concealed from the user.

A human problem of importance to systems designers is that many firms now contain staff in flexible roles with wide decision-making responsibilities. This, together with the recognition that there are many decision-taking styles, is another factor increasing the challenge of the systems designer's task. He or she may have to create systems which appeal both to the systematic individual who likes logical routines and to the creative, intuitive person who prefers 'ideas' to 'proof'. The computer system of the future should not place restrictions on its users. It must be able to cater for individual differences and personal preferences.

Systems designers require a good theoretical and pratical understanding of how firms are organized and structured, how they interact with their business environments, and how both of these are becoming increasingly dynamic and complex. They also need to appreciate the variety and complexity of the users of their systems. People with different roles, responsibilities and personalities will want to use information in very different ways.

Design Processes

Systems design has its own complexity. The designer has to be able to identify and set appropriate goals for the new system, consider different strategies for achieving these, and turn the selected strategy into a model of a system incorporating new technology and tasks, redefined roles and relationships and new job and organizational structures. This system then has to be implemented and the affected parts of the firm moved to a new post-change way of working. Finally, the newly introduced system must be closely monitored to ensure that it is operating effectively. This requires its significant parts to be well integrated and working smoothly and easily with each other. The technology must be functioning efficiently, easy to use and providing the information that is required. The surrounding organization of activities and jobs must enable the firm to meet its business objectives more easily and, most important, the people who use the system should be experiencing high job satisfaction and an enhanced quality of working life.

The attainment of a well functioning system of this kind requires the ability to solve difficult problems and to get individuals and groups working cooperatively together. It also requires the skill to generate support in interested groups—particularly top management. And the designers must be able to continually increase and use effectively their own knowledge and experience.

The essence of successful systems design is generating processes that will assist the successful attainment of an acceptable and accepted system. Processes are much more than methods or methodologies—they are concerned with visions, interests, intentions, attitudes and emotions. They are also about involvement, communication, motivation and timing. They are the means for making things happen, the 'levers' which enable change to be successfully introduced.

The road to change is long, hard and, with pioneering systems, little travelled. Making progress requires an ability to anticipate the route ahead and to avoid or overcome difficulties; to decide which path to take when a number of alternatives present themselves; to plan, replan and even abandon plans as the nature of the situation changes, and to continually learn from these fast-flowing experiences. The systems designer requires theory, methods and language to understand, describe and handle the processes of change.

The travellers along this road to 'change' will not just be those responsible for designing the system. At least part of the route will also be traversed by other groups. Top management will be one as the future business success of the firm may be related to the successful introduction of the new system. Middle management will also be there as they will be responsible for the system's eventual operation. The future users of the system are likely to be enthusiastic or reluctant travellers, depending on whether they see the journey's end as an improvement or a worsening of their present situation. And there will be other groups—customers, suppliers, other departments in the firm—who may not be actively involved in the 'changing' process but who have a considerable interest in the nature of the 'promised land' that is eventually reached.

VALUES, CONCEPTS AND METHODS

Systems design in the past has been influenced by two important attitudes which no longer fit with the needs of modern industry. It has suffered from the 'cult of the expert' and from a view of the world that was almost entirely technical. Computer systems designers, although a relatively new group, have associated themselves with disciplines such as engineering and science and tried to create a role and aura in which their knowledge would not be questioned by the outside world. They saw themselves as technical specialists and denied other groups, particularly the users of their systems, the right to challenge their activities. This definition of the systems design task as an expert one was reinforced by the development of a 'jargon' language which made it more difficult for the man in the street to comprehend what they were doing.

The desire to be regarded as an acknowledged expert is understandable. It enables a group to be viewed with high esteem and seen as a valuable community commodity. It also contributes to a less stressful working environment by ensuring that the group's role is not often questioned. It is not a new phenomenon for similar behaviour has been encountered from very early times. In societies such as Egypt, China and India groups of men, often of a priestly character, came together, formed associations and passed on their knowledge to a carefully selected group of younger men. This knowledge was protected from outsiders and often viewed as sacred. These early men of knowledge saw themselves as discovering absolute truths (Znaniecki, 1940). This behaviour is not very different from that of today's experts who also seek 'truth', protect their knowledge from outsiders and are reluctant to abandon theories they believe to be correct until there is incontrovertible evidence from their own group that new theories are required.

This identification of systems designers with the role of the scientist led to a belief that they knew how to design valid systems and did not need to consult with other groups, especially users. Because most of the early administrative computer systems used by industry handled simple tasks and affected the work of clerks rather than managers, they were infrequently challenged. The systems might be technically inefficient and produce routinized and segmented jobs but the clerical workers who used them were in no position to protest. It is only in recent years, with middle and senior management becoming influential users, that the right of the user to question the system and participate in its design has been accepted. Today it is difficult to keep the user away. Also, the fact that computers are now being used to contribute to the solution of complex business problems means that few technical experts have the level of business knowledge that the user possesses. The business expertise of the user is as critical to successful systems design as the technical knowledge of the computer expert.

The other powerful influence on systems design, and one that is related to the 'cult of the expert' has been the belief that systems design is a technical activity concerned only with technical factors. In this view, people are not its concern. Here again it is interesting to go back in history and identify where this belief came from. One important influence was the ideas of the eighteenth-century European economists and philosophers who believed that knowledge led to development and progress and produced greater human happiness.

The British economist Jeremy Bentham was one of these eighteenth-century intellectuals. He wanted to establish morals as an exact science and subject it to the rule of reason and he was attracted by the idea of a machine-like man who could be made to work scientifically. Bentham was one of the originators of ideas on economic planning and social engineering which are still in use today. He saw the individual as being wholly egoistic—seeking pleasure and avoiding pain (Carroll, 1974). He believed that the happiness of a community was a product of the economic sufficiency of its members.

Bentham's ideas were given practical form by the engineering innovators of the time—Watt and Newcomen who invented the steam engine, for example. These technical developments reinforced and gave practical form to the new philosophical ideas of economic efficiency. There was a strong desire for order and control and great importance was placed on virtues such as perseverance, energy, thoroughness and self-reliance.

During the later part of the second half of the nineteenth-century and the early part of the twentieth the process of rationalization and mechanization began to speed up. This period saw the beginning of mass production industry. It also saw the appearance in the United States of the scientific management movement. Pioneers such as Taylor and Gilbreth applied scientific method to what they saw as the muddle and inefficiency of industry. Improved profitability and higher earnings for employees were to be achieved by separating 'doing' from 'thinking' and allocating the first to workers and the second to management. The role of management was to study scientifically the best methods for carrying out tasks and for measuring the level of performance reached. The role of the workers was to do what they were told. Taylor's principles were applied by Henry Ford when, in 1914, he established the first car assembly line at Highland Park, Michigan.

The increased efficiency that resulted from scientific management led to a powerful set of values, many of which are still with us today. First, there was the belief that the human being could be treated as an operating unit which could be adjusted by training and incentives to meet the needs of the organization. Second, there was the view that a majority of people were unreliable, with narrow capabilities and limited usefulness. They should therefore be given small, low discretion jobs. Third, labour was a commodity to be bought and sold by the organization and, fourth, a materialistic ethic suggested that if the end of increased material comfort was achieved, then this justified the means to achieve it. These ideas on efficiency had considerable influence on the organization of industry and on the design of jobs. In the twentieth century they still influence many engineers and technologists.

The design of computer systems in the office and on the shop floor has, up to now, been largely the responsibility of computer technologists. These, until recently, have followed the traditional engineering philosophy of focusing on the technical design of a new system and paying little attention to the needs of the human being who would work with the system. There has been a tendency to undervalue human skills and abilities and to try and build skill, control and judgement into the machine.

In the early days of computer development few users were allowed to intervene in any meaningful way in the systems design process and little attention was paid to their needs and interests. Clerks and machine operatives might not like the new systems they received but their lack of power meant that the design philosophy behind them was rarely questioned.

This technical orientation made life easier for the systems designer. It enabled him to concentrate on the complexity of the technology without having to spend a great deal of time considering the complexity of the human being. It helped him to simplify the design process by reducing the number of variables he had to handle. When the system was finally implemented he could evaluate it in terms of its technical rather than its sociotechnical success. But there were disadvantages. Computers were received unenthusiastically in many offices when clerks found that their work had been deskilled or made redundant.

Today, the situation is changing rapidly. Systems designers are now working for senior managers and important specialist groups. These will not accept unsatisfactory, 'hard-to-use' computer systems and insist that their views are taken account of when the system is being designed. The systems designer is now recognizing that systems will not be accepted unless they are efficient and user friendly. They must serve the needs of the users and enable them to work more efficiently, with more responsibility, challenge and interest. The values of systems designers are also undergoing a major change. These now increasingly reflect the values of the firms they work for and of the groups for whom they design systems.

Their identification with the values of the scientific community is becoming weaker. Systems design is now so complex that it requires multidisciplinary values and a partnership between designers and users. This is leading to a search for new ways of designing systems.

The Search for Method

Methods and methodologies have always been seen by systems designers as a useful means for bringing order and logic into the design process and as devices to assist training. Following the definition of systems design as a technical activity, traditional methods have been tools and procedures for designing technical systems. The analyst has not seen his role as managing difficult change, rather he has viewed himself as a neutral person operating in a cooperative environment. The practice of systems design has been broken down into a number of sequential operations which are often referred to as a 'system life-cycle'. Typically these include analysis—gaining an understanding of the problem and describing the activities, data and information flow which it contains. This leads to a requirements definition. Next comes a functional specification or description of the functions to be performed by the system to process the required data. Design follows and this covers the development of the internal structure of the software which will provide the functions that have been specified. Implementation is the development of the computer code that will enable the system to produce data. Validation checks that each stage is successfully accomplished and 'evolution' is the correction of errors or modification of the system to meet new needs (Wasserman *et al.*, 1983).

The human user of the system figured very little in this technical approach. If the user was considered at all he or she was seen as predictable, rational and part of a group who all required the same information and solved problems in the same way. Consideration was not given to the issues discussed earlier—complex business goals, needs and structures, competing demands, multiple interest groups, dynamic business environments.

There is now increasing recognition that a narrow technical approach to systems design is not sufficient. A great deal of attention is being paid to the development of methods that will assist the systems designer to take better account of business and organizational issues. A number of these already exist. One is sociotechnical design, which has been available since the 1950s for the creation of new work systems. It has been used in the United States, Europe, Australia and India.

Sociotechnical design was developed by a group of psychologists at the Tavistock Institute of Human Relations in London. Their aim was to ameliorate the adverse human effects of new technical systems in industries such as coal-mining by introducing good organizational design. This included the building of small, multiskilled teams of operatives who assumed responsibility for a great deal of their own work planning. These psychologists believed that technical and organizational design were complementary and should reinforce each other (Trist, 1981). The result would be a work system which provided high technical and human efficiency together with interesting and challenging jobs. Surprisingly, despite its clear benefits, this approach has not yet been given serious consideration by many of those responsible for the design of computer-based systems. Other methods which take account of organizational and technical factors in systems design are the 'soft systems methodology' developed by Checkland and Enid Mumford's ETHIC's method (Checkland, 1981; Mumford, 1986). Sociotechnical design and the ETHIC's approach will be described in the next chapter.

It has to be recognized that methods are useful tools that help the systems designer to systematically tackle difficult problems, but they are not neutral. They embody particular visions of the world and incorporate the values of their creators. Those who see systems design as a technical process concerned primarily with the production of computer-mediated data will develop and use methods which help them to do this. Those who see design as a complex, multidisciplinary activity which must take account of social, organizational and technical factors will want a set of comprehensive tools which assist them to do all of these things. Few of these yet exist and there is an urgent need for more to be developed.

THE DESIGN OF EXPERT SYSTEMS

What is an Expert System?

This book is the story of a pioneering expert system developed by the Digital Equipment Corporation in the United States to solve a major business problem. It may therefore be helpful to begin this section by explaining to readers unfamiliar with artificial intelligence what an expert system is.

Artificial intelligence has been described by Sell as having two different products: models of human cognition and intelligent computer programs. Expert systems belong to the latter category. He tells us:

> 'They were created not so much to model how experts set about solving problems and, hence, to understand better the workings of an expert's mind, but for the practical purpose of reaping the benefits from the expert thought embedded in a computer system.' (Sell, 1985)

Intelligent computer programs are developed primarily to solve problems and this is the main reason for building expert systems. Normally, these problems are specific rather than general. That is, they address problems that are well defined and associated with discrete areas of specialist activity. For example, medical expert systems do not address a range of diseases, they take one disease, or even one aspect of a disease and provide a tool that assists the doctor with diagnosis and treatment.

Expert systems depend on knowledge that has been acquired for human experts. This is the reason that they are sometimes called knowledge-based systems, or even intelligent knowledge-based systems. They provide expertise— the detailed knowledge of a particular subject area. At present they address one problem at a time and are competent in narrow areas of expertise, although the knowledge they contain may be considerable. In the future they may be able to solve a number of problems simultaneously and in depth. They ask questions of their users or collect information from their environment, and they then arrive at a conclusion which may be given as advice or as a statement of fact. Sell's definition of an expert system is:

> 'A knowledge-based system that emulates expert thought to solve significant problems in a particular domain of expertise.'

Expert systems, if they are to be used, must possess certain characteristics. First of all they must perform well on difficult problems. At present large expert systems, which can produce major benefits, are expensive to build and this expense would not be justified for something trivial and unimportant. At the same time it is unreasonable to expect that their performance will be better than that of a human expert, although this is sometimes the case. Expert systems must also be accurate—nothing can be more dangerous than an expert who is relied on yet provides the wrong answers. But we cannot expect them to be one hundred per cent accurate. In their early stages a great deal of time is likely to be spent by programmers identifying and correcting errors. They will only be correct if they are regularly updated as the knowledge which they handle changes.

It must also be possible to obtain the required knowledge from an expert. This means that the expert, or more likely experts, must be willing to give it. Some specialists may be reluctant to hand over to a machine knowledge which has been slowly, and perhaps painfully, acquired through many years of study and experience. The whole area of knowledge acquisition presents many problems and requires a great deal of research. Experts do not always know why they do things in certain ways. They may find it difficult to formalize their knowledge and put it into words. Experts in the same discipline may not always agree with each other. These are all difficulties which have yet to be solved. Expert systems, once designed, have to be used, and acceptance by users is not always forthcoming. The users, if they are a different group from the experts, may not want the system. They may see it as threatening their skills or even their jobs.

An expert system must be able to converse with the person using it in terms that the user can understand. This is particularly important if the system has been built to solve problems such as fault identification—for example, to tell plant operators about hazards that may require a fast emergency response. A UK expert system of this kind has had to have the information which it gives to operators rewritten to incorporate the words which the operators actually use on the job.

And, the expert system must be able to explain itself. It is this characteristic more than any other that distinguishes an expert system from other kinds of computer-based system. An expert system must be able to explain how it reaches its conclusion from the facts that have been given it, and provide this explanation through reasoning that mimics the mental processes of a human being. Only if it does this can the human user judge its correctness and credibility. It must be able to justify why it wants a particular piece of information from the user. It is also helpful if the expert system can explain why it had not reached a particular conclusion, or made a particular recommendation. This may be more valuable to a user than knowing why it has.

Lastly, expert systems need to work at the speed that the situation requires. This means that they should proceed at a conversational pace when interacting with human beings although they can work at a much faster pace when talking to other systems and machines. It must also be easy to augment the knowledge of an expert system. Knowledge is not a static thing but something that is constantly developing and changing. The expert system must be able to accommodate new knowledge and to receive it from users in a simple and direct way.

Almost everything in this description of an expert system and its characteristics, except the 'explanation' requirement, would apply to any well designed system, expert or non-expert.

Expert Systems Design versus Traditional Systems Design

How does the design of an expert system differ from that of a traditional system? There are, of course, many similarities but expert systems appear to have important differences. Problems may be less clearly defined and more difficult to solve. Whereas the earlier data processing systems handled simple, well understood, procedures, the problems expert systems address are less well structured in that there can be more than one right answer. They can also affect powerful specialist groups who may reject them if they are seen as unhelpful or threatening.

The design process for an expert system is a complex one which progresses through a number of different stages. These can be broadly categorised as 'problem identification', 'decision to build', 'resource creation', 'experiment', 'learning', implementation' and 'evaluation'. Each stage has its own managerial and process requirements and problems. Although the stages are presented here as a sequence of activities, in reality all of the activities may occur to some extent at each stage.

The most critical part of the design process is stage one 'problem identification'—finding a suitable problem for an expert system. This should be a problem that is both costing the company money and likely to be present for some time, say the next five years. Trivial and short-term problems can provide an opportunity for learning how to build expert systems, although the ensuing system may never be used for real. But it must be recognized that any serious project will cost money and only be worth while if it can be shown to have a significant pay-off. It is also crucial that the system is wanted by the future users.

A choice has to be made between automating strategic but well understood problems and automating problems which are more complex and less well understood. If the system is to be a success it is essential that the problem selected should be located where the future users believe that automated assistance will be helpful to them. The processes which are used to maintain this positive attitude will be crucial to the system's acceptance.

Once a 'decision to build' is taken, other managerial issues become important. There must clearly be an expert who is willing to divulge his or her knowledge; also a sponsor and supporter in the AI area so that the necessary technical resources will be available. If the expert system is to be used by a group other than that with the expert knowledge then it is vitally important to have an enthusiastic senior user manager who will eventually accept ownership of the system and ensure that it is implemented, supported and used.

The next important step is 'resource creation'. The building of an expert system requires cash, time, technical skills, business knowledge, social skills, motivation and participation. It is wise to ensure that all these resources are available before going ahead.

The cash and time required will be difficult to estimate with any precision but it is best to assume that the system will take longer to design and implement than early forecasts suggest. Over-optimism is a common, and perhaps desirable, condition at the start of the system-building process. But few systems are completed on time and this is even more unlikely to happen if the company is a novice in the expert system area.

Technical skills may be difficult to acquire now that so many firms are becoming interested in expert systems. Specialists with experience of building expert systems are in short supply and firms may be well advised to grow their own by developing small pilot systems as a means for acquiring knowledge. It must be recognized that technical skills are important but never enough. The technologists can physically build the expert system but business experts will be required to ensure that it is the right system to solve the business problem which it addresses. Ideally, these will be the future users of the system and their managers. They may be a totally different group from the experts with the knowledge that is built into the computer's knowledge base. Three kinds of expert can be required to build a large system. These are a group with expert knowledge of the problem area; a group who encounter the problem in their day-to-day activities—who are likely to be the principal users of the system; and a group called knowledge engineers who are able to take the knowledge provided by the human experts and translate it into a form which can be handled by the computer. A major expert system will also require programmers and project managers.

Social skills are required to handle the difficult and time-consuming group processes that are involved in the design and implementation activities. If the system is designed participatively by both the experts in the problem and the future users of the system, these groups will have to be kept interested and motivated throughout the long and sometimes difficult design process. This requires skills of leadership, understanding and encouragement. It also requires the ability to consult and communicate with those participating in the design task, with their managers and with other interested groups who may be affected by the new system or wish to build an expert system of their own.

An important resource is the one or more groups created to handle the design task. There are a number of options here. The most common approach is to set up a technical group who will at some stage hand over the expert system to the users for testing and acceptance. But this can be a risky strategy. Users who are not involved with the system at an early stage will probably feel little sense of ownership, will probably not want the system and may use it with reluctance or not at all. If the experts are not also the future users then a better strategy is to create a design group which contains technical specialists, problem experts and future users. These will work together as a team, jointly developing the system and shaping it to the users needs.

In many situations the technical members of the design group will form a development team which is part of the design group and takes its instructions from it but does a great deal of the actual software creation. If the development team responsible for building the expert system is new to the task or the system is one that has not been built before, the next stage is one of 'experiment' and testing. There will be a need to seek out tools and methods that can assist the design of the expert system. There will be a need to evaluate AI languages and other expert system building tools. There will also be a need to assess techniques for obtaining an expert's knowledge, for specifying business requirements and for designing work organization. All of these require a mix of knowledge derived from both the behavioural and the computer sciences.

A difficulty in selecting tools and methods is that many are new and untested. The group making the choice embarks on a voyage into the unknown never sure where the approach is taking them or if another would have served them better. This problem may be avoided if the design group has a very clear idea of the kind of system that they are trying to build and the extent to which technical, business, organizational and human factors have to be taken account of in the building process. A broad vision of this kind will enable the design group to recognize that technical tools alone will not solve all their problems. They must also have methods that enable them to address human and organizational needs and problems.

Once the design task is underway the design group moves into a 'learning' period in which they have to get used to coping with a great deal of complexity and uncertainty. They will have to decide when to stop searching for new methods and options; when to make choices; how to deal with constraints—things which they would like to do but cannot—and how to cope with the sudden arrival of problems that were totally unforeseen. They will frequently have to do all of these things without any clear vision of the outcome of their decisions.

Some of the ideas of the cyberneticians on how to manage complexity and variety can be of use at this stage. Complexity means problems that are difficult to solve—usually, but not necessarily, because they contain many different factors and relationships. Variety means having a large number of different activities or problems to handle, although these will not always be complex.

In the 1950s a prestigious cybernetician, W. Ross Ashby, postulated the law of 'requisite variety' (Ashby, 1956). This states that 'only variety can destroy variety'. In terms of systems design this law can be restated as 'variety can only be handled successfully if those coping with it have an equal amount of variety in the approach which they use to manage the activity or problem'. For example, the parts of the design task that require both organizational and technical solutions cannot be managed satisfactorily if only technical tools are used to solve problems. When the variety contained in a problem is identified and specified an optimal solution may prove impossible and a compromise may have to be accepted. Design teams should not be criticized for this. It may be the only way of proceeding and avoiding failure.

The complexity and variety contained in the design task will not be solely concerned with structural factors such as technology and organization. Design will also be influenced by less clear-cut phenomena such as attitudes, aspirations and emotions, many of which express themselves as company politics. These too have to be managed and may be the factors that most influence the success or failure of an expert system. A characteristic of these systems is that they tend to affect those located at senior positions in the company more than those lower down. This is in contrast to earlier office computer systems where the principal impact was on clerks and secretaries. The designers of expert systems therefore need to have a strong awareness of company attitudes and to make determined efforts to gain support for what they are doing, particularly from top management.

After design comes 'implementation' and there can be as many problems at this stage as at any other. Many non-expert systems have foundered at implementation even though they were good systems that could meet the business objectives set for them.

A characteristic of expert systems created to solve strategic problems in international companies is that they may be used on a world-wide basis. This means that the system's introduction has to take account of different cultures, attitudes and needs while at the same time ensuring that it is installed and commences operation without undue confusion and trauma. The management of large-scale change of this kind is particularly difficult and requires well thought out strategies for securing acceptance and a planned and easy implementation.

Once an expert system is in and working there is a need for systematic 'evaluation'. How effective is the system? How well is it solving the business problem? How acceptable is it to the users? These are all questions that need to be asked before its future is assured.

To sum up, the design and implementation of an expert system is a complex process but one that if well managed can contribute a great deal to business success and human welfare. Along the route there will be numerous difficulties, many of them human. The knowledge elicitation process is one of these. We need to ensure that experts are able to provide knowledge in a logical, accurate and comprehensive form. An expert system that is built on poor knowledge is better done without.

Another essential task is ensuring that expert systems are wanted and acceptable to the future users. This requires both the involvement of these users in the design process and the ability of the expert system to fill a knowledge gap or help solve an urgent business problem. Users must also not feel threatened by these systems. Expert systems should act as automated experts which add to human knowledge like a good teacher. They should assist, not displace, the human being who associates with them.

. . . I intend to go along with this good man, and to cast in my lot with him. But my good companion do you know the way to this desired place?

John Bunyan

Chapter 2

PARTICIPATION AND SYSTEMS DESIGN

The later chapters of this book contain a description of the design processes associated with the development of an expert system that was built and introduced participatively. The authors believe strongly in the benefits of a participative approach and in this chapter they discuss participation as a general strategy for systems design, describing its history, use, problems and advantages.

WHAT IS PARTICIPATIVE DESIGN?

Participative systems design means giving responsibility for all, or part, of the design of a new system to the group who will eventually use it. There are four principal arguments for the use of such an approach. The first states that people have a moral right to control their own destinies and that this applies as much in the work situation as elsewhere. In many countries this philosophy is now part of the policy of the main political parties. The second is based on expediency rather than values. It states that people who do not have a say in decisions may refuse to implement the decisions of others if they see these as misguided or unnecessary. The third relates to the location of knowledge and states that the experts on how work is, and should be, carried out are the workers themselves. The fourth is that involvement acts as a motivator and leads to more productivity and efficiency. Companies which use participative design probably do so for reasons which include some or all of these arguments.

Participative design requires the future users of a new system to think hard about their business needs and problems and decide how the system can best help with these. They will also consider their working environment and decide how their quality of working life can be improved through the removal of frustrations and by making tasks and responsibilities more interesting and rewarding. The design task will be a collaborative exercise between users and technical systems designers. The end-product should be a system that users like and find helpful, and which makes a major contribution to the efficient and effective running of their department and firm.

THE HISTORY OF PARTICIPATION

Participation is not new. The Greeks used community decision taking and the concept was popular in eighteenth- and nineteenth-century Europe. The French philosopher, Jean-Jacques Rousseau, was interested in the Greek notion of a 'participatory society' and believed that governmental action should reflect the views of all citizens. British thinkers Jeremy Bentham and John Stuart Mill thought participation could help voters protect their interests and exercise control over their parliamentary representatives (Nelson, 1980). Mill also saw participation assisting personal development and the general advancement of the community, with industry as one area where the individual could gain experience of managing collective affairs (Poole, 1982). He believed that cooperative forms of industrial organization could lead to a 'moral transformation of those that took part in them' so that relationships became based on a 'friendly rivalry in pursuit of a good common to all' (Pateman, 1970).

Similar ideas were to be found in the United States. President Thomas Jefferson, one of the eighteenth-century fathers of democracy, believed in freedom, feared ignorance and had great confidence in the intelligence and good sense of ordinary people. Many followed in his footsteps including John Dewey, born in 1859, thirty-three years after Jefferson's death. Dewey was a prestigious philosopher and academic whose ideas were similar to those of John Stuart Mill. He saw democracy and participation as a means for bringing people together in a situation which would provide opportunities for learning and intellectual growth. He believed that it was the duty of society to provide individuals with conditions that would enable them to continually enlarge their experience.

Later writers on participation were of a different kind from these early philosophers. Many were contributors to the American 'human relations' movement in industry and they include such famous names as Mayo, McGregor, and Likert. The Tavistock Institute in England had a major influence on organizational participation from the 1950s onwards, working in close association with Norwegian social scientists. These groups and individuals moved away from ideas of a 'common good' to simpler questions about authority, motivation and job satisfaction. They believed that the quality of working life could be increased through greater employee participation in decisions which concerned their day-to-day activities.

The American social scientists all had their own definitions of participation. Elton Mayo saw it as a democratic form of organization with no fixed concentration of authority at the top (Mayo, 1949). It could not easily be represented in an organizational chart or engineering blueprint for the locus of authority moved from place to place according to the demands of the situation.

Douglas McGregor defined participation as 'creating opportunities, under suitable conditions, for people to influence decisions which affect them'

(McGregor, 1960). Rensis Likert held a similar view, describing it as a process in which 'all subordinates in a work group who are affected by a decision are involved in it'. Likert included the supervisor in his definition of a work group (Likert, 1961).

Other writers were less willing to have management as co-partners in decision taking. Participation was variously described as 'any or all of the processes by which employees other than managers contribute positively towards the reaching of managerial decisions which affect their work' (Sawtell). And, 'the totality of such forms of upwards exertion of powers by subordinates in organizations as are perceived to be legitimate by themselves and their superiors'. This last definition implied that there was some shared notion of what were legitimate and illegitimate topics for participation.

A definition favoured by the authors is less open-ended. This definition describes participation as:

> 'A process in which two or more parties influence each other in making plans, policies or decisions. It is restricted to decisions that have future effects on all those making the decisions or on those represented by them.' (French *et al.*, 1960)

These definitions of participation vary considerably although they have two elements in common. They all recognize that participation involves more than one set of interests and that it is concerned with decision taking.

WHY IS PARTICIPATION WORTH CONSIDERING?

Systems analysts and behavioural scientists have an important common interest— they are both concerned with the problems of implementing technical change. But the two specialisms have different approaches and objectives. The systems analyst is primarily concerned with designing and introducing new technical systems while the behavioural scientist is interested in the consequences of these new systems for the work groups associated with them, and in ensuring that they are designed and implemented in such a way that human beings are not degraded or made to suffer undue stress and anxiety.

The behavioural scientist believes that companies will achieve their business objectives more easily and effectively if change is introduced in a way that does not cause resistance in groups that experience it. Resistance to change is also of the utmost importance to the systems analyst for sophisticated technology becomes an expensive white elephant if people refuse to work with it.

User attitudes to new technology are influenced by a large number of different factors. One is the stability of the existing system. By this is meant the extent to which the current departmental organization fits the needs and aspirations of the staff employed there. Another is how users perceive change. Do they see a proposed new system as a threat or an opportunity? These perceptions will not necessarily bear any relation to the realities of the change. A third is the strategy used for introducing change—the levers used by the innovating group to change the user department from an existing organization of work to a new one. Lastly, there is how the innovating group responsible for designing and introducing the new technology perceives its role, and is perceived by the users, and how these perceptions affect attitudes and strategies.

Figure 2.1 provides a model of what is meant when we talk of the 'stability' of the user department.

The model can be explained in the following way. At work we all try to meet a large number of personal needs. The nature of these needs depends upon many factors related to our upbringing, personality, education and responsibilities. For example, the needs of clerks are likely to be different in many respects, although not all, from the needs of highly qualified scientists. We all require adequate financial rewards for the level of work we are asked to perform. Most of us want status—and some of us, in addition, want power and responsibility. We want interesting work and pleasant social relationships within the work situation and most of us want job security. But the extent to which we, as individuals, want some or all of these will depend on the kinds of people we are and on our personal circumstances.

The degree to which our needs within work are satisfied affects our attitudes to our work and our behaviour in work. If the needs of individuals and groups are being adequately met then the work situation is stable. People are getting satisfaction from work and there should be little conflict. Managers will talk about running departments in which morale is high. But employee needs in work can only be met if the work situation is designed to permit this. Whether this happens depends on a number of factors related to the structure and organization of the department. These are set out in Figure 2.2.

All departments in a firm will have some sort of technology, although this can range from a simple manual system to a complex form of automation. The nature of this technology will influence the way work is carried out, the kinds of controls that are used to ensure that it is carried out and the social structure

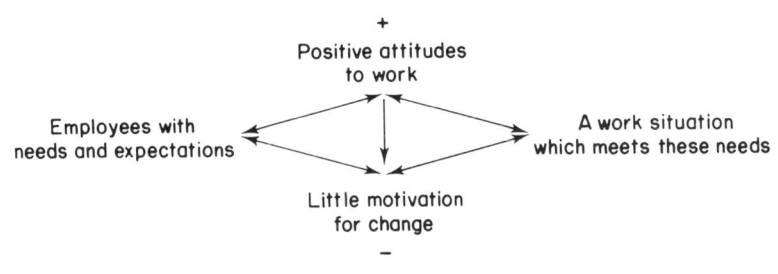

FIGURE 2.1

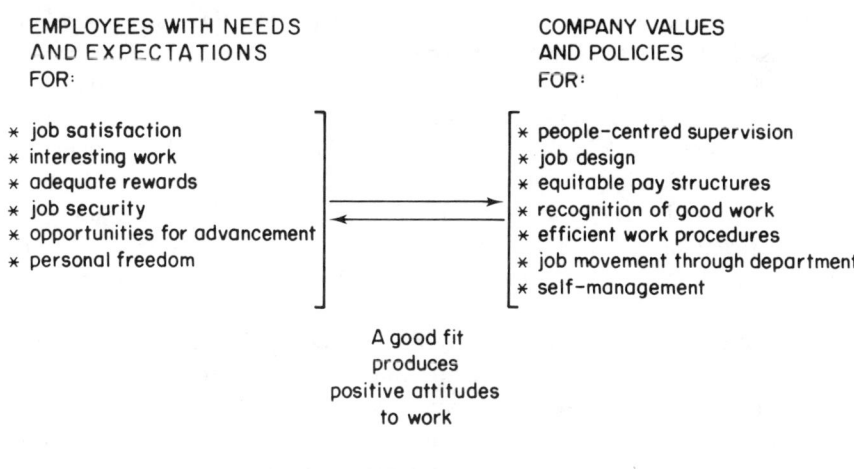

FIGURE 2.2

of the groups in which it is carried out. If the nature of the technology leads to dull, routine or stressful jobs while the needs of the workforce are for interesting and varied jobs then, inevitably, there will be conflict and employees will take some kind of action to try and change an unpleasant situation. This action may take the form of labour disputes, low productivity, absenteeism or departures from the company.

Technology is probably the most constraining factor on the way work is organized, but there are others. Three of them are the nature of departmental targets and goals, the leadership style of supervision and the rewards system— the methods which are used to reimburse employees financially for their effort. If targets are tight and difficult to meet, then management may introduce tight controls, and these may thwart employee needs for freedom and responsibility. Again, if a work group wishes to be consulted but has an authoritarian manager, then communication needs will not be met and there is likely to be conflict and low morale. Similarly, reward systems based on output may lead to high production but do this at the expense of quality, work interest, and social relationships.

If the situation in a department or firm is stable—with people liking their work and having the majority of their needs met, then there may be no internal dynamic for change. People will want the comfortable and satisfying situation to continue. The problem for the innovator is then how to change disinterest in change into enthusiasm. If, in contrast, the situation is unstable and employees have grievances because of unfulfilled needs, then a new system may be responded to in one of two ways. Either it will be seen as making an already undesirable situation worse, or it will be seen as a means for improvement.

When presented with the prospect of technical change the first question most people ask is 'how is this new arrangement going to affect me?'. The nature of their answer will depend on their attitudes to technology—many of which will have been derived from books, TV and films, and from their own experiences and those of colleagues in other departments. They will also be influenced by their relations with the development group. If this group adopts a technical/rational role and pays little attention to the views of the future users then negative reactions will increase. The weak department will retaliate by non-cooperation and poor performance, the strong by militant resistance to unwanted change.

Many of these problems can be avoided if participation and involvement is used as a change strategy. The relationship between users and technologists now becomes a collaborative one and the final system will embody tasks, procedures and controls which meet individual and group needs. Change will be introduced in an atmosphere of knowledge and approval, uncertainty and resistance will be reduced and the user department will recognize that gains rather than losses can be a product of new technology.

Creating acceptable and accepted systems is a major gain but there are other reasons for adopting a participative approach. One is the complexity of organizational life today. This makes it very difficult for any group of technical specialists, no matter how expert, to design a new system that precisely meets the needs of a user group. Specialists cannot easily obtain a detailed knowledge of user requirements in situations where work is highly skilled and subject to constant change. The employees in such departments already have this knowledge and they are more likely to get the kind of system they need and want if they contribute to the design task. This is especially true of systems used by groups at higher levels in the company, for example, information systems for top management.

Also, many different groups—senior and middle management, departments which work closely with the principal users, and external groups such as customers and suppliers—will also have an interest in a new system and its functions. These too can benefit from a participative approach by being invited to attend design meetings whenever their interests are being discussed.

Another factor is the increasing shortage of technical specialists. These experts are a scarce resource and the involvement of users in design can relieve them of some traditional responsibilities and provide them with more time to take on other projects. There are also sound psychological reasons for a participative approach. Good evidence exists that if those who will use a system can influence its development, then anxiety and uncertainty is reduced. The users see themselves as the 'owners' of the system and have a vested interest in its successful operation.

Participation also helps overcome problems of conflicting interests. Not all members of a user group will have identical interests. It is likely that staff from different grades, jobs and functions will have their own problems, needs and objectives. The opportunity for discussion that a participative approach provides means that differences can be recognized and reconciled. In this way serious conflict that might threaten the acceptance of the system can be avoided.

But it is important to recognize that in most situations participation is a means to an end and not an end in itself. It is there to assist the creation of good systems that work efficiently, increase human effectiveness and contribute to a stimulating and satisfying work environment. There are companies which have participation as a major organizational value and share decision making with their staff on a wide variety of issues. Such firms have a democratic philosophy and believe that participation is the right way to run a business. Firms of this kind are admirable but unusual. In this book the emphasis is on participation as a means for assisting the successful introduction of major change.

THE STRUCTURE OF PARTICIPATION

Participation can take many different forms. It can be a product of an institutionalized democratic system such as a workers' committee with elected representatives. Or it can be a formally organized vote such as a referendum. It can also take the form of pressure groups which make their views known through legitimate channels such as the media or political representatives. Alternatively, it can be a pressure group prepared to use means such as strikes or other militant action to make its view known.

A firm with an interest in developing participation will be less concerned with the options described above than with deciding whether to have a direct or indirect form of participation. Direct participation means trying to involve all users at intervals throughout the design process in some aspects of decision taking. There will still be a selected or elected design group but it will work very democratically. It will continually seek ideas and inputs from colleagues and constituents while passing on information and holding regular meetings open to all. The final decision on how to organize the user area around new technology will be discussed by the department as a whole. This approach works particularly well in small departments or firms.

Indirect participation is when a representative group becomes the sole vehicle for decision taking. This approach requires that all major interest groups— roles, functions, grades—are represented in the design group, together with the technical specialists. Decisions have to be taken on whether these representatives are selected or elected and on whether more than one design group is required. This may be necessary if a number of different departments will be using the new system.

Design groups can be vertically organized incorporating representatives from different levels, or they can be horizontally organized—a group of clerks designing their own word processing system, for example.

Participative design works best when there is both a steering group and a design group. The steering group should consist of senior managers with a stake in the project. Its role is to set guidelines, ensure that design group decisions are in line with company policy and provide encouragement and advice.

There is also a need for a change 'facilitator'—someone who can assist the design group to carry out its task. The role of the facilitator is to help the design group work effectively.

THE CONTENT OF PARTICIPATION

The content of participation is the nature of the issues about which decisions are taken. It involves a consideration of decision boundaries—the subjects which can be considered participatively and those which are seen as the prerogative of management. Participative design can be broad or narrow. That is, it can encompass all decisions from whether to embark on a new strategy or a new technology to the final implementation. Or it can be associated with a more limited range of decision-taking—for example, what needs to be changed and what should go in its place.

Participative design can involve all or some of the following decisions:

1. The initiation of the project and agreeing that it shall go ahead.
2. The setting up of the design group and the steering committee.
3. The diagnosis and specification of existing problems and needs.
4. The identification of alternative strategies and solutions.
5. The evaluation of these alternatives and choice of one for implementation.
6. The detailed design of the selected system.
7. The implementation of the system.
8. The evaluation of the system in operation.
9. Modifications and adjustments.

THE PROCESS OF PARTICIPATION

Participation in the design of a new system requires a process over time. It involves the acquisition of knowledge so that decisions are taken from an informed position; it involves learning, the development of effective working relationships, the setting and achieving of goals and the implementation of solutions. It is also concerned with power, and it has been suggested that in true participation all the parties will have equal power. If power within a participative group is not equal, then the interests of a faction can unduly influence decisions. Where power is equal but there are conflicts of interest, the outcome has to be negotiated and is likely to be a compromise. Occasionally it is possible to develop a solution that is so good it meets the objectives of all concerned. At other times a group may find it impossible to arrive at a solution.

The Role of the Change Facilitator

The facilitator is an important part of the processes of change. He or she will guide the design group along the route to successful change and provide helpful intervention and advice when this is required. The facilitator must understand the design methodology that is being used and be able to guide the group through the design task, including the reorganization of the user department and the redesign of jobs.

One of the important tasks of the facilitator is to help the design group examine organizational options—different ways of organizing work around new technology that can help the user group more easily achieve its business mission and key tasks, while at the same time meeting the specific objectives set by the design group for the new system.

The facilitator also has to help the design group stay motivated and interested in its design task, ensure that communications about the group's activities are established with all interested people, and help the group handle the inevitable 'process' problems which it will experience at some point in its activities. These problems may be disagreements between group members, or between the design group and the steering group, or unanticipated events that impact on the group's work. The facilitator must also provide instruction in any organizational design methodology that is being used.

The design group will need to be guided by the facilitator more at the start of a project than later on. Design group members normally take some time to learn how to work together and to understand the nature of the task they have embarked on. Once this initial hurdle is over they will progress quite rapidly with the analysis of needs and problems because they are all familiar with these. Design can prove more difficult when they are creating their vision of the new system. This step is a difficult one for most design groups and it is helpful if the facilitator lets them know that a drop in effectiveness is not uncommon at this time.

If a new work system is being introduced and technologists do not form part of the design group, then a technical adviser may be necessary. This will be the case, for example, when participation is being used to increase departmental productivity. New technology may not necessarily form part of this change but advice from a technical expert can help the group decide if it should be considered.

When technologists do form part of the design group their role is very different from that of traditional systems analysts. In the past, the systems analyst has seen himself or herself, and has been seen by the users, as the designer of the system. In contrast the role of the technical members of a design group is to help the users make informed choices between available technical solutions.

This kind of role is not always easy. The technical members may receive pressure from technical colleagues to justify a participative approach. There may be accusations of time and money wasting because the lead time for a participatively designed system is seen as longer than that for a system designed in the conventional way. All of these things can cause stress, particularly if the technical specialist is not receiving encouragement and support from top management.

The Role of the Steering Committee

Participative design works best when there is both a design group and a steering committee. The steering committee will consist of senior managers with a direct interest in the new systems and, in some companies, senior trade union officials. The design task or contract will normally be agreed between the steering committee and the design group. The steering committee will set the broad framework within which the project is to be carried out. This will take account of company policy on particular issues, sensitive decision areas, design boundaries and other matters viewed as important by senior management. In turn, the facilitator working with a new design group will point out to the steering committee the importance of their interest in, and commitment to, the project. The facilitator will ask them to meet regularly with the design group to discuss progress and problems. The facilitator will also ask for individual members to be available to give advice, when this is required, and for them to inform the design group if they hear of other projects which may overlap with the design group's work. In principal, these responsibilities are quite straightforward and most steering committees provide their design groups with the necessary help and encouragement. But there can be problems and some steering committees may find it difficult to fully comprehend the nature of their role. They may 'forget' what the project is about and be intolerant of the time required to do a high quality job. They may have heavy workloads and find it difficult to meet regularly. Key members may miss meetings because unexpected problems arise. These lapses can cause problems for a design group who may begin to doubt the steering committee's interest and commitment.

The challenge for the firm using participation as a strategy is to create the kinds of structures and processes that will assist all the different stakeholders to obtain some gains from using this approach. These gains will not necessarily be all of the same kind but they should enable each interest group to say with conviction 'participation has clear benefits for us'.

THE ETHICS METHOD

Effective participative design requires decisions to be taken on content, structure and process. One way of facilitating the process of design and enabling a design group to make rapid progress from a diagnosis of its needs to the design of the new system, is to provide them with a set of analytical tools. One of the two authors of this book, Enid Mumford, has developed a method called ETHICS (Effective Technical and Human Implementation of Computer-based Systems) which was used in the XSEL project. ETHICS assists a design group to do the following: identify their own efficiency and job satisfaction needs, set specific objectives for the new system, rethink the organization of work in their department and contribute to the design of the technical part of the system. The method is set out in some detail here in case readers wish to use it themselves. The steps involved in designing a system participatively, using the ETHICS approach, are set out below.

Step 1—Diagnosis of Needs

Describing the Business Mission

The introduction of new technology provides an opportunity for taking a fresh look at the business mission of the group who will use the system and establishing clearly the primary objectives and key tasks of the department or function accepting the new technology. This preliminary examination of business mission and key tasks is called analysis of the 'primary' system. It describes the reason the department exists and the fundamental activities it must undertake irrespective of how it is organized or the technology it uses.

A design group using ETHICS will proceed through the following steps.

a. Specify the nature of the *presenting problem or opportunity*. Why should the existing system be redesigned?

b. Identify the group or groups with a major *interest* in how the problem is solved. These should be represented on the design group. They will be using the new system in their day-to-day activities once it is operational.

 Identify the indirect users of the system—groups who will be affected by it without being major users.

c. Define the *boundaries* of the system. Where does the design task begin and end? Is it restricted to one department or a number of departments or does it take a narrow track through the firm, crossing many departmental boundaries?

d. Describe clearly the *business mission and key tasks* of the future users. The principal objective of the new system will be to enable users to achieve their business mission more easily and effectively. It is important to establish agreement on the business mission before proceeding further.

Key tasks are the integrated sets of activities that contribute to the achievement of the business mission and must take place irrespective of how the department is organized or what technology is used. It is useful to prioritize the key tasks in terms of their criticality to the accomplishment of the business mission.

This early statement of the business mission and key tasks helps the members of a design group to free themselves from focusing on the existing organization of work and assists them to logically think through the basic activities which their department must carry out if it is to achieve its primary objectives. Unless the department is given a major new role the business mission and key tasks will remain the same irrespective of the level of technology or the nature of work procedures.

Describing the Existing Work System

Once the business mission and key tasks have been identified the design group should spend some time examining the present organization of work. It is advisable to understand how the existing system is functioning before redesigning it, and this analysis will provide important information on problems and needs. The description should cover the following:

● *Operational activities*—the day-to-day tasks which are being carried out at present to achieve the business mission. Many of these will be changed when the new system is created.

● *Efficiency needs*—problems which are impeding the easy achievement of the business mission through slowing work down, causing errors and increasing costs. This kind of problem can be called a 'variance'. A variance is defined as a tendency for a system or subsystem to deviate from some desired or expected norm or standard. These kinds of problem can be categorized in terms of their ability to disturb the system. Critical variances will be those which are difficult to avoid and correct. These frequently occur at the interface between the department and other groups such as customers and suppliers. Operational variances are less serious and generally due to inefficient procedures, a poorly functioning form of work organization, or inadequate controls.

● *Effectiveness needs*—These are identified by examining the key tasks, establishing which contribute most to the achievement of the business mission and asking two questions. Are some of these being performed less effectively than they could be? Are there key tasks which are not being performed at all and should be introduced? Effectiveness is often related to the coordination of activities with other internal and external groups and to the department's ability to accommodate and adjust to change.

● *Future change*—A note should be made of likely or possible changes that will affect the user area in the future. The new system will need to be flexible enough to accept these.

● *Job satisfaction needs*—the ETHICS method always make an improvement in job satisfaction an important design objective. This means that job satisfaction needs and objectives must be made explicit as part of the system description. All the future users of the system are asked to state the level and kinds of satisfaction they enjoy in their present jobs, the frustrations they experience and their views on how job satisfaction could be increased. Unless a very small group is involved this information is best collected through the completion of questionnaires. This data can then form the basis of small group discussions on how work and the work situation can be redesigned so as to improve job satisfaction.

Job satisfaction has been defined by Mumford as the 'fit between what an individual or group is seeking from the work situation and what they are receiving'. It is seen as being achieved when three kinds of needs are successfully met. These are personality needs, competence and efficiency needs and needs associated with personal values. The ETHICS method ensures that these needs are ascertained and discussed with users before the new system is introduced. The following information is obtained on the ideal versus the present situation.

Needs associated with personality

● *Knowledge needs.* How, ideally, would each individual or group like their existing skills and knowledge to be used? What opportunities for developing these further would be advantageous to them?

How well are these needs being met at present?

● *Psychological needs.* What are their needs for responsibility, status, esteem, security and advancement, and how do they define these needs?

How well are these needs being met at present?

Needs associated with competence, control and efficiency

● *Support/control needs.* What kind of support services would enable them to carry out their work responsibilities more efficienctly? These support services will include the information and materials necessary to work at a high level of competence as well as supervisory assistance and good working conditions.

What kind of control systems do they think would assist their motivation and efficiency? The level and structure of wages and salaries is an important part of any control system.

The extent to which these are provided at present.

● *Task needs.* What kinds of task structures and role responsibilities do different kinds of users find motivating, interesting and challenging. For example, to what extent do they want jobs that include the following: opportunities for self-management, for developing new methods, services or products, for coordinating their own activities and taking organizational decisions, for solving their own problems and monitoring their own progress.

The extent to which they already have these.

Needs associated with personal values

● *Ethical needs.* How do they wish to be treated by management? Do the firm's policies on communication, consultation and participation meet their expectations? Do other kinds of policy also meet these expectations?

Although this diagnosis is being carried out by the design group all members of a user area can make a contribution to the analysis of variances and job satisfaction needs.

Step 2—Discrepancy Analysis

● *What must be changed.* The job satisfaction survey has compared the present with the ideal situation and this now needs to be done with the efficiency and effectiveness analyses. A note should be made of those parts of the present system which are working well and contributing to the successful achievement of the business mission. Changes may not need to be made here. Those parts of the system that are not performing well and need improving should be noted and ranked in order of priority. This analysis will cover key variances which require better control, operational variances which should be eliminated if possible and critical tasks which can be carried out more effectively. The criterion for prioritisation will be the extent to which deficiencies are frustrating the easy achievement of the business mission and the key tasks associated with this.

Step 3—Agreeing Objectives

● *Setting objectives and evaluating strategies*—The design group must now set clear, precise objectives for the new system. These will be listed under four headings— efficiency objectives, effectiveness objectives, job satisfaction objectives, future change objectives.

This part of the design task often becomes a negotiating process, for the representatives of the different interest groups will not necessarily agree on which objectives should be given highest priority. The ideal solution is to find a design that meets each group's most important objectives. But this is not always possible and disagreements can arise. These must be brought out into the open and rationally discussed. The aim should be to achieve a consensus on the most important objectives for the new system.

A strategy for achieving the objectives must now be chosen. This will incorporate both organizational and technical solutions for the problems that have been identified. It is advantageous to examine a number of possible organizational/technical solutions and to select the ones which best contribute to the achievement of the system objectives and the department's business mission.

The facilitator now has an important role in explaining available options to the group and the implications of each of these for the organization of work in the user area. The choice of strategy will be made by the design group after consultation with the steering group. It is important to check that the selected organizational and technical solutions fit well together and reinforce each other.

Once a strategy has been chosen the design group must think it through in detail, even considering such matters as the physical layout of the department, training, implementation and evaluation, as well as the new organizational/technical structure.

Step 4—Designing the Organizational System

● *Sociotechnical design*—There are a number of approaches to work design which design groups may want to consider. The two most frequently used are 'job enrichment' and 'sociotechnical' design. Job enrichment focuses on the individual worker and tries to build up a job in such a way that it increases in interest, responsibility and challenge. The aim of job enrichment is to improve the relationship between the individual and his or her work.

The sociotechnical method was originally developed by the Tavistock Institute of Human Relations in Great Britain and this takes a very different approach. The concept of a sociotechnical system is derived from the premise that any production system requires both a technology and a social structure, with the two linked together and reinforcing each other in the accomplishment of a common task or goal (Trist, 1981). For example, in an office the technical system consists of the tools, techniques and procedures to process the raw materials of information. The social structure is the network of roles, relationships and tasks which interact with the technical system and form the organizational structure. The purpose of the sociotechnical approach is to produce technical and social structures which have a high capacity to achieve technical and social goals and which reinforce each other in the achievement of these goals.

Sociotechnical analysis incorporates a logical analysis of the technical components of work (machines, procedures, information) and the grouping of these into logically integrated sets of tasks—one set being separated from the next by a change of state of the input or product. Work design which uses a sociotechnical approach identifies sets of integrated tasks and allocates one or more to each work group. The work group then has responsibility for allocating tasks amoungst its members and for training its members so that each individual is competent to carry out all tasks. This form of work organization is often referred to as 'autonomous' or 'semi-autonomous' groups.

Step 5—Implementing the System

Once a system has been designed it has to be implemented and this involves a set of change processes in which an existing system is assisted to move smoothly and successfully from one organizational state to another. The new work structure and level of technology have to be established in such a way that they fit well with employee expectations and values. The result should be a set of social, technical and administrative relationships which lead to greater efficiency and provide opportunities for job satisfaction and personal development.

This relationship between tasks, technology, human needs and organizational goals must be stable but it should not be static. A department must be able to respond to new demands and inputs, while at the same time maintaining a state of internal equilibrium. An ability to accept and adjust to new pressures will assist the avoidance of stress and conflict.

A system that has been participatively designed can still encounter serious problems if the way it is introduced does not fit with user ideas of what is an acceptable implementation strategy. All groups concerned with the change processes, including senior and departmental management, the design group, the staff they represent and, if they are affected, external groups such as customers and suppliers, must understand the nature and logic of the proposed change, must approve and like the change strategies that are to be used and must regard the results of these as beneficial to their own interests.

Implementation involves developing user commitment to the new system, and providing users with an understanding of how it functions and with the skills to operate it effectively. Commitment is facilitated by user involvement in the design process and by a belief that the system will increase job satisfaction and provide an improvement on previous work methods. This belief must not be jeopardized through poor implementation, as change will only prove successful if groups which experience it can adapt easily to the new situation and feel comfortable with it.

Participation requires thought, knowledge and competence. It is more than joint discussion—it is joint problem solving. It also requires a humanistic value system, a methodology that assists the acquisition of knowledge on how to design good organizational and technical systems and a democratic structure that enables effective design to be realized.

The different analysis and design steps incorporated into ETHICS provide a systematic route along which a design group can proceed. Each step is a learning opportunity and also a means for achieving further progress towards the completion of the design task. Clearly, the steps described here are not the only means for achieving design competence, but they are an example of useful tools that assist learning (Mumford, 1986).

THE PROBLEMS OF PARTICIPATION

Participative systems design has its problems and these have to be understood for it to be successfully managed. Here are some of them.

Creating the Design Group

The composition of the user design group is one of the first problems that has to be faced. Ideally, this group should be representative of all the different functions and subgroups with a major interest in the new system and be drawn from several organizational levels. Taking a 'diagonal' slice of the firm in this way ensures that a considerable breadth and depth of knowledge is located in the group. Members also have to be people who have a stake in the project, are actively interested in it, have the time available to work on it, can express their views clearly while thinking broadly and creatively, and have good interpersonal skills. If a group cannot be found which already possesses these skills, then the next best thing is the selection of team members who are willing to develop them.

Learning to Design

All design groups develop and increase their skills over time and they need more help and guidance at the start of a project than later on. The biggest hurdle can be learning to work together as a team. Once this is accomplished the group is usually able to progress rapidly with an analysis of current problems because each member is very familiar with these. Nevertheless some design groups become overwhelmed with the complexity of the analysis task at this stage. If more than one design group is involved in the project then encouraging one team to support another by comparing problems and progress is a way of handling these difficult periods.

Design is also complex when ideas for change, and a vision of a new system to replace an existing one, have to be created. Some design groups find it difficult to think creatively and the facilitator can assist this process by encouraging them to identify and evaluate organizational options.

Relations with Line Management

An important question for a design group is how best to involve management in participative design. Managers are typically interested in any approach that will improve productivity and they normally value the efforts of their staff to increase this. Once having set a project in motion, however, they may forget long-term objectives and focus on immediate problems. Or they may press for results in a shorter time frame than originally anticipated. Or have incorrect expectations of the scope and length of the project. Pressures of this kind can cause a design group to experience conflict between the project and their day-to-day activities. The facilitator can help the avoidance of these kinds of problems by inviting the manager to meetings of the design group and ensuring he or she always has information on the latest stage of the project.

All supervisors who are not members of the design group or steering committee but have an interest in the project must be kept regularly informed of the design group's activities through minutes and invitations to meetings. Their viewpoint should be an important input into the design group's thinking and they should share in the sense of project ownership.

Other problems that can occur are a reluctance to change establishment methods of work for new, improved, but unfamiliar ones. Also, the opportunity for discussion that participation provides may bring to the surface organizational, technical and human issues that are not directly relevant to the project in hand. And the design group members may have difficulty in keeping their constituents and other interested groups informed about what they are doing. Formalizing communication through a wide circulation of minutes after each meeting can assist this problem, as can the occasional 'open' meeting which any interested person can attend. Lastly, design group members may suffer from having 'no place to hide'. Whereas a professional group of technical systems designers can escape to their own department when relations with users become difficult, user members of a design group may suffer stress through continually having to explain and defend their design decisions to their colleagues.

THE ADVANTAGES OF PARTICIPATION

These are numerous and appear to greatly outweigh the disadvantages. Here are some of the arguments for participation.

Participation can Act as a Statement of Company Philosophy

Many companies today are trying to introduce a more employee-centred style of management. They are striving for open communication, the opportunity for debate and question at every level, and a high emphasis on personal reponsibility and development. Participative systems design is one means for demonstrating management's commitment to this employee-centred philosophy.

Participation can Stimulate the Sharing of Knowledge

A design task shared between the future users of a system and the computer specialists responsible for technical solutions should assist good design. The users are expert in the operation of their department and aware of all its faults and problems. They have a great deal of practical knowledge to contribute to the design of a new system. But they are better able to express this knowledge if they can share ideas with technical specialists in a group situation. The department can then be looked at as a whole and the contributions of different roles and functions identified and examined.

Participation can Provide a Learning Experience

When the design task is shared both users and computer specialists learn from each other. Regular group discussions help technical participants to get a deep level of knowledge about the user department and its needs that is difficult to achieve using the traditional approach of individual interviews. They can discover, not only how the department does work, but also how it could work and, perhaps, should work.

Similarly, the future users of the system learn a great deal from the technical specialists. Users can participate in the evaluation of hardware and software options, relate what is on offer to the department's needs and contribute to the design of the human–computer interface.

Both users and technical experts leave a participative experience with greater knowledge and understanding than they had before, and with sympathy for each others point of view. This will be of considerable benefit when they come to design their next system.

Participation is a Means for Giving a Sense of Ownership to the Future Users of New Systems

Many books and lectures on systems design stress the need to make users feel that they 'own' the system—that it is theirs to operate and manage. But it is not easy to give a sense of ownership when one group designs a system for another. With participative design users can really claim ownership of a system that they have developed themselves; that they fully understand because they have helped it to grow and mature, and that they feel is their 'baby'.

Participation can Increase the Effective Use of a System

Participation means that not only do users want to use their new work system effectively, they have the knowledge to do so. Because they have lived with the development of the system over many months they will have an excellent understanding of how it works, what it has to offer and of its advantages and limitations.

Participation is a Means for Developing Good Human Relations

It is difficult, if not impossible, to introduce new systems easily in a situation where there is conflict between management and employees. Either the new system will be used reluctantly and seen as yet another imposition by an uncaring management, or, if the firm is unionized, it will become a victim of protracted industrial relations feuding. It may eventually have to be abandoned or else bought in at a price. User participation in systems design can help avoid conflict arising or, if it does occur, enable it to be brought into the open and dealt with through reasoned discussion.

Even in firms with good management/employee relations major change can cause stress and conflict and damage relationships. Participation can act as a means for improving and cementing these. It provides an opportunity for collaboration between technical specialists and users, and for consultation and discussion between managers and those lower down. Everyone is then involved, as a team, in overcoming the inevitable problems associated with change and in jointly striving towards the accepted goal of a viable and working system. Change then becomes an exciting integrator and not an unwelcome disrupter.

Participation is a Developer of Change Skills

Participation means that users become increasingly expert in managing their own change. They come to understand how to analyse their own needs, how to design new systems and how to introduce these successfully. User involvement can help ensure that the management of change is carried out with interest and enthusiasm, and a minimum of human problems.

Participative design enables employees to mould their own futures and create the kind of environment that is both efficient and stimulating. By taking part in a process that is creative yet directed at a specific task-based goal they acquire confidence in their ability to contribute to the management of their own change.

The system that emerges from a participative design process will be seen by the users as very much their own system. Employees will have identified their own problems and arrived at their own solution. In doing this they will have been assisted by the computer professionals whose focus of attention is on how the user area can receive the most help from technical back-up. A good human solution will emerge from the knowledge and skills of the design group, assisted by the 'change facilitator'.

But for participation to succeed, the company as an institution must offer something. Its expert groups must be willing to share the design task with non-experts; its top management must be willing to delegate some responsibility to those lower down. The firm as a whole must be flexible and adaptive and not caught up in rigid bureaucratic procedures.

Participation requires a methodology, management and leadership. The change facilitator will provide many of these and the person in the role needs to exercise considerable social skills, understand group processes and be able to help resolve conflicts of interest, as and when these arise. Design groups which have successfully completed a project are often anxious to continue working together as a team. They can make an important contribution to the successful operation of the new system by monitoring its use and helping with future developments and modifications. Any system should be critically evaluated at intervals to ensure that it continues to meet efficiency, effectiveness and job satisfaction needs. Design groups can also help to spread the participative message by advising other groups who are embarking on new projects.

. . . a pleasant place where was builded
a stately palace, beautiful to behold; at
the sight of which Christian was clearly
delighted; he saw also upon the top thereof
certain persons walked who were clothed all
in gold.

John Bunyan

Chapter 3

INNOVATION AND THE DIGITAL CULTURE

PROBLEMS AND OPPORTUNITIES

The Digital Equipment Corporation became interested in expert systems at the end of the 1970s. As a high-tech company it was keen to play a leading role in new computer developments and for some time had worked closely with researchers at Carnegie–Mellon University. Here artificial intelligence and expert systems were being pioneered by John McDermott and his colleagues (McDermott, 1984).

At this time Digital had a serious and continuing problem that there had been many unsuccessful attempts to solve. This was associated with the process of 'configuring'—the name given by the manufacturing plants to the specification of the different components required to create a computer system, and the relationships between these. Digital's sales policy has always been to give the customer what he or she wants, within very broad limits. In order to do this the company provides a very considerable range of products and options. This is in contrast to other computer manufacturers which market a smaller number of standard systems.

This range of options made life very difficult for the Digital manufacturing plants. Systems might contain as many as 100 components, each of which could relate with the others in a number of different ways. The possibilities for error were therefore considerable and great knowledge and skill was required to ensure that hardware could be assembled correctly. Some of these errors originated in the manufacturing plants but the majority occurred earlier in the order process. Components selected by customers might not fit together and the salesperson would not always be aware of this. Also, it was easy for the salesperson to omit parts from the order. The components selection process was so complex that few people had the knowledge to do it correctly. This problem was experienced to some extent by all firms in the minicomputer industry at this time (O'Connor, 1984).

Prior to the arrival of AI and expert systems a number of human checks took place to ensure that the configuring process was handled without error. Each order, when it arrived in the manufacturing plant, was examined by two people called technical editors. The first check was to ensure that the order was complete—that it contained all the parts necessary for the required system. The second examination double-checked this but also made sure that the relationships between the components were clearly stated and correct. But the growth in Digital's business in the early 1980s meant that the existing group of technical editors was finding it difficult to cope with the amount of work and it was becoming necessary to recruit and train a larger number. This would have been expensive. It would also have been unsatisfactory since, despite the skill and experience of the technical editors, many configuring mistakes still got through to the shop floor.

The Digital configuring problem had many of the characteristics which AI experts suggest should lead managers to consider building an expert system. The configuring task required knowledge which could be clearly and logically specified. This meant it could be built into the knowledge base of a computer. It also required either the existence of human experts who had the knowledge, or of documents in which the knowledge was contained. In Digital this knowledge existed in both forms. Also, the configuring task was well understood and complex only because of the number of components involved. There was also a clearly identifiable pay-off in solving the problem. In doing so, Digital would both reduce its costs and please its customers (Waterman, 1985).

Here then was an excellent problem to address with an expert system. This led to the development of R1, later called XCON, a system designed to assist the technical editor in the manufacturing plants by providing information on the mix of components required by a particular application and on the ways in which these components had to relate to each other.

XCON proved to be a highly successful system. Its two principal benefits were, first, it accurately verified customer orders and, second, it enabled correct systems to be consistently built in all manufacturing plants. Today, all VAX family system orders are configured by XCON in the United States and European manufacturing plants. Orders, after they have been checked by XCON, are now 98 per cent correct, and manufacturing can commence assembling a system confident that it has accurate instructions.

But many of the configuring errors experienced by the manufacturing plants originated in the Digital sales offices and costs would be reduced further if these mistakes could be prevented. The sales force had to configure the system to meet customer needs, and to provide him or her with a cost quotation. They also had to send an accurately configured order through the order processing system to one of the manufacturing plants. XCON solved the problem of errors occurring at the manufacturing stage but it did nothing to prevent errors arising earlier in the process. Many of these originated at the point of sale through staff omitting items of equipment from quotations and orders or indicating the wrong piece of equipment.

Although XCON did check order accuracy at the manufacturing plants, the technical edit group there could not take responsibility for changing an order that was incorrect. They sent it back to the salesperson who had originated it.

This movement of orders from sales to manufacturing and back again increased administrative costs and annoyed customers whose orders could be delayed. The expert system described in this book, XSEL, was built to solve the configuring problem in the sales offices. Digital would experience a major saving in costs if an expert system could ensure that configuring in sales offices was always correct.

There were other factors in the sales offices that made a configuring expert system an attractive proposition. Whereas experienced sales staff might be expert configurers and not require automated assistance, the company's business was expanding, the sales force was growing in numbers and new salespersons were being recruited. New sales staff did not know how to configure and it could take a long time before they were able to do so with confidence. An expert system would be of great value to this group. Also, even for experienced sales staff, the configuring task was a time-consuming one and this time could be better spent selling equipment to customers. Other advantages would appear in the future although these were only dimly perceived at the start of the XSEL design process.

XSEL developed and expanded many of the capabilities of the XCON program although its users were very different from those of XCON. XCON's users were a number of physically close technical edit groups located in Digital's manufacturing plants. The sales offices, in contrast, were small establishments, dominated by a 'selling' culture but likely to differ in the kinds of customers they serviced and in their approach to the selling activity. They were distributed around the United States, Europe and the rest of the world.

Configuring was selected as a suitable problem to address with expert systems for very good commercial reasons. XCON and XSEL could help solve very expensive problems which arose because people had difficulty in remembering accurately large numbers of facts. These problems were expensive because configuring errors in the manufacturing plants caused production delays. They also caused financial problems with customers if an application did not work because an item of equipment had been omitted. Similarly configuring mistakes by the sales force added to administrative costs and also made Digital's image suffer with customers.

Configuring was an ambitious problem for Digital to choose for an expert system as the task was company-wide and critical to business success. But if XCON and XSEL were both successful then the financial pay-off would be enormous.

HOW DIGITAL BEGAN

The Digital Equipment Corporation was the creation of Ken Olsen—an entrepreneurial American engineering graduate with an exciting vision of the future—one in which small, widely distributed machines replaced large computers. In this way computing could reach all levels of society and leave the rarefied atmosphere of the technical laboratory and the MIS department.

Ken Olsen was born in 1926, the second of four children, to a family with little money, a belief in traditional values and a great interest in making things. His father was a machine-tool designer and the basement of the family house in Stratford, Connecticut, contained many tools which he and his younger brother were encouraged to use. The two brothers, like many other young boys, were excited by the possibilities of electricity and became expert at assembling and repairing radios. Engineering was in their blood and an important part of their everyday environment (Rifkin, 1986).

After leaving school, Ken Olsen joined the US navy and became involved with the advanced work in electronics which was helping the US war effort. This fascinated him and he became determined to study it professionally. So, when his war service was completed, he enrolled as an undergraduate at MIT. Here he came into contact with the early development of large-scale data processing and worked in the Digital Computer Laboratory helping design a machine called the MIT Whirlwind 1. This was a first generation, stored program device sponsored by the US navy. Stored program computers made it possible, for the first time, to build instructions into, and store operating programs in computers. This made large-scale real-time computing feasible.

After graduating he stayed on at MIT and worked at the university's Lincoln Laboratory on the first large real-time computing system—the US Government's SAGE (Semi-automatic Ground Environment) air defence system. The Lincoln laboratory had been established in 1951 with a charter to work towards a computer-based air defence system. Sage was an interactive time-sharing system which allowed military operators at separate consoles to request and receive information from the central computing system simultaneously. This system demonstrated the feasibility of processing radar data through a central computer for air defence.

These early experiences with military computing made Ken Olsen and his MIT associates appreciate the potential of the technology for civilian use. If computer-linked communication networks with men and machines talking to each other could be used by the military, they could also be used by civilians. They decided to set up a business to exploit the potential of computers. Unfortunately, although their engineering knowledge was excellent, their understanding of how to create a new business was less good and the initiative failed.

Harlan Anderson, one of the group involved in the first unsuccessful project then approached Ken Olsen and suggested that the two of them start a company of a less ambitious kind—something small and easy to manage but with interactive computing as a key concept. This time they spent many hours in libraries getting an understanding of accounting principles and eventually they succeeded in persuading a venture capital group, American Research and

Development, to provide initial funding of $70,000. Interestingly, in view of Digital's subsequent development, this was given on the understanding that what they built was not called a computer. In the 1950s a number of major American companies were experiencing severe problems with their computer divisions and the financial sponsor believed that there was no future in selling these machines.

The new was linked to the traditional by renting space in an old woollen mill in Maynard, Massachusetts, where a discount store had just moved out. The early Digital managers did everything themselves, from building the offices to moving the equipment (Olsen, 1986). At the same time they learnt from practical experience about accounting and manufacturing. They responded to their sponsor's restriction by producing printed circuit logic modules instead of computers. In 1957, at the end of their first year, they found that they had made a profit. Ken Olsen had now taken control of engineering, assisted by his brother, while Harlan Anderson looked after finance and accounting.

Because they were engineers, they starting hiring other engineers and their twelfth employee, who later became Digital's senior vice-president of Engineering, was hired in 1958. Another old colleague from MIT joined the company as its first computer engineer. They recognized that they could not run a growing company on engineering knowledge alone and they began bringing in other kinds of management expertise to fill their knowledge gaps in manufacturing, marketing and other business functions. In 1960 Digital's PDP-1 was launched on the market. PDP stood for Program Data Processor— a name that was intended to conceal the fact that the machine was actually a general-purpose computer. The PDP-1's success was helped by ITT who purchased large numbers for message switching and made the product a standard for this activity.

NEW MACHINES

Since its creation Digital has directed its efforts at providing computing for the individual specialist and manager. Whereas IBM and other major computer manufacturers have focused on making large mainframes that produced vast amounts of data and required specialist teams for their operation, Digital has concentrated on small machines that could be used by a variety of staff for their everyday tasks.

In the 1960s Digital attracted more and more first class engineers, all excited at the prospect of working for an innovative and rapidly developing company. The PDP-1 was soon followed by others, including the PDP-4—a machine developed in association with the Foxboro Corporation as a real-time process controller. This took the company into the new market of OEMs. OEM stands for 'other equipment manufacturer' and refers to companies which use Digital equipment as part of their own products. Later the PDP-5 and the PDP-8 emerged, with the PDP-8, released in 1965, leading the field as the world's first minicomputer.

After the PDP-8 came the PDP-9 and 10 and then, in 1970, the very successful PDP-11. This was a 16-bit machine that helped Digital to establish and maintain its stake in the profitable OEM business throughout the early 1970s. But by 1974 it had become apparent that the PDP-11 did not have the capability that customers required and this led to the development of the first VAX systems. The letters VAX stand for Virtual Address Extension and refer to the greater memory capacity of the new machines over the PDP-11s. The VAX-11/780 machine was introduced in 1977 and reinforced Digital's position as leader in the minicomputer industry. The company now decided to concentrate on producing VAX machines and to make these the centre of an integrated product strategy. By the beginning of the 1980s Digital could pride itself on being the world's number two computer manufacturer, with IBM as number one.

Most major companies have problems as well as successes and Digital now experienced some commerical setbacks and for a short time lost its clear vision of where it was going. Senior management recognized the need for innovative thinking and developed a new and effective marketing strategy. Digital's prosperity was firmly reestablished in 1985 with the launch of the VAX 8600 and the Microvax series. It was believed that these new products would keep the Company a market leader well into the 1990s. While these products were being developed, Digital's System Research Center in Palo Alto, California, was carrying out advanced research on networks and computer architectures. This too was a major contribution to future commercial success.

DIGITAL ORGANIZATION

Considerable thought must be given to the best way of structuring the activities of any company and this was a problem that Ken Olsen and his senior managers had to address at intervals over the years. Initially the company was run like a research project. Everybody got together and made decisions. But as the scientific and technical community purchased more and more Digital machines the company began to grow rapidly in size. This required it to move from its first loosely connected network of managers who were primarily engineers to a structure more appropriate for a rapidly developing company.

In 1966 Digital became a $20 million dollar company and went public. Ken Olsen now introduced a new organizational structure based on product lines, with each product group responsible for its own profit and loss account. The product managers made the budgets and everybody else budgeted to serve them. Major functions such as sales, manufacturing and R and D were shared at a corporate level. This decentralized form of organization proved very successful and has become a model for many other companies. It enabled decision-taking and control to be clearly located in the individual product groups, yet avoided the duplication of services which all needed. Each senior manager now had responsibility for a product line—from development to marketing (Petre, 1986).

Company organizational structures become obsolete as environments alter and circumstances change. Digital encountered this problem nineteen years after the decentralized structure was first introduced. By the 1980s the product line form of organization had become bureaucratic and top heavy. Managers were competing too aggressively with each other for resources and the company contained more than thirty semi-autonomous groups. Changes had to be made.

Digital began to rethink its organization and went through a period that proved highly traumatic for many of its staff. Ken Olsen's objective was to make the company as effective as possible in its marketing activities and to provide customers with an excellent service that precisely met their needs. Digital was now producing a vast range of products and moving into new areas such as artificial intelligence and the development of software. Senior management knew that the company could make these products, they were less certain that it could sell them effectively. They decided to create a unified marketing organization that was capable of handling all new products. This required major change.

In 1983 profit and loss responsibility was finally removed from the product managers and Digital became a more conventional, functionally organized company—simpler and leaner than before. Ken Olsen now had the problem of ensuring that the new structure provided the opportunities for personal responsibility, creativity and use of initiative that he valued so highly. He did this by ensuring that decisions were taken at the lowest possible organizational level and by insisting that staff did not stay too long in any particular job. They were required to regularly acquire new skills and experience. He maintained organizational fluidity through the use of committees and task groups. These enabled problems to be thoroughly investigated from many different points of view before solutions were agreed. And so the organizational structure of Digital changed but care was taken to see that its values and culture did not.

THE ORGANIZATION OF ARTIFICIAL INTELLIGENCE IN DIGITAL

During the 1970s Digital's AI activities were located in its engineering laboratories. Then as interest in AI increased other groups and departments began to get involved. An organizational structure had to be created which would bring these together, provide them with resources, and enable them to flourish. The first initiative was the creation of a knowledge engineering group to build expert systems. In early 1981 Manufacturing requested that such a group should be formed. In July of that year the Knowledge Engineering Advanced Development Group came into existence with a staff of four AI professionals.

The goals of this group were to:

1. Obtain new knowledge engineering techniques.
2. Identify problems within Digital that might be solved by knowledge engineering.
3. Demonstrate the feasibility of the proposed solutions by creating working prototypes.
4. Collaborate with other groups in Digital to develop the prototypes into production quality software.
5. Assist in the installation of the systems into the appropriate department.
6. Evolve a plan for the organization of knowledge engineering technology within Digital.

In addition to these goals the group was to import and support various knowledge engineering tools from outside Digital; and to support and develop the LISP language for use internally.

A knowledge engineering steering group was also formed. This was a loose coalition of people interested in knowledge engineering and related subjects. Its purpose was to encourage the exchange of information about topics relevant to AI and knowledge engineering; help the members to learn about knowledge engineering, and help any others in Digital who wished to learn about the subject.

The Knowledge Engineering Advanced Development Group financed itself by obtaining funding from groups within the company who wanted expert systems built. It created two successful systems—one to assist VLSI (very large system integration), the other to assist hardware fault diagnosis.

But there was a need for a much large AI group that had its own budget and could undertake long-term as well as short-term projects. In 1982 an AI Technology Centre was set up to develop engineering, manufacturing and customer service expert system applications. This had a board of directors of senior managers so that the idea of AI could be spread across the company. It was split into a loose federation of three groups—an engineering applications group; a systems manufacturing applications group, and a customer service applications group (Polit, 1985).

The systems manufacturing applications group was headed by Dennis O'Conner, an entrepreneurial manager who had spent most of his Digital career in Manufacturing. Here he had played a major role in designing the production line for the PDP-8. He was one of the first people in Digital to recognize the great potential of AI. The systems manufacturing group later changed its name to the Intelligent Systems Technology Group (ISTG). It started with five individuals, only one of whom had an AI background. This was a deliberate policy on Dennis O'Connor's part. Because AI was new he wanted to create a real spirit of innovation—to move away from the traditional data processing professional and recruit new kinds of people with new mind sets. By 1984 the Group had grown to 77 people responsible for eight different knowledge-based systems—two of these were XCON and XSEL.

By 1987 the AI Technology Centre had a staff of 196. In addition to XCON and XSEL there were fifteen other projects. ISTG employed 119 people, 35 of whom worked on XSEL. XSEL itself contained two groups—one was a technical group, the other a development team whose primary role was to ensure that a product was developed that fully met the needs of the future users. Bruce Macdonald joined Digital in 1981 as project manager of this team.

COMPANY VALUES

The first impression that a visitor receives is of a workplace full of vitality, with many different kinds of activity taking place. There is a belief in 'action'—identifying problems, coming up with solutions, then implementing these solutions as rapidly as possible. The second impression is of an enthusiastic, creative and dedicated staff who are strongly identified with the company and its values. Digital wants leaders and innovators. It also wants employees who can learn and go on learning. Individuals are respected and the views of employees at all levels are sought and acted upon. The company nurtures its 'insubordinate minority'—the group that continually questions and challenges existing ways of doing things.

Good communication is regarded as vitally important. Staff are not encouraged to hide themselves away behind closed doors. Everything is open plan and everyone available and accessible. Status is kept in its place. Friendliness and informality are the norm and the expectation is that all employees will strive to give of their best.

Digital also tries to maintain close contact with customers—it solicits their views, respects their knowledge and works hard to establish good working relationships. The company regards their experience and needs as an important source of information for planning new hardware and software developments.

The third impression is that company values are not solely to do with business success, although this is clearly of great importance. Digital is very concerned with relationships, attitudes and behaviour as these affect employees and the outside world. This philosophy contributes to business success but does not depend on this success. Values run deeper and are an important part of the company's ethos in both good times and bad (Peters and Waterman, 1982).

Management recognizes that personal opportunity must be accompanied by an acceptance of common objectives and a willingness to work together to achieve these. Consensus is achieved through discussion and argument between everyone with an interest in a particular subject, and staff are sometimes hard to contact because they are so frequently in meetings. Digital places a high value on its employees and they in turn value their association with the company.

Digital makes its values explicit in a booklet, which it gives to employees, called *Representing Digital*. This book describes the kind of company it wants to be in terms of honesty, profit, quality, responsibility and management. Some quotes will show the company's emphasis on ethical behaviour. On 'honesty': 'when we make a commitment to customers or to employees, we feel an obligation to see that it happens'. On 'quality': 'our goal is to be a quality oganization and do a quality job which means that we will be proud of our product and of our work for years to come'. On 'management': 'meeting financial targets is only one measure of a plan; other measures are satisfied customers, development of people, meeting long-range needs of the corporation, development of new products, opening new markets, and meeting commitments made to others in the Company'.

Ken Olsen expressed his personal values in an address to the American Newcomen Society in Boston in 1982. He ended his presentation with the words,

> "Computers are making work more interesting, making it more fun, making it more satisfying. That's the business we're in—we're having more fun at it than ever before, and there is no end in sight."

EXPERIMENTS IN PARTICIPATIVE DESIGN

Forward movements in organizations often happen as a result of informal and unplanned activities. A particular manager becomes interested in a subject and creates a social network of others with similar interests—which may embrace people inside and outside the firm—and something new is started. Digital's style has always been to encourage these kinds of contact and they had an influence on the acceptance of participative design within the company.

In March 1981, Enid Mumford received a telephone call from a senior Digital manager. The caller was Gerhard Friedrich who was in the UK speaking at a conference organized by the British Psychological Society. Gerhard was the leader of a US team associated with the company's office systems program. He had trained as a Gestalt psychologist and had a great interest in fostering opportunities for personal development in the work situation. Gerhard had heard of Enid's interest in systems design and was curious about what she called 'participative design'—the involvement of the future users of a system in the systems design process (Mumford, 1983). He wanted to talk about this as he believed the approach fitted with both his own personal philosophy and with company values.

This first meeting led Gerhard to return to England in June 1981, to gather more information about participative design. In order to do this he went to visit the Tetley Walker Brewery in Warrington where a group of personnel clerks were working hard to design their own management information system. He was impressed with the systematic analysis of information needs that the clerks were carrying out in the brewery. He returned from the visit full of enthusiasm for more user involvement in systems design but anxious for additional evidence of its value. He next went to talk with Don Henshall, a systems expert who had commissioned a participative design project which Enid had managed in Rolls-Royce's Aeroengine Division in Derby, England. Don was now working with a British government agency—the Centre for National Academic Awards. He was helping its staff of one hundred to analyse their own information needs and design a new, computer-assisted, information system. Don reinforced Gerhard's growing belief that participation should be an important input into systems design and that it had relevance for Digital's internal projects in the US.

On his return to the States, Gerhard arranged for Enid to come to Digital at the beginning of September 1981. While there she visited the Concord plant and talked with a number of people who were associated with data processing and with organizational and employee development. Interestingly, the company did not appear to separate these two things. Data processing and office automation were viewed as a means for assisting the personal development and work interest of employees. They were not used as bureaucratic weapons for tightening controls or making work more routine. During the visit she gave a number of seminars on participative design and showed groups of staff video-films made during her UK projects. Her aim was to persuade them of the advantages and logic of using a participative approach.

These examples of participative design were well received; there were many expressions of interest and questions on how Digital could involve staff more closely in its own projects. One person present at this discussion was Bruce MacDonald, the new project manager for XSEL. He had joined Digital three weeks previously after a career in school administration. Bruce was an example of imaginative recruitment policy for AI initiated by Dennis O'Connor. Dennis wanted staff with fresh minds and new ideas and with the kinds of background and experience that would enable them to build and manage interdisciplinary teams and cross-functional relationships. Many of these new staff, like Bruce, came from teaching backgrounds; others were from walks of life far removed from computers and computer systems. Digital knew it was strong in technical skills. It now had a conscious policy to become equally strong in non-technical areas.

Bruce was as interested in participative design as Gerhard and this led to two streams of participative projects beginning in Digital in 1981. One was XSEL, the other was a group of projects sponsored by Gerhard and the Office Systems Group.

PARTICIPATIVE DESIGN AND OFFICE SYSTEMS

These projects were not concerned with AI but used the ETHICS method to assist a number of departments develop strategies for increasing their productivity. In 1982 and 1983 there were six projects of this kind. They were managed by members of the Office System's Group who acted as facilitators.

These early projects were less concerned with introducing new technical systems than with increasing departmental efficiency. The Office Systems team decided that this was a particularly appropriate problem area for a participative approach. As a result a business group located in Manufacturing examined how its work could be streamlined and responsibilities better aligned with authority; a group of administrative purchasing staff looked at how they could more effectively manage their information needs; district sales staff looked critically at their own performance and made recommendations for better communication and improved coordination of the sales effort; field sales staff developed a new procedure for ordering computers on-line which saved time and increased order accuracy, and a group of Headquarters sales and systems staff, working in two interfacing departments, integrated their business planning processes. This enabled them to reduce redundant operations and enhance teamwork (Mumford *et al.*, 1983).

The Office Systems Group believed that participation was helping the company to achieve good solutions to difficult problems, to avoid 'resistance to change' and to get innovation easily and enthusiastically introduced.

In the AI group Bruce MacDonald was already using the same participative approach in the XSEL project. From the start he had involved the sales force users in its development. He saw himself as both facilitator and project manager. In 1983 Gerhard Friedrich moved from Office Systems to the intelligent Systems Technology Group (ISTG) which had responsibility for the XSEL project. This meant that there were now two managers in the AI area with strong interests in participation. This contributed to the acceptance and spread of the approach within Digital.

Those concerned with the participative design projects defined their role as providing strategies, advice, resources and management to address the organizational factors that could affect the design and use of office systems. They were keen to ensure that new systems were developed and used to improve the business effectiveness of the group which owned them. They also wanted to build bridges between technology and the behavioural sciences. It was hoped that experience in using a participative approach would lead to a clear set of design and implementation principles and guidelines, and generate a user or 'customer' focus to systems design.

Digital started on the road to AI and expert systems with a strong humanistic philosophy, a belief in the value of participation and a recognition that good technical design will not, alone, solve problems. The Company recognized that the most difficult problems were likely to be those concerned with people— their attitudes, behaviour and aspirations.

Part 2
THE US DEVELOPMENT OF XSEL

Here have been swallowed up
at least twenty thousand
cart loads; yea, millions of
wholsome instructions.

John Bunyan

Chapter 4

THE TECHNICAL DEVELOPMENT OF XSEL

In 1978 Dennis O'Connor, Head of Systems Manufacturing Technology, was asked by the Vice-President of Manufacturing if he could find a solution to the configuring problem. Attempts to do this had been made since 1974 but none of these had proved very successful. Dennis had discussions with John McDermott, a professor at Carnegie-Mellon University, and John began developing a problem-solving strategy which incorporated an AI solution. At this time Digital had little idea of the skills required for developing AI technology. There were only a few seasoned practitioners in the field and so a link with a University was necessary. The company could provide John McDermott and Carnegie-Mellon with an understanding of business needs and concepts. In return CMU would provide the tools to build an expert system.

The first initiatives in building both XCON and XSEL were carried out at CMU with John McDermott acting as principal researcher. Digital had always had a close relationship with the Computer Science department at Carnegie-Mellon and work began on XCON (known as R1 at that time) in 1978. DEC began supporting the project in January 1980.

By 1980 CMU had already acquired a reputation as a pioneer in the artificial intelligence field and had made considerable progress in the development of the new languages which AI required. OPS5, the language in which XCON and XSEL were written, was the product of earlier research sponsored by the Defense Advanced Research Projects Agency (DARPA). It was a rule-based language especially suited to programs that evolved as the database was increased and new functions added (McDermott, 1982).

Both CMU and Digital believed that if artificial intelligence was to become acceptable and useful to industry, development needed to be based on a collaboration between academics and industrial companies. The academics would produce the new tools, industry would test them out and assist their own staff to acquire familiarity with the technology.

The problem initially addressed at CMU was the configuring of the VAX machines which in 1980 were forecast to be the Company's main-line family of minicomputer systems. Whether performed manually or with the assistance of an expert system, the configuration design task had two parts.

1. Component selection—identifying the set of components which were both necessary and sufficient to meet the requirements of a particular computer application.
2. Component organization—the set of components selected must be put together to form a system that satisfied the requirements of the computer application.

XCON was designed to handle component organization.

XCON was created to assist the manufacturing plants and worked in the following way. A Manufacturing 'technical editor' input to a terminal the names of the components on a customer's purchase order required to assemble a VAX machine. XCON's knowledge base was built in such a way that the system was able to recognize the required relationships between these components—which component had to fit with another and how they must fit together. It could also spot if components were missing from the list which it had received. Its output was a set of diagrams showing what the spatial relationships between the components should be, and what components needed to be added.

The language used for XCON, OPS5, was a general purpose, rule-based language related to LISP—an AI language that is much used in the US. It was developed by Charles Forgy of Carnegie-Mellon University and it provided a rule memory, a global working memory and an interpreter that tested the rules to determine which ones were satisfied by a set of descriptions in the working memory. Rules are IF-THEN statements that are checked against a collection of facts about the current situation. When the IF portion of a rule is satisfied by the facts, then the action or conclusion specified by the THEN portion is performed or stated. A medical example would be 'if the patient has spots, then the diagnosis includes measles'. A rule interpreter compares the IF portions of rules with the facts and executes the rule whose IF portion matches the facts. The rule's action may modify the set of facts in the knowledge base, for example by adding a new fact.

Examples of XCON rules for placing a power supply in a computer cabinet are:

Rule 1
IF
- the context is layout and assigning a power supply
- an sbi (system bus interconnect—boards that plug in backplanes) module of any type has been put in a cabinet
- the position it occupies in the cabinet is known
- there is space available in the cabinet for a power supply
- there is no available power supply
- the voltage and frequency of the components is known

THEN
- add an appropriate power supply

Rule 2
IF
- the context is layout and assigning a power supply (the other conditions are as in rule 1)
- there is an available power supply
THEN
- put the power supply in the cabinet in the available space

When designing XCON, OPS5's two memories were augmented by a third. This memory, the database, at first contained descriptions of each of the more than 750 components required to assemble a VAX. Each database entry consisted of the name of the component and a set of eighteen or so attribute/ value pairs that indicated the properties of the component which were relevant to the configuration task. As XCON began to configure an order, it retrieved the relevant component descriptions. As the configuration was produced, the working memory grew to contain descriptions of partial configurations, the results of various computations, and context symbols that identified the current subtask.

XCON's production memory contained the knowledge required to configure all VAX systems and some other machines. In the early days of its development this consisted of about 850 rules. By 1986 it had over 4,000 rules and a database containing more than 10,000 items. But, when it was first built it lacked certain pieces of information. All the information it received from the user was the set of components associated with a customer order. It had no knowledge of the physical characteristics of the room or rooms where the system was to be housed.

This meant that XCON could not produce a realistic floor layout even though it had the capability to do so. For example, it could not determine the precise lengths of cable required to connect certain pairs of components. It also did not know if there were any physical or other constraints that would affect the use of the system. Because of this lack of information XCON did not necessarily produce configurations that were the best, and most economical, for the customer. This only became possible as XSEL was developed. Today XCON covers the following stages of the configuration task.

1. Checking the order, looking for mismatched items and missing components.
2. Laying out the processor in cabinets.
3. Placing boxes in the input/output cabinets, and placing components in these boxes.

4. Placing panels in the input/output cabinets.
5. Laying out the floor plan.
6. Doing the cabling.

The designers of XCON had many problems to solve as they moved through the development process. Four examples were: the proliferation of cables associated with different pieces of hardware; the difficulty of ensuring that the XCON group were always informed when new items of equipment were released so that they could put these into the knowledge base; the difficulty of getting good feedback from the people testing the pilot system, and the initial slowness of the system.

The cable problem caused major frustrations. The disk and tape designers were accused of designing as if their device was the only one that Digital was concerned with. The updating problem was eventually overcome through the AI engineering group under Dennis O'Connor accepting responsibility for keeping XCON up to date. The engineers learnt how to handle the data and rule knowledge acquisition tasks on their own and were able to supply good information to XCON. A great deal of attention was also paid to the best way of getting feedback from XCON users, and many different approaches were tried. The XCON team wanted to know who were the people in manufacturing that really dealt with the XCON information, and how manufacturing actually did handle orders as opposed to how it was supposed to handle orders or how the people working there thought orders were handled. An error reporting and correcting process called XCAR was created and used with success with XCON.

Throughout XCON's development every care was taken to ensure that the need to communicate was never forgotten—there were continual discussions, visits and feedback. New members of the configuration group, used to the poor communication practices of other companies, were often surprised at the dedication to communication and consultation. They appreciated the weekly meeting of the XCON group, seeing it as a means for talking over sensitive issues and 'clearing the air'. It provided an opportunity for resolving, and dissecting all the pertinent matters in the XCON project.

In January 1980 the system was tested out in a manufacturing plant in Salem, New Hampshire. It worked well and XCON was handed over to the manufacturing plants early in 1981. The plan was to have five plants—Salem, Westminster, Marlboro, Kanata and Ayr in Scotland—start to use it by the end of January, with other plants receiving it soon after. This plan was broadly adhered to although it took each manufacturing plant some months to become familiar with XCON. As expected, there were teething problems, particularly in the Ayr plant, but these were overcome and the response to XCON was very favourable. The manufacturing plants recognized its value as a means for solving the configuration problems that had previously caused them so much anxiety.

During 1981 the implementation and development of XCON continued. The design emphasis was now on improving the system's speed, accuracy and performance. Particular attention was paid to ensuring that graphic output was produced in a form that met the users needs.

In 1981 a Vax New Products Committee was set up to check that new products conformed to VAX standards. Members of the XCON group were on this committee and this meant that they knew when new products were released and were more easily able to ensure that XCON was up to date. Between July and September of this year, 200 new products and packages were added to the XCON rule and data base and XCON grew in size at a rapid rate. The XCON group now realized that the development of an expert system was a continuous process. There would never be a time when they could say 'this system is now complete'.

DEVELOPING XSEL

While XCON was being developed Dennis O'Connor and John McDermott, became increasingly aware that the configuring problem originated in the sales offices and that while XCON helped Manufacturing it did nothing to assist Sales. There was an urgent need for an on-line configuration checking system which would make it easy for the sales force to give accurate quotes, and prevent orders travelling to and fro between Manufacturing and the sales offices because they contained errors.

John McDermott was once again asked if he could help create a prototype. The proposed system would be called XSEL, standing for eXpert SELling. XSEL would complement XCON. Its task would be to select the set of components required to assemble a particular hardware configuration. It would then inform XCON of its selection and provide any other information that XCON needed to configure the application.

One of XCON's attributes made XSEL's task considerably easier than it would otherwise have been. Much of the problem of component selection arose because salespeople, in addition to having to select components relevant to the intended uses of the system, also had to specify support components—boxes, panels, cabinets, cables etc. Part of XCON's task was to make sure that all such support components were included in the saleperson's order, and to add them if they were not. This XCON facility meant that XSEL did not need to concern itself with support components.

XSEL, in its early days, was little more than a front-end for XCON. It allowed a user to specify a central processing unit, an amount of primary memory, necessary software, and additional equipment such as tape drives, terminals, printers etc. This skeletal order was passed to XCON to be fleshed out and configured. The user interacted with the system by responding to XSEL's questions. For example:

1. XSEL asked
   'What operating system will the system use?
   Is the power 120V 50h or 240V 60h?'
2. XSEL then asked the user what components he or she wanted to order.
3. XSEL asked the user to give it the information it required in order to provide a floor layout. It also asked for any special configuration constraints that would result from the way the system would be used when operational.

Stage 1 was simple and straightforward. Stages 2 and 3 were more complex.

When asked what components were required the user could, if he or she wished, enter their names and quantities. XSEL then performed a few simple consistency checks to make sure that the components were compatible with each other and moved on to stage 3. But Digital's component naming conventions are not always easy to understand and remember and so the user was given the option of specifying the components by 'subtype' instead of name. Other options were also provided. For example, the user could identify components by their capabilities.

The provision of these options meant that XSEL had to have the knowledge of how to select among subtypes and from descriptions of capabilities. When first developed XSEL did not do this very expertly. It had a number of rules that enabled it to avoid making poor choices, but these performed only marginally well. Since then its ability to choose between alternatives has become much more discriminating.

Once the user had specified the components that were required, XSEL went on to the third stage. This involved asking a number of questions about the room or rooms in which the system would be housed. XSEL asked for the dimensions of the rooms and the positions of doorways and obstructions. The user could now state how some or all of the components on the order were to be positioned, and do this either precisely or approximately. After the floor layout information had been provided, the user could then give other configuration information—how devices were to be distributed amongst controllers, the type and length of cable to be used to connect pairs of devices; the position of boxes and panels in the cabinets. XSEL then passed to XCON the set of components ordered and any other information which the user had entered. All of XSEL's knowledge was represented in the form of rules for two reasons. First, the configuring task is applying a set of rules. Second, human beings find it easy to think in this way.

Much of the knowledge built into XSEL in its early days was not about configuring but about how to lead a user through a selection process. XSEL had to be flexible. It was important that the user could take as much or as little advantage of XSEL's expertise as he or she wanted at any point in a particular man–machine dialogue. This was a central concept in the design of XSEL. Sales force users would have different levels of configuring knowledge. New salespersons would want to make comprehensive use of XSEL as they learned how to configure. Experienced salespersons might need its assistance only for complex orders.

XSEL and XCON—What They Are and What They Do

XSEL and XCON are knowledge-based expert assistant systems designed to assist sales and manufacturing organizations in configuring computer systems from DEC's vast and rapidly changing range of products.

XSEL and XCON have five basic components:

- *The XCON knowledge base.* This is the heart of XSEL/XCON and consists of product-specific information (the component base) and Engineering and Marketing configuration rules and restrictions (the rule base).

- *The XSEL rule-base* which consists of knowledge about how saleable components can, from generic or specific input, be combined into sets of items to be submitted to XCON.

- *The inference engine* which selects the appropriate knowledge (rules and data) and applies it to the configuration sub-tasks.

- *The user-interface* software which allows users to enter and modify orders and review the system output.

- The traditional software which provides access to the data-base management system and collects performance statistics on functional accuracy and hardware utilization.

XSEL/XCON have a shared data-base which is maintained by the Intelligent Systems Technologies Group in the USA.

XSEL (the eXpert SELling assistant)

XSEL is an interactive system designed to aid the sales force in creating technically correct configurations at the pre-quote stage and thereby reduce or eliminate incorrect orders and their associated costs.

Since XSEL recognizes generic names for the components of a computer system it allows the user to build a complete system using only common terms for the functional parts. The user does not need to know details such as cables, controllers, formatters, boxes or backplanes since XSEL will add these as required.

XSEL checks marketing and technical restrictions for each component as it is entered and then when all items have been entered checks that the resulting system is complete and accurate.

XSEL includes an aid to computer room layout design. Output from XSEL is passed to XCON for further processing.

XCON (the eXpert CONfigurer)

XCON was designed for use by DEC manufacturing plants to produce configuration information for building systems. XCON carries out a more detailed validation and completeness check than XSEL. Because of its more detailed configuration knowledge XCON may suggest some changes to the set of items proposed by XSEL. If this is the case then XCON will inform the user either by adding components to the list or identifying the components on the list which could not be configured.

The output produced by XCON includes:

- Configuration layout diagrams.
- Details of additional components required to build the order.
- A list of the components which could not be configured (with reasons why).
- Details of switch settings for component addressing and vectoring.
- System cabling information.
- Unused capacity of the system.

XSEL's early knowledge also had to provide a base that would support the more specific knowledge on how to perform the component selection task that would be added later. Expert systems grow rapidly as more knowledge is put into them, and so their initial structure needs to be built in a way that enables it to support this much larger amount of knowledge. XSEL also needed to be able to systematically examine its own decision processes so that it could provide explanations of why it was taking certain decisions.

A considerable amount of knowledge was required for the configuration design task because there was no small set of principles that could be used as the basis for component selection. A customer is often not completely sure of the uses to which he will put his computer system. The best he can do is provide a general description of the requirements of each of his proposed applications. Although the component selection process was made difficult because of a lack of exact knowledge, the task of selection could be split into three subtasks. These were:

- *Decide* if a particular component is necessary for a proposed configuration.
- If one is required, *select* from among the subtypes available the subtype that best meets the need.
- If a subtype has been selected, *select* from among the variations available that variation that best meets the need.

This was mainly a *recognition* task—that of recognizing what questions must be asked before a selection could be made.

The fact that component selection was primarily a question of recognition made XSEL conceptually quite simple. XSEL's dialogue with a user moved from the general to the particular. XSEL first found out what general classes of components the user had in mind and questioned him or her about these. XSEL then determined if a particular type of component was necessary. Once the component type was determined XSEL questioned the user further until it was able to recognize the subtype (and later the variation) which best satisfied the requirements of the customer's application.

An XSEL dialogue might take the following form.

XSEL to user 'what kind of disk do you need—fixed or removable?'
The user replies 'a fixed disk'.
XSEL then asks 'what size of fixed disk?' and so on.

By the beginning of 1982 XSEL was able to do the following:

1. Guide and assist the user (normally the salesperson) in selecting a set of components to be configured.
2. Allow an order to be modified by the deletion or addition of any item, or by changing the quantity of the item.
3. Allow the entry of information about the room in which the system would be placed.
4. Allow the user to place components in the room in arrangements conforming to customer preferences.
5. Provide the user with a fully configured system based on the components ordered through XSEL.

6. Permit easy additions and deletions to configurations ordered through XSEL.

The first version of XSEL provided:

1. A configuration of a system from line items or components typed in by the user.
2. Power and electrical systems requirements and BTUs produced by the system configured.
3. A map of the system components in the customer's proposed site, given information supplied by the user.
4. Short descriptions of the line items ordered.
5. Current prices for the components listed.

Facilities planned for XSEL, version 2, included:

1. The ability to accept input regarding intended customer applications and to build a configuration based on those applications.
2. The ability to provide information about the estimated data of component availability.

The XSEL program was structured to:

1. Provide help, if the user wanted this, whenever a choice must be made.
2. Allow the user to skip any portion of the program not suited to his or her needs.
3. Permit the user to quit the system at the end of any subroutine without losing data, and in the middle of a subroutine with the maximum loss of one line of work.
4. Make it possible to shift from one part of the program to another.

Today, the user interacts with the system by reading and choosing items from a series of menus, and by entering data at appropriate points. Defaults (statements suggesting what is likely to be the correct answer) are presented at each point that requires a user response. Defaults regarding equipment choice are derived from engineering data, or from typical marketplace choices on component selection.

Most expert systems have a explanation facility—an ability to explain how the system arrives at its answers. In the early days of expert systems development many of these explanations were rudimentary and difficult for the user to understand. Little attention was paid to the kind of information that a user was likely to require when an explanation was asked for.

XSEL's explanations are still being developed and are intended to both provide the reasoning behind a particular inference or decision that the system has made, and to provide the kind of explanation that the user can easily understand and considers relevant. The kinds of explanations provided by XSEL will cover the following areas:

- Descriptions of components, definitions of properties of components, definitions of terms used in formulas.
- Values of the properties of components, data entered by the user and inferences drawn from that data, components selected, configuration constraints generated.
- Significant differences among components of the same subtype, significant differences among subtypes of the same type.

Digital management has always been keen that XSEL should incorporate a 'sizing' capability. If XSEL was given certain information about an intended application by a salesperson—for example, desired operating system, desired programming languages, desired data management capabilities, desired data communication capabilities, number and type of users, expected growth in these and desired central processing unit—then, using the sizer, it would be able to determine how many kilobytes of memory were required, how many megabytes of disk, number and type of tape drives, printers, terminals, and any other components that could be required for data communication. XSEL would then select the appropriate components to fit these specifications.

This facility is still a hope rather than a reality for the sizer has proved to be extremely difficult to develop. If it can be built in the future it will greatly extend XSEL's performance.

From the start of the XSEL design process it was agreed that the system must be 'friendly' and easy to use by a novice. To accomplish this, XSEL had a built in on-line comments facility. Users noted their frustrations and successes and these were monitored and collected by the XSEL development group. They sent back explanations of the reasons for problems and suggestions on how these might be avoided in the future. A 'help' function was also provided at every point where the user had to make a decision. Also, error messages were short, free of jargon, and told the user what corrective action to take. Very short response times, similar to those in normal conversation, were used when interactive dialogue was taking place.

XSEL, therefore, had two main functions. It was a repository of permanent information on Digital's component database, and on the configuration rules guiding the ways in which these components could be related to each other. It also had an 'advisory' role. It provided users with configurations of computer systems, and it suggested plausible ways of laying these systems out on the floor. But, like XCON, its reliability depended on accurate information reaching the XSEL database from Engineering.

XSEL, also like XCON, had to be designed so that it could easily be developed and altered to meet changes in the sales environment, and to accommodate the addition of new products. Its success depended on its ability to work efficiently but also on a number of outside factors. As well as the importance of keeping it up to date through the receipt of accurate, timely information from Engineering, and the product lines for newly engineered or newly marketed products, the sales offices had to have computers on which they could run XSEL; they had to be willing to bear the cost of doing this, and the sales force had to approve of, and want to use, this new tool.

DIGITAL'S DESIGN PHILOSOPHY FOR EXPERT SYSTEMS

In 1988 Digital published a *Guide to Expert Systems Program Management*. This was initiated by Gerhard Friedrich and prepared by Wendy Wilkerson, a member of the Intelligent Systems Technology Group (ISTG). She talked to project managers who were developing, or had developed, expert systems and produced a set of guidelines which expressed their philosophy and practice. These are summarized below.

Within Digital the expert systems design task is seen as covering the following stages:

1. The identification of a suitable business problem.
2. The initial prototyping of the solution to check its feasibility.
3. The creation of a project team. This normally consists of a mix of experts, knowledge engineers—who act as the link between the human expert and the computer—and future users.
4. The creation of a steering committee. This is very important if the expert system is to be used within Digital. The steering committee needs to include representatives from top management, particularly top management of the user area.
5. The development of a project plan.
6. The training of project team members in the technology, problem area and methods of expert systems design.
7. The creation of an initial design.
8. The development of a basic shell. A shell is an expert system structure without the comprehensive knowledge base which will enable it to operate as an expert.
9. The testing of this in the user environment.
10. Installing the system in the user environment and training the users.
11. Enhancing the system.
12. Adapting it to changing business needs.

Digital would, of course, include many of these steps in its normal systems design procedures. They are not specific to the design of expert systems.

The Guide suggests that the successful completion of the twelve stages requires interdisciplinary skills, particularly those associated with the behavioural sciences. Technical knowledge of how to build expert systems will not, on its own, lead to the creation of usable and acceptable systems.

It also states that the design and implementation of expert systems should incorporate three perspectives. These are:

1. The business/strategic perspective. This covers the identification of the business issue or problem, the analysis of risks, costs and benefits and the writing of business plans to obtain commitment and funding.

   Placing this perspective first emphasizes the crucial point that expert systems must have a pay-off in business terms.
2. The technical perspective. This ensures that the system is using the appropriate technology and that all of the technical aspects of systems design are identified and planned.
3. The human resource/organization perspective. This enables the system to be successfully transferred from the design to the operational stage, and to be smoothly introduced and acceptable to the users. It requires the identification of all users, decisions on how to involve them in design and an assessment of the potential impact of the system on them.

The most important decision in the design of an expert system is the first perspective—what problem or issue to address. Digital has always paid great attention to this question. A great deal of money has been, and will be, spent on the development of expert systems, therefore a good strategy for a confident company could be to select business problems that are already costing the firm a great deal of money.

But, the urgency of the business problem, although the most important, is not the only factor to consider at the start of the design process. There also has to be a perceived solution—and one that can be contributed to by an expert system. Expert systems are particularly good at handling problems which are complex, rapidly changing and have few human experts.

In addition, the users must be favourably disposed to the idea of an expert system and the human risks and costs must be outweighed by the potential benefits.

Digital believes that the project teams concerned with the design of expert systems must be interdisciplinary and contain a mix of skills. The members must have business knowledge and skills; also technical skills and organizational and behavioural skills. These last are concerned with motivation and participation, team building and the general management of change.

The training of the project team is seen as crucial to success and a training plan should be worked out for each team member. Key roles in the team are the project manager, the senior knowledge engineer, user representatives and a human resource/organizational development consultant. All members of the team should receive technology training—the issues, principles and tools of artificial intelligence; technical training—how to use a number of AI tools; problem domain training—the nature of the problem or business issue that is being addressed, and training in participative design and the management of change. Managing change covers problem and decision analysis—how to identify, assess and handle problems, how to interview experts and how to involve users in the design task. Digital is keen to ensure that project teams have the competence to involve users in the design of their own expert systems.

The users may be the experts who have contributed to the design of the system or they may be a completely different group. Often an expert system will have a number of users all of whom wish to make use of it in different ways. These users need to be identified at an early stage so that the needs of all of them can be reflected in the design of the system.

ISTG experience has been that during participative design the contribution of experts and future users will vary at different stages of the design task. When the objective knowledge required to solve a problem is being identified the views of the experts are likely to dominate, as they are the possessors of this knowledge. When consideration is being given to how the system can be most effectively used, then the views of the users will carry great weight.

With some complex systems different experts and different users will be required to contribute at different stages of systems development. However, ideally, expert systems design should be a group not an individual activity. A single programmer can write a program for an expert system but this is unlikely to work well unless there has been extensive consulting with the experts. Experts do not always agree and group meetings will enable them to argue through points of dissension. Similarly, users do not all want the same kinds of information, and discussion in groups will enable them to identify what information is required by all, and what is of specific interest to a particular user group.

The importance of training cannot be overstressed. The need for a training programme for the design group at the start of the project has already been mentioned. But once the expert system becomes operational there is a need for a systematic programme of user training. All users will have to understand how to work with the system effectively and be given the responsibility for identifying its errors and weaknesses.

It is very important that users should feel that they own the expert system. The use of a participative design approach can help avoid the dangerous split that sometimes occurs between active technical designers and passive user recipients. Participation should have ensured that the users have accepted ownership of the system. But the responsibilities of ownership have to be made clear. The users must accept that they can now no longer rely on the development group for all initiatives. A continuing dialogue between technologists and users must take place about problems and improvements.

IMPORTANT QUESTIONS

There are always three important questions that the designers, implementers and users of an expert system must answer. (1) Who will own and be responsible for the system throughout its existence? The system will need updating, revising and maintaining throughout its life. It should be the user's responsibility to see this is efficiently carried out.

The other questions are (2) Is the system a generic tool that will be used on more than one site? And (3) is the business problem that the system addresses one that changes rapidly? If the system is to be used on more than one site careful planning for implementation will be necessary and a wide range of support services may be required. If the business problem is a dynamic one then care must be taken to ensure that the knowledge base is always accurate and up to date.

Careful attention must also be paid to the reorganization of work. Once the expert system nears implementation the design group must give careful thought to how work is to be organized around it, and how existing roles and functions need to change. A brand-new system cannot just be dropped into an existing work organization and expected to function optimally in a situation that was never designed to receive it. If this happens the result is likely to be more confusion and less efficiency instead of vice versa.

Following the ETHICS approach, the opportunity provided by change should be used to look hard at the business mission of the user area—the primary objective of the department or function—and to answer the question 'how can we work more efficiently and effectively to achieve our mission?' A first reorganization should be directed at achieving this essential business improvement and then later adjustments can be made to accommodate the expert system and enable staff to work with it easily and comfortably. If some existing human skills are going to be lost because of the introduction of the expert system then thought must be given to the design or redesign of jobs.

It is important that new technology, and particularly that associated with expert systems should, whenever possible, be used to enhance an existing situation. Jobs should become more interesting and responsible, not less. Expert systems should therefore enable people to become more not less expert. The Digital philosophy recognizes this point very clearly and most expert systems are known as 'expert assistants'.

Lastly, new systems should always be evaluated to check that they are achieving the objectives that were set for them. Before an expert system is implemented success criteria need to be worked out and documented—the operation of the system can then be checked against these. These criteria should again be interdisciplinary. They should cover business and financial targets—the achievement of business goals and expected financial benefits; organizational goals—the creation of a well functioning work system that better achieves the business mission; job satisfaction and quality of working life goals—an increase in employee satisfaction with work and an improved work environment; and greater flexibility—an improved organizational and human ability to introduce and respond to change.

This evaluation should be carried out at regular intervals to ensure that the system is being developed in the right direction and continues to achieve those of the original goals that are still relevant.

In a large international company even a participatively designed expert system may encounter problems when it is transferred to another location where the users have not played any part in its development. An element of participation can still be introduced at this late stage. First, the new users must familiarize themselves with the system and what it has to offer, and decide how *they* want to use it. Their preferred use may be quite different from that of existing users. Second, they must decide how they want to reorganize so as to work more effectively and use the system optimally. Third, they must take part in the evaluation and their comments and reactions must form an important part of the feedback. Fourth, if they do not like it and want it, it should not be forced on them.

The Guide, therefore, at an early stage in Digital's development and use of expert systems, made the company's values very clear. Digital wished to associate a strong humanistic philosophy with the development of new technology and to recognize the need of users to influence the design of systems that they would eventually operate and own.

*Yes, there are many ways butt
down upon this; and they are
crooked and wide; but thus thou
may'st distinguish the right
from the wrong, that only being
straight and narrow.*

John Bunyan

Chapter 5

STARTING THE DESIGN TASK

POTENTIAL PROBLEMS

Embarking on the design of a major system is like setting off, in poor light, on a route that is unfamiliar to a place which has never been visited before. To arrive successfully may be difficult, even impossible. It will not be a Cook's tour with everything planned and tested beforehand. It will be more like the journey described by John Bunyan in *The Pilgrim's Progress* with many difficult and dangerous obstacles to be overcome before the promised land is reached. There may also be disappointment. The promised land may fall below expectations. The hoped for benefits may not be as great as anticipated and the automated 'expert' may find that its arrival is not greeted with a great deal of enthusiasm.

And, although great financial benefits may result from the successful application of an expert system, the fact that it is associated with an important business function means that it can easily become caught up in the internal politics of the firm. It is also likely to affect the activities and responsibilities of powerful managers and groups. The result is that its political and human effect may be as great as its business impact; it can arouse strong emotions of either resistance or support.

Another complicating factor is that large, complex expert systems take time to design and implement. The design of XSEL began in 1980 but it was not until 1988 that XSEL was fully operational in the European sales offices. During this eight-year period there were many changes of business policy within Digital and some of these impinged on XSEL and influenced attitudes towards it. The group responsible for the development of XSEL had to be aware of these changes in policy. They had to assess how they would affect top management attitudes to XSEL, and play an important communication role in showing how XSEL still fitted the new situation. This required both political and communication skills.

Problems also arose because XCON and XSEL were pioneering efforts and when XSEL was in its infancy few people had any knowledge of how to build expert systems. There was little awareness of the technical problems that would be encountered and the time it would take to solve these. Even with today's level of knowledge of how to design expert systems such problems would be considerable.

This mix of different kinds of complex problem required the understanding and management of a task containing high variety which was taking place in an extremely volatile environment. The XSEL team had to continually revise its plans, abandon selected options and choose new ones. It had to obtain support from new managers and new groups as internal organizational changes removed old activities and brought in new. It had to review its design and implementation objectives and strategies and change these to fit new business objectives.

This has been the reality of designing large, complex expert systems in all pioneering companies since the early eighties and there is no reason why the situation should change in the future. Even if technical problems become better understood, the most critical and difficult to handle problems are those resulting from a rapidly changing business environment and from internal company politics. These will continue to occur in the future. Unlike most previous computer applications, expert systems affect powerful individuals and groups. They will therefore evoke powerful positive and negative reactions. Considerable management skill will be required to manage the change process.

In July 1981 Carnegie–Mellon University provided Digital with a demonstration version of XSEL which could be used as an early pilot for testing user reaction. In July this prototype had its first public showing—to a meeting of the Digital Worldwide Automated Quotes System Steering Group held in Lexington. This was very successful. It confirmed that the OPS language worked well and created a responsive interactive software for the configuring task. The demonstration also included XFL (Xpert Floor Layout), an expert system program which showed how hardware could be most effectively situated in a customer's computer room. ISTG (Intelligent Systems Technology Group), the AI team responsible for building XSEL, aimed to have a trial version of XSEL working in the Digital engineering plant at Tewksbury, Massachusetts by September.

But already, at this very early stage, there were some anxieties about the long-term viability of XSEL. Dennis O'Connor was worried that Sales—the future users—were not showing enough interest in its progress. He saw the need for a senior sales manager to assume responsibility for XSEL, support its development and demonstrate its importance to Sales. This did not seem to be happening. Dennis's view was, 'We have been pushing the sales force, now they must start to pull'.

Dennis was concerned that Sales had made no hard commitment to implement XSEL and that the sales offices were not purchasing the necessary hardware. He wrote a note in which he stressed the need to do this, pointing out:

> 'One of the major requirements for the entire program is the installation of the VAX 11/780 computers by the sales department for their regional computer centres.

We have yet to see evidence that these have been ordered and that plans have been made to have them implemented on schedule. The absence of these computers could cause a major slip in the entire schedule to the detriment of the Company.'

Here were the first signs of a problem that affects the success of many computer-based systems—how to get the future users interested in, and committed to, a solution that another group is creating for them.

Bruce MacDonald joined Digital as Project Manager of XSEL on 17 August 1981. This was his first contact with expert systems. He arrived with some doubts on how he would make-out in a dynamic, technological environment. He saw himself as a quiet, philosophical kind of person, very different from the 'get up and go' personality usually associated with the computer industry. Digital's first step was to send him on a crash course on salesmanship. This involved going out on calls with salespeople and talking to field service staff and sales secretaries. It was a completely different world from his previous job in education—selling computers had short-term objectives and much pressure.

When Bruce arrived the XSEL team split into two groups—a technical team and a development team. Bruce was in charge of the development team. Its primary role was to gain an understanding of user needs and ensure that XSEL was designed and built to meet these. The technical team was working exclusively on XCON at this early stage.

In September the total team consisted of fourteen people. Six of these were knowledge engineers—their task was to transfer configuring knowledge from the professional engineers to the computer. Two were professional engineers, one was a data analyst. The others had management roles—project manager, software development manager, program and data-base manager. Between September and December the XCON/XSEL team expanded in size by another twelve people. At this time the annual budget of $1,200,000 required by XSEL and XCON was shared equally by four functions—Engineering, Manufacturing, Sales and Field Service.

INVOLVING THE USERS

From the start of the project it was clear to Bruce and his team that the views of the future sales office users must be important inputs to the design process. This was even more important for XSEL than it had been for XCON. XCON, located in the manufacturing plants, was used by staff with technical backgrounds. The principal requirement was that it should be accurate. The information for XCON's knowledge base had been derived from engineers, and engineers and technical editors remained responsible for maintaining its accuracy and adding to its knowledge. XSEL, however, was a tool for the sales force, many of whom did not have engineering backgrounds. XSEL had therefore to be both accurate and helpful and only the future users of the system would be able to say what kinds of attributes were either helpful or unhelpful.

Like Bruce, many of the XSEL development team members were new to Digital and new to AI. Most did not have computer science training or come from traditional software backgrounds. They include people who had previously been secretaries, technologists and school teachers. Digital provided them with informal opportunities for training—talks from John McDermott and learning on the job. Later, this training was formalized into fourteen-week courses which staff from many departments and also customers attended.

The XSEL development team recognized that user participation was the key to producing an acceptable system but early on none were very clear on how this participation could best be achieved. A strong participative philosophy is not commonly found in design groups located in a technical department. It emerged in ISTG as a result of Bruce's influence and the varied backgrounds of the development team members. These attitudes were reinforced by the company culture. Digital believed in open management and encouraged debate and discussion.

A participative approach of this kind is very different from the knowledge elicitation practice carried out with most expert systems. This relies upon obtaining knowledge for the knowledge base from experts alone, and often single experts. Future users of a system are rarely involved in its development. This selective approach to the elicitation of knowledge is very susceptible to failure. Experts do not always agree and group discussion seems essential if a consensus view is to be formed. Also, when the experts are not the users, the participation of users in systems design will assist the systems acceptance.

The XSEL team were also reluctant to develop a new system on the basis of formal written specifications alone. They believed strongly that prototyping was the way to proceed. They would provide a simple test version of the system, first obtaining an understanding of the problem from the engineer—the 'domain' expert, and from the user—the salesperson. They would then program the problem and its answer into XSEL and have the engineer and the user test it out—a 'try it and see what happens' approach.

During his first weeks as XSEL project manager, Bruce received a friendly memo from a colleague giving some good advice on how XSEL should be developed. The colleague first emphasized the importance of user involvement in the design of the system, writing,

> 'It is essential we involve the actual sales force in XSEL's design, so that we don't end up building something that the sales force can't, or won't, use.'

This statement fitted very well with Bruce's own values and intentions.

The memo then set out what a salesperson needed to know—the capabilities of hardware, its cost and availability and the technical support services which it required. It described the kind of expert system that would be acceptable to a salesperson. This must be:

1. simple to use,
2. be interruptible at any time, either by choice (i.e. a command from the user) or randomly (if the system crashed the salesperson did not lose data),
3. it must minimize the amount of time the salesperson had to spend at the keyboard,
4. it must minimize the amount of time the salesperson had to wait for information.

The memo described in detail how the system should work and continued with some general requirements for the user interface. This should be:

1. easy to learn,
2. helpful,
3. forgiving,
4. responsive,
5. and it must display the maximum amount of information in a readable way.

It must be 'easy to learn' because a busy salesperson is not going to have the time to read a 400-page manual on how to use XSEL. If XSEL is not easy to learn the sales force will not use it.

It must be 'helpful' so that if a salesperson forgets what hardware options he or she has at a particular point in the configuration process, the system will provide a reminder.

It must be 'forgiving'. If the salesperson by mistake types a command that wipes out the entire configuration he or she has been working on, then there should be a way to get it back.

It must be 'responsive' in the sense that it responds immediately to the keyboard. If it is in the middle of a lengthy computation then it will acknowledge the new command and indicate when it has finished the computation. It must display as much information as possible at all times, with the user having the option of choosing what he or she wants displayed. A window approach would enable this to happen.

As Bruce was still new to the computer industry and to XSEL, he was happy to receive this good advice and grateful to his colleague for giving it. He regarded it as a helpful contribution to the development of XSEL and one that pointed him in the right direction.

When Bruce received this memo the idea of user involvement had not been translated into action and Bruce had to create a strategy for achieving it. He now visited the Washington sales office and found that the sales force there were very keen to be involved in the design of XSEL and already had some very specific requests. For example, they wanted XSEL to be linked to AQS—

an automated quotes system that told the salesman how much a particular application would cost the customer. They wanted a means for inputting their own data into the XSEL database. They also wanted a short English language description of Digital products and an easy to use interface with the system.

After this meeting Bruce made a summary of the XSEL goals—the objectives which the system was being designed to achieve. He also began a search for a machine on which the prototype XSEL could be run and tried out by the future users. But he was still not sure how best to involve the sales force in the design of XSEL.

MOVING INTO PARTICIPATIVE DESIGN

In September 1981, Enid paid her first visit to Digital and talked about participation and the ETHICS approach. It suddenly became clear to Bruce that ETHICS was a way of solving the participation problem. He began thinking how it could be adapted to meet the needs of the XSEL development process.

Enid had developed ETHICS to assist user participation in systems design. Like Gerhard and Bruce, she was philosophically committed to this, believing that it helped produce good, acceptable systems. As influential members of the design team, users could influence business and quality of working-life objectives. They could ensure that the system they would eventually have to operate really did meet their needs.

ETHICS had first been used in a number of British companies at the beginning of the 1970s and it had gradually evolved over time. Its purpose was to assist the participation process by providing users who had not previously been involved in systems design with a set of simple analytical tools. Bruce believed that ETHICS would help the sales force approach the XSEL design task systematically through asking and answering the following questions:

a. 'Why do we need to change. What are the problems or opportunities which an expert system could solve or prevent?' If the answer to this question was 'there are none' then systems design would proceed no further.
b. 'What is our business mission in Sales? What important business objectives are we trying to achieve through the design of the system? This question was of great importance. An expert system could be an expensive white elephant unless it was seen as helping solve an important business problem, and the nature of this problem was clearly defined.'
c. 'Given this business mission, what are the key tasks that the expert system must help us carry out? Again, these must be thought through in depth and in detail or the expert system might not prove worth while.'

d. 'How is work organized at present? What are the problems that are preventing the efficient carrying out of the key tasks? How can an expert system remove or reduce these?'

Here it was important to distinguish critical problems from less important ones so that particular attention could be focused on these.

e. 'How can the goal that the expert system is directed at—more accurate and faster configuring—be achieved most effectively?' This required an examination of methods and procedures which might already be working quite well to see if they could be improved even more with the assistance of an expert system. Some tasks which could contribute to the business mission of the sales offices might not be being carried out at all and consideration should be given to incorporating these in the expert system.

SUMMARY OF ETHICS

In ETHICS the systems design activity is defined as,

> the process of creating and introducing new systems which incorporate technical and organizational components to improve business efficiency and effectiveness and the quality of working life of the employees who use or are affected by them.

By efficiency is meant removing or reducing problems so that costs are also reduced and the business works in a flexible, dynamic and streamlined manner.

By effectiveness is meant carrying out critical business activities at a higher, and more successful, level than before and introducing new activities which contribute to the better achievement of the business mission.

The ETHICS approach requires a design team, normally user led, to proceed through the following diagnostic and design steps. The members must:

1. Examine their business needs and problems and decide to consider organizational change incorporating a computer-based system.

2. Agree a clear specification of the business mission of the firm as a whole and of the department or departments which will be using, or affected by, a new computer-based system.

3. Make an analysis of efficiency needs—problems which are increasing costs and reducing the ability to achieve the business mission.

4. Make an analysis of effectiveness needs—critical tasks and functions which will 'add value' to the work of a department if existing ones are improved and new ones introduced.

5. Make an analysis of job satisfaction and quality of work needs. Aspects of work and of the work situation which are lowering morale and causing frustration.

6. Make an analysis of future change needs. Likely or planned change to which a new system must adapt.

This is similar to the 'requirements analysis' normally carried out in systems design but it has the important difference that it is a 'business' and not a 'technical' requirements analysis.

This business requirements analysis leads to the specification of *system objectives*. This step translates the needs which have been identified into a series of precise objectives which the new system must be designed to meet. It requires the:

7. Specification of efficiency, effectiveness, job satisfaction and future change objectives.

The next step is,

8. Systems design.

This will have two components—technical and organizational. Both must contribute to the objectives which have been set in step 7.

Technical design requires the acquisition or development of software and hardware that will enable a computer system to provide the information or data that the business efficiency and effectiveness objectives require.

Organizational design is the creation of a viable work structure that will facilitate the achievement of the business mission, contribute to the efficiency and effectiveness objectives that have been set for the new 'business' system, provide job satisfaction and accept easily the new technical system.

As organizational design is directly related to the achievement of the business mission, ideally it should precede technical design. The technical system should be designed to fit with it and not vice versa.

This analysis of business needs and problems at the systems requirements stage, and combination of organizational and technical factors at the design stage is the basis of the ETHICS design methodology.

f. 'What factors are causing user frustration and lowering job satisfaction?' 'How can the expert system contribute to the removal or reduction of these?'
g. 'How is the configuring activity likely to change in the future?' The answer to this question would provide an early understanding of how the expert system would need to be developed in the future.

ETHICS provided a number of methodological tools to help this analysis. A tool called 'variance anlaysis' assisted the identification of problems that were hindering efficiency. Another tool provided a means for defining and measuring job satisfaction needs.

The answers to these seven questions would provide a 'diagnosis of needs'. This diagnosis would ensure that the design of the system was not seriously commenced until the nature of the business and human problems that the expert system was to address had been carefully thought through. This step-by-step diagnostic approach would help users to cope with the complexity of the design process, but it would also provide important information which would help ensure the relevance and contribution of the final system.

ETHICS assumed that the future users of the system were the best group to collect this data. Only they had the detailed information. There was considerable evidence that the design of computer systems by technical experts alone had never worked well. It was probable that this single discipline approach was unlikely to work any better with expert systems.

Once the 'diagnosis' of needs was completed a second set of questions must be asked. These were to enable clear objectives to be set for the design of the expert system.

h. 'What specific efficiency, effectiveness and job satisfaction objectives do we want to achieve through this expert system?' These objectives would be principally derived from the diagnosis of needs but others could be added because they fitted with the business mission of the company and current or future strategy for achieving this.

Setting objectives in this way provided an evaluation tool against which the expert system could be measured once it was in use. 'Has it achieved all the business and human objectives set for it? If it has not does it need redesigning to enable it to do so?' One great advantage of expert systems is their flexibility and ease of amendment. This means that improvement is not difficult and development need never stop.

Once clear objectives had been set the last question was:

i. 'How do we achieve these objectives?'

This would lead to a consideration of different approaches to solving problems, different technical solutions, different ways of presenting and accessing data. It was the information necessary to create a usable and useful knowledge base.

As design progressed many other questions would have to be asked and answered. These included the major question 'how do we implement the system?' Experience has shown that even the best designed system may fail through poor implementation. Expert systems may be particularly vulnerable to failure at this point because of their impact on the power structure of the company. Other important questions would concern training, the organization of work around the system and updating, support and development resources.

CREATING THE USER DESIGN GROUP

Bruce was very keen to try ETHICS as a means for assisting user participation in the XSEL project. In October 1981, he began considering how best to set up a formal participation structure and create a user design group from the XSEL development team and members of the sales force. Enid had said that ETHICS worked well with different levels of participation. User involvement could be 'consultative', with user opinion being sought but the technical design group retaining total design responsibility. It could be 'representative', with elected or selected members of different user interest groups coming together with the technical specialists to form a design group. Or it could be 'consensus', with all users taking part in design meetings. This implied that the user group was a small one. Where it was large it was best to have a representative design group taking decisions, although all or most users could be given an opportunity to express their opinions as part of the decision process.

It was this last approach that Bruce thought the most appropriate. More comprehensive user involvement was not possible because XSEL development work was taking place in two physically separate locations—the Tewksbury, Massachusetts, facility and Carnegie–Mellon University in Pittsburgh. Also, the potential XSEL users in the US sales force were too scattered and too many in number to bring together as one large user design group.

It was therefore decided to create a representative design group. This would be drawn from people known to the XSEL team as interested in new tools and methods; or recommended because they were bright and energetic. The aim was to create a group which was as representative as possible of the diversity of the sales force.

Bruce first sent a letter to all those who were candidates for membership of the user design group, explaining:

> 'The plan for XSEL specifies that the product be built with the fullest possible involvement of the end users in the design of the program. This is being implemented in the US area through the User Design Group, made up of salespersons and members of the XSEL staff. Our intent in establishing such a

group is to utilize the skills and knowledge of the sales force. We are doing this to demonstrate our commitment to meeting the real needs of the ultimate user of the XSEL program, to provide the design team with insight into the salesperson's job satisfaction needs, and to help build a sense of ownership of XSEL within the sales force. EDP systems that are built without the involvement of the end user are often misunderstood, misused, or ignored.

Since this approach may differ from traditional systems design processes, and since in the short run it may add operating expense to the design phase, we include here a thumbnail sketch of the purpose and advantages of this approach.'

He went on to describe the philosophy behind ETHICS, pointing out that traditional systems design had been characterized by some or all of the following:

'Technical design has preceded and taken priority over social design; technical, not social, constraints and alternatives have been considered; the impact of technology on organizational structures has been neglected and not seen as part of the design task, and systems objectives have not included human needs such as the desire for increased job satisfaction and an improved quality of working life.'

He explained that the participative systems design process which was to be associated with XSEL, with the User Design Group at its core, was an attempt to integrate the various organizational, human, technical and task-related factors into the design process in a formal and organized manner, so that the final product brought improvement in all these areas. He told the recipients of the letter:

'We do not want to optimize one factor only, with unplanned or undesirable consequences affecting the others.'

He also listed some of the tasks that the User Design Group must contribute to:

- Improving the human/machine interface.
- Ensuring that XSEL does what is required of it.
- Checking documentation.
- Ensuring that XSEL can talk to other automated systems that affect the sales function.

And he provided a description of the composition of the User Design Group. This would have the following types of members:

- A Convenor/Facilitator. I will fill this role and act in a manner similar to that of an outside consultant. I will help define agenda items, keep the group focused on its task; ask critical questions; mediate conflict, and ensure that the group meets its work objectives and time targets.
- Representatives of the sales community. These will form a majority in the group and should come from the sales offices chosen to test the prototype XSEL program.
- Technical designers. These will include representatives from the development group at Carnegie–Mellon and from the configuration group at Tewksbury.

At the same time as writing this letter, Bruce also sent a letter to interested groups in Europe, telling them about XSEL and asking for their future help and cooperation. He had hoped to restrict the size of the User Design Group to six to eight members. This would permit one facilitator, five user representatives and one or two technical design people. But he found that the Group could not be restricted to these small numbers. Soon after the US letter went out in October 1981, just prior to the first meeting, its numbers had grown to 24; including fifteen salespeople, one field service representative and eight development team members. It was decided that the group should meet regularly and that members should visit each others sales offices to compare practice and progress with XSEL.

Although proposing to adhere closely to Enid's ETHICS methodology Bruce recognized that the XSEL project differed from the kinds of projects with which she had been involved in the UK. XSEL was a much larger software development task than any of the English projects. The User Design Group had to tackle the organizational problem of ensuring that the new technology fitted easily and smoothly into the work of sales offices and into the jobs of the sales staff. It also had to create an excellent technical tool that would do the job required of it. In many of the English projects the software was given. Here, the design task had been restricted to creating a work system and individual job roles that would assist business effectiveness and job satisfaction while at the same time accommodating the new technology. Software design had not been part of the design brief.

There were some risks in adopting a participate approach. It was asking the future users of XSEL to involve themselves in the design of a tool which had already been under development for nearly a year and which had a prototype already working. If the users rejected this prototype then the development team would have to build an entirely new tool. This was a risk that had to be taken.

Also, the participation process was likely to be an extensive one. Organizing a representative design group for the US was only a first step. As XSEL moved out into Europe and the rest of the world, user groups there would need to be involved in redesigning XSEL to meet their needs. This would require the support and understanding of management in these other areas and this might be difficult to achieve. Finally, if participation was successful with XSEL, might be possible to diffuse it to other projects. These were problems and opportunities that would have to be addressed in the future.

THE FIRST USER DESIGN GROUP MEETING

The first meeting of the User Design Group was held on 10 November 1981. The day before the meeting Bruce had strong feelings of confusion, uncertainty and unreality. He still hardly knew what XSEL was. He was supposed to be the project manager, and this sounded important. Yet he found himself crawling round the conference room on hands and knees with a screwdriver installing jacks for the phones. As he inserted the last screw and carried in the last load of equipment, he wondered how acting as an electrician and porter fitted in with his grand purpose of meeting the users and helping them to create a major new piece of software.

His anxiety continued the next day and he went into the meeting with a number of major concerns. He was worried that the sales force would reject the idea of XSEL altogether, seeing it as irrelevant to their main concern of 'selling'. He thought they might reject the approach of building XSEL as a front-end to XCON—a tool designed to solve a manufacturing problem. And he was afraid that they would see XSEL as potentially threatening since it might automate the whole task of selecting and configuring a computer system. XSEL could rob the technically oriented salesperson of the pleasure of configuring systems. In 1981 many of Digital's salespeople had technical degrees or had done engineering work before moving into Sales. Also, Digital's customers at that time were very technically oriented, and the salesperson enjoyed talking 'bits and bytes', as well as cables, hex slots, vectors and addresses.

Bruce had other anxieties. The XSEL development process was already underway, for the ISTG team had commenced work six months earlier. Would the sales force resent not being asked to participate at the very beginning of the project? He was also concerned about the use of the ETHICS methodology. He knew, from Enid, that it had been successfully applied in the UK. But it had been used in a different context—one in which secretaries or clerks designed the elements of a work system into which a new application would be embedded, but did not design the new application itself. He thought the User Design Group members might find the approach too complicated. He imagined them saying 'forget all this job satisfaction stuff, and let's just get on with building a system'. Bruce recognized that because he had come from an educational environment he might be taking too academic an approach in using an analytical methodology. Would it be better to be more results oriented, more focused on hard returns?

Even though Bruce had previously talked with each of the invitees, in some cases at great length, he felt as nervous standing in front of them that first morning as he had in front of his first class as a teacher. All of his anxieties raced through his mind as the meeting began. He had made overheads of all the questions in ETHICS, with each question on a separate sheet. He proposed to show each foil, restate the question, ask for responses and write each one down.

He began with question one from ETHICS, 'what is the problem?'. There was an immediate explosion of comments from the floor. '*It takes us months to get the right information*'. '*I get killed by my customer because I always have to go back with a change in the configuration*'. '*It takes me forever to do a configuration and then I always get it wrong because we don't have the latest rules'. 'The systems are getting so complicated now I can't keep up with them'.*

There were so many comments that Bruce had difficulty in capturing and recording them. Discussion became more and more excited. Question two from ETHICS was 'why change from our present methods?'. Bruce said, *"I think I can guess your views, but let me have them anyway."* This produced another avalanche of comment. *'The manual methods are too slow'. 'The documentation is wrong'. 'I don't have the time'. 'I need to go and sell, not read volumes of configuration data'.*

The most dramatic moment of the morning came when an energetic young member of the Boston office sales force responded to the question of how XSEL could help meet the job satisfaction needs of the salesperson. He spoke for everyone present when he said. *"Bruce, we get no satisfaction out of the present process. It's full of pain for us. Give us some help"*. His colleagues responded with murmurs of approval, a waving of arms and exhortations to *'go for it'*, and *'You've heard us, let's get moving'*.

It was now clear to Bruce that configuration was a serious problem for the sales force and that he was receiving an early vote of confidence from a wide variety of people, drawn from all over the US.

The day was made even more memorable by the successful launch of one of the early American space shuttles. Everyone cheered when they heard that the shuttle had successfully reached the stratosphere and this event seemed to reinforce the group's emerging feelings of identity and togetherness. That evening, as Bruce and the group sat down together for dinner, the mood was expansive and upbeat.

But it was later to turn out that many of Bruce's concerns were valid. They would surface again in future meetings and cause problems that had to be resolved.

XSEL AND EUROPE

In December Bruce made his first trip to Europe to discuss the means by which XSEL could be redesigned by European sales people for their own use. He was now acting as a 'seller'—trying hard to persuade European sales management that XSEL was something they really ought to buy. He visited Geneva, where Digital's European Sales headquarters was located, and also FMIC at Ayr in Scotland, FMIC (Field/Manufacturing Information Centre) was responsible for seeing that all orders given to the Manufacturing plant were correct. This technical editing function involved checking that no items of hardware, such as cables, had been omitted and that the relationships between one item of equipment and another had been set out correctly. An important aspect of FMIC's role was answering the queries of the European sales force about configuring problems. Most of these came from the UK sales offices. If Ayr found orders to be incorrect it returned these to the sales office and salesperson who had originated them.

Bruce found that some of the staff in Ayr were apprehensive about XCON and XSEL and associating expert systems with possible loss of employment. This was a not too surprising reaction as new technology has always been seen as a threat to jobs by vulnerable groups. It was very understandable in Scotland where unemployment was high in 1981, and in Ayr where Digital was one of the few large employers of labour.

The participation of the US users in the XSEL design task was going well, however. Each member of the User Design Group had now been given access to the prototype XSEL program into which John McDermott had introduced a comment facility. This meant that any member of the sales force who was testing XSEL out in practice could comment immediately he or she found anything they particularly liked or disliked about it. There was a utility program that would sweep these comments out of the system every few days so that they could be read and responded to by the XSEL development team. All the comments and responses were batched and sent back to the users. Issues that could not be easily resolved were to provide agenda items for the next User Design Group meeting. Bruce had decided that if any issues came to a formal vote he would recognize a two-thirds majority as providing the final answer. But he was to find that there was unaminity on most issues.

The development of XSEL was now successfully underway, helped by an enthusiastic group of future users who were looking forward to participating in the design of their new 'expert' tool.

STARTING THE DESIGN TASK—LESSONS TO BE LEARNT

What can be learnt from this early period in the design of XSEL—the beginning of 1980 until the end of 1981? First *the choice of problem* to address with an expert system had clearly been a good one. Configuring caused financial and public relations difficulties for the company as a whole and the first User Design Group meeting showed that it was also a difficult and serious problem for the sales force. Attempts at a solution should have high legitimacy and elicit support from both senior management and the sales force.

Second, the *choice of an individual* as project leader who had administrative rather than technical skills also seemed to have been effective. Bruce's early anxieties demonstrated that he understood some of the complexities of the situation he was going to manage. His belief in participation fitted well with the Digital open management philosophy and was favourably received by the sales force.

Third, the *use of participation* as an important part of the design process produced a situation which reflected the view of management theorist Douglas McGregor that:

'the essential task of management is to arrange organizational conditions and methods of working so that people can achieve their own goals best by directing their own efforts towards organizational objectives'. (McGregor, 1960)

The first User Design Group meeting gave the sales force an opportunity for showing their frustration with the configuring problem, providing some of the reasons for this frustration, and demonstrating their willingness to help solve it.

Bruce chose to take on the dual task of project manager and facilitator of the User Design Group. The combination of these two activities was not easy and in other situations might be best kept separate. The management role required that XSEL made efficient progress; the facilitator role that the sales force members of the User Design Group were kept interested and motivated. The ISTG development team members had also to be persuaded that they were partners and not leaders in the design task. Their role was to respond to the requests of the sales force, to build the kind of system that the sales force wanted, and to help the sales people test the early XSEL prototypes. This mix of control and facilitation is difficult to manage and firms using participative design often prefer to have as facilitator someone from another area who does not have any vested interest in the new system.

When major change is being introduced good social skills are required in both the facilitator and the managerial roles. Participation does not happen of its own accord, it requires encouragement, nurturing, knowledge transfer and good administration. Communication to the User Design Group members, to their constituents and to the steering committee has to be excellent. Conflicts have to be recognized and resolved. But the benefits of successful participation are likely to be great. In Digital it was not only a means for getting sales people interested in XSEL. It was also a way of bringing technical and business factors together and ensuring that business issues were not forgotten as the system was being designed.

The principal challenge is the effective management of social processes, but there are also technical and organizational problems that have to be managed. There is the technical challenge of selecting and mastering new hardware and software. There is the organizational challenge of creating a major new system in a dynamic culture. Difficult problems have to be coped with in environments which are both complex and in a state of rapid change. Tools, such as methods, techniques and procedures are helpful but the real demands lie in the successful management of relations within and between the different groups with an interest in the building of a new system.

In Digital this early period was the beginning of the excitement and challenge that was to be associated with XSEL throughout its development in the US. The User Design Group members initially saw themselves as visionaries and entrepreneurs. They were supremely optimistic. Everything was starting well, surely it would continue to remain so and the creation of XSEL would soon be achieved. Bruce's only uncertainty at this time came from the visit to Ayr. Was Europe somewhat ambivalent? Did the FMIC group perhaps see XSEL as a threat rather than an aid?

But, as often happens with large projects, this early optimism was to prove ill- founded and premature. Political and economic problems were to affect XSEL's progress in the US. Ayr was not to use XSEL operationally until five years later and it is possible that Bruce's visit aroused fears that were to linger, unresolved, for a considerable period of time.

Looking back it is apparent that much of the confidence displayed in 1980/ 81 was premature and based on unrealistic assumptions about the speed at which XSEL could be developed. Such over-optimism is a characteristic of the development of many new technical systems. It has the positive function of generating enthusiasm and motivation at the start of a project. Too many, and too strong, beliefs in fast progress can, however, lead to unacceptable pressure, disappointed expectations, frustration and low morale. Enthusiasm needs to be tempered with reality, but only experience can show what is realistic.

It is interesting to compare Digital's early expert system strategy with that of other firms. In XSEL and XCON Digital chose a business problem to address that was important and costing money. The person who became the XSEL project manager was an administrator, not a technologist. The sales force users of the system were active participants in the design process. The pattern in the UK has been almost entirely the opposite. Firms have moved into expert systems through tackling small, simple problems; technologists were placed in charge, and the potential users of the system were often ignored until a late stage, if not altogether. The result has been a large number of systems that have never been implemented. This has not been a complete waste of time as many firms have gained valuable experience of the technical problems of designing expert systems. The early days of XSEL suggest however that the successful design of major expert systems requires great attention to be paid to social processes. These may well be the critical factors in the successful management of technical change.

Is this the happiness you have
told me all this while of?
If we have such ill speed at
our first setting out, what
may we expect 'twixt this and
our journey's end?

John Bunyan

Chapter 6

LEARNING BY DESIGN

THE SECOND USER DESIGN GROUP MEETING

At the beginning of February 1982, XSEL was demonstrated to Digital's Sales Management Committee—the senior members of the future user group. They responded favourably and Bruce asked them if they would help the project by preparing a firm hardware plan for the sales offices so that the XSEL development group could be clear which offices had machines that would run XSEL.

He was now spending a great deal of his time becoming thoroughly familiar with XSEL and with the configuring task. As project manager he felt that he needed to know the system better than anyone else. He checked with the sales office representatives on the User Design Group to find out how many configurations sales staff did per quote; the number of quotes that were associated with an order, and the time it took them to do configurations. This information would enable the efficiency of XSEL to be evaluated. It turned out that configuring took up a considerable amount of a salesperson's time— three hours per configuration was not unusual for systems that were not packages. And as many as a dozen configurations could be completed before a final quote was given to the customer. This did, of course, vary from one salesperson to another and from product line to product line.

Bruce spent much of the early part of February preparing for the second User Design Group meeting which was to be held on the 18th and 19th of that month. He was most anxious for this to be a success as he saw each meeting helping XSEL to move a step forward. He needed to establish excellent relations with the sales force so that he could eventually visit a large number of the sales offices, demonstrate XSEL and talk with the managers about its implementation.

Any apprehension he had proved to be without foundation as the meeting was very positive and stimulating. The sales people present turned out to be a most energetic and motivated group of people. They had all spent considerable time and energy in the preceding weeks testing the first version of XSEL— using terminals linked to a VAX owned by the development team. Many comments and suggestions had arrived via the XSEL 'COMMENT' facility. At the meeting they indicated that they were keen to make fast progress with XSEL's development and testing. They wanted to discuss how best to do this.

Before the meeting all of those attending had been sent a questionnaire to complete. They had again been asked to answer a number of the questions in the ETHICS methodology. These included 'why do we need to change'?, 'what problems are preventing our working efficiently?' and 'what objectives should XSEL help us achieve?' Participants were asked to bring their completed questionnaires with them so that their views could form the basis of group discussion. At the meeting the views expressed in the questionnaires were collated and discussed.

The following reasons were given for changing from present methods:

- to improve Digital's image in the marketplace
- to improve customer satisfaction
- to improve communication and coordination between different Digital departments—e.g. Field Service and Sales
- to provide more historical and environmental information
- to reduce frustration and make jobs more fun

Problems that were seen as impeding efficiency were,

- unprofessional configuring methods
- not enough time available for configuring
- unreliable data
- information coming from different sources
- information not available, accurate or timely.

All of these problems were said to reduce the job satisfaction of sales personnel. The principal objectives of XSEL were seen as:

- to provide customers, or prospective customers, with configuration and pricing information in an efficient and timely manner
- to provide this in a form the customer can understand
- to create a user friendly system

In the discussion many suggestions were made on the kinds of improvement that would increase XSEL's value. The salespeople told Bruce that the LISP-based code was too slow and that the system, in its present form, created a barrage of output files. These would quickly swamp sales office machines when the system was implemented. There were also many comments about the user interface. This was built to run on hard copy as well as video terminals and was therefore simple and slow. A salesperson from the Washington DC office made these criticisms clear, saying, "This does not feel like an expert system to me. Where's the expertise?" This was a theme the User Design Group would return to in the future. Although XSEL was called an expert system and had a growing rule-based knowledge base, it was a very slow expert. *"Why does it take so long?"* asked the User Design Group members.

There was also a continuing series of questions about XSEL's ability to provide information and the mystery of the process underlying this. Bruce told the group that the development team had decided to provide, initially, only essential information. This would save time for the user. "But we need to know something about what is happening underneath", said the Washington salesperson. "We can use that with the customer. And it will help new users learn from the system." Bruce noted the point, which everyone in the group agreed was important.

He next asked the Group for their views on XSEL's general performance. A Houston salesperson was vehement about this. "You will not make it in the sales environment with the performance of the system as it is. It just takes too many cpu cycles to get to the bottom line." The development group had always known that the LISP-based code would be a problem, and Bruce acknowledged this fact and promised to work on it. He knew that it would mean developing a new compiler for OPS5 as OPS5 was compiled into LISP for execution. He also knew that this problem was not going to be quickly solved. The Houston salesperson, who was technically qualified, knew this too. "This is going to be a hard one, isn't it?", he said. The development team member responsible for handling this aspect of software design was present at the meeting. He replied "you're right. It will take some time".

The early XSEL incorporated a prototype delivery estimator, which told the users when items of equipment could be delivered to customers. This had been achieved by transferring data that was supplied through an existing manual process into electronically readable format. After XSEL had selected components and configured them, the user could ask to see a set of delivery dates for the chosen configuration. The development team had seen this innovation as a very good idea and Bruce was pleased that this new feature had been built into the prototype so quickly. The sales force had said that it would be a useful thing to have.

It was shown to the users at the second User Design Group meeting. There was immediate trouble. "Where do you get the data for this thing?", asked a member of the Washington DC sales office. Bruce told him that it came from the paper 'delivery estimator' that went out to the sales offices every two weeks or so. The Washington salesperson turned to his colleagues with a look of amazement. "You took that!", he exclaimed. "If that is what you're using take it out of XSEL straightaway" said someone else. "It has never been accurate, it is not now, and it never will be so far as I can tell."

Bruce defended his innovation by saying that the development group knew the data was not accurate at the moment, but that they wanted to test the concept and the way the feature might work in the system. A senior salesperson was not impressed. "Don't waste your time on things that might be nice to have if only they worked. Get the basics of the system right. Make it fast and accurate. You don't need all these other things." The clarity, force and impact of this user input had a powerful impact on Bruce. He decided to remove the delivery estimator section of the code from the prototype immediately.

Despite these comments, the general consensus was that XSEL would become a useful tool and that the User Design Group's first priority should be to make it as robust as possible before allowing it to be used by a larger group of sales staff. They decided to try and get XSEL close to handling 10 per cent of all US VAX quotes by the end of March.

At the end of the meeting all those present were asked to give some thought to how XSEL could be financially evaluated. Bruce asked "how can today's practice be compared with tomorrow's when XSEL is operational? What tangible and intangible factors can be measured. Will you think about this and let us know?"

The User Design Group decided to meet again in early July. The purpose of this meeting would be to tell the XSEL development team whether it should extend the field test to other users. Before doing this it was crucial to establish that XSEL was stable and capable of handling a large number of less sophisticated users who might not have the dedication and zeal of the first group. There was a feeling that it was unreasonable to involve more sales-people in the tests before July, because the January to March period required a great deal of concentrated sales effort. The plan was to have XSEL operational in the sales offices in 1983.

Reviewing the meeting afterwards Bruce came to the conclusion that systems design was a very complex process. To be successful there must be a good integration between the technology, the users and their tasks and responsibilities and the needs of the company. The choice and design of the technology must help the successful performance of the selling task; the nature of this task must provide the users with job satisfaction, and the interaction of the technology, task and people variables must be a positive one that helped the sales offices to achieve their 'mission' of more effective selling and improved customer satisfaction.

He had also discovered that the selling operation was not necessarily carried out in exactly the same way in each sales office. It varied with management style, length of service and knowledge of the system ordered. He wondered if these differences should be resolved and a common approach agreed before the design of XSEL progressed too far? Or should the system be built to accept a variety of work practice?

This absence of a common way of performing tasks or solving problems is a difficulty frequently experienced when expert systems are being developed and a participative design approach greatly helps its solution. Because different interest groups are represented in the design meetings, procedural variations can be talked through and agreement reached on what needs to be standardized and what can be left flexible.

During 1982 the development of XSEL made progress although difficulties were encountered—some unexpected and some expected. For example, few sales staff had personal terminals. This meant that, at first, the salespeople in the User Design Group could not test XSEL out in the form in which it would finally be used. The development team therefore had to provide terminals for the members of the group. There was discussion of the tasks that XSEL should be able to perform and a request that it should 'size' systems by indicating the amount of memory, size of disks etc. that a particular system required to cater for its users. Some work was done on sizing but it was too early in XSEL's life to bring this to fruition. There were also database and systems problems that had to be solved. It took longer to get XSEL into a robust state than either Bruce, his team, or John McDermott had anticipated. The goal of using XSEL for 10 per cent of VAX orders slipped from the end of March to the end of September.

But problems were compensated for by successes and, at the end of February, 1982, there was a major technical breakthrough when a BLISS version of the original OPS compiler went into operation. BLISS was a higher level language than LISP and it enabled XSEL to run more efficiently. XSEL's speed became twice as fast. "BLISS is bliss" said the XSEL development team.

The need for XSEL was increasingly being recognized within Digital. There was no reduction in the number of order errors arriving at the manufacturing plants. In the United States 25 per cent of orders had these errors. In Europe the error figure was 35 per cent.

Digital now began to get some press publicity for its AI efforts. On 8 March 1982, an article appeared in *Business Week* under the title, 'Artificial Intelligence: the second computer age begins'. The author wrote,

> 'The world stands on the threshold of a second computer age. New technology now moving out of the laboratory is starting to change the computer from a fantastically fast calculating machine to a device that mimics human thought processes—giving machines the capability to reason, make judgements, and even learn.
>
> A program called XCON, for example, helps Digital Equipment Corporation select components and put together large computer systems to meet specific customer needs at the lowest possible cost.
>
> And now businessmen are beginning to recognize that research in A.I. could have big payoffs. The cutting edge of applied A.I. is now the expert system.'

PREPARING FOR IMPLEMENTATION

By March a few high volume sales offices were online for testing XSEL and it was hoped to release XSEL to the US sales offices in the fall of 1982. Bruce began to make plans for a 'get on board with XSEL' trip round the sales offices and prepared a release schedule. Washington DC would receive XSEL in August and thirteen other offices would receive the system in turn between August 1982 and September 1983. This plan was very optimistic and for it to be realized many of the existing problems would need to be rapidly solved. Not all of these could be addressed by Bruce for a great deal of XSEL's development was still taking place at Carnegie–Mellon University. Ownership was not officially transferred to Digital until July 1982.

In June, Bruce produced a draft XSEL implementation plan for the sales offices and made preparations for the third User Design Group meeting to be held in July. The implementation plan was a substantial document which covered the resources and procedures that would be used, XSEL's training requirements and future changes in the system. The plan covered implementation in both the US and Europe. It listed four crucial factors on which successful implementation depended. These were:

1. the provision of VAX machines to support XSEL in the sales offices,
2. the commitment of area management to install XSEL on these machines,
3. the willingness of management to budget for hardware purchases and operating expenses,
4. the development of the planned software links between XSEL and AQS— the automated quote system.

The plan also had a number of appendices. These described the design philosophy used with XSEL; the tasks that had to be completed to make it operational; how it would be tested initially; a user procedures guide, and a data centre procedures guide.

Bruce recognized that all was not yet cut and dried. Many technical, economic and administrative uncertainties would have to be quickly resolved if the proposed implementation schedule was to work. In the event he found that hardware availability could not be guaranteed. His team experienced great difficulty in getting the sales offices to buy VAXs to support XSEL. They had thought that they could convince Sales to do this more easily than proved to be the case. An even more serious problem was that senior sales management still did not seem to have an active interest in XSEL. The development team was concerned that Sales Administration was doing very little about XSEL's implementation.

At the end of June Bruce began to prepare for the next User Design Group meeting. Except in those parts of the meeting which would be devoted to a discussion of the technical aspects of the configuration task, he proposed to once again use the ETHICS method framework to organize discussion on the development of XSEL. The previous meetings had shown that the methodology covered all the substantive matters related to the development of an automated configuration tool.

Because senior sales management was not taking the initiative with XSEL, the User Design Group assumed an increasingly important role in XSEL's development. It was proving to be an excellent vehicle for ensuring that XSEL was built with the needs of the user in mind. Unfortunately, only a relatively small group of users could be present at any Design Group meeting. This meant that there had to be a constant check that those attending really did represent the majority viewpoint of the sales force.

Bruce found that one of the most difficult aspects of using a participative approach was setting the tasks for, and the expectations of, the User Design Group. The members were all very busy, pressurized salespeople who were not normally involved in the design stage of software development. He had to stress, and repeat many times, the nature of their commitment as members of a design team. Their previous experience as users of software designed by others had conditioned them to reject, and not use, systems which they did not find useful. They had never been in a situation where it was their responsibility to develop software.

As User Design Group members their role was now fundamentally different. It was to help uncover problems in the design and coding of the program itself. Bruce had to constantly remind them of this point. They must avoid rapid reactions and change to an approach involving thought, the weighing of alternatives, and the suspension of judgement. Hopefully, the result would be an expert system designed by them and for them which would exactly meet their needs.

The third User Design Group meeting was held on the 8th and 9th of July in the Hilton-Colonial Hotel, Boston. The group attending was a large one. Forty-four people were present of whom fourteen were from sales and twenty from the XSEL development team. The remainder were from Field Service, New Products Marketing and other interested groups. Dennis O'Connor and John McDermott were also present.

Bruce began the meeting with some introductory remarks, saying:

> "There is now a great deal of expert systems activity taking place in Digital. This reflects an increased awareness that artificial intelligence and expert systems can help us solve a number of problems that we have previously seen as intractable. XCON and XSEL are receiving increased attention both within the company and in the outside world.
>
> At this meeting we want to work on a production version of XSEL that can be tested in the sales offices."

The User Design Group then spent a great deal of time discussing XSEL's current state. Dennis O'Conner, for example, wanted definite information on when XSEL would be released. He was concerned that other groups in the company should be able to plan how and when to hook into it. He also wanted to ensure that XSEL would integrate with all the other automated systems that were being developed by Digital for its own use.

Another important issue was how XSEL could be regularly updated so that the data base was always complete and correct. A number of groups had first knowledge of new products—design engineers, product managers etc.—but they did not always pass this knowledge on. The XSEL development team needed to create a system for acquiring this information; checking its accuracy, and inputting it into XSEL as soon as it was available.

Other questions were concerned with how the sales force could be helped to use XSEL. Some users would be experienced configurers, others complete novices. Could the system have a beginner mode and an advanced mode? What would happen if a number of sales staff were trying to use XSEL simultaneously? Who had line responsibility in each sales office for sorting problems out?

There were also a number of questions on the human and organizational impact of XSEL. A salesperson expressed anxiety about whether expert systems could remove human skills. He asked:

> "Will it make us less technically efficient? The 'intelligence' needed to do the task is built into the system and we need never learn to configure on our own".

This was a difficult question and Bruce had to make a diplomatic reply. He said what he believed to be true—that everything could not be put into the system. An informed sales force was still very necessary.

The User Design Group next spent some time restating and confirming what they saw as the desirable characteristics for XSEL. XSEL should be:

- based on a sales view of the configuring problem.
- Knowledge acquisition should be done at the 'front end'—information should be obtained from the salesperson.
- XSEL should provide answers on the basis of a reasonable amount of dialogue.
- There must be a natural language interface.
- Knowledge must be collected from several domains.
- XSEL must have the ability to explain why it does what it does.
- It must be easily implemented and rapidly developed.
- It must be used as a teaching/learning vehicle.

Finally, discussion was focused on how XSEL could best be moved from its development status to a production tool. Bruce referred to some of the problems that had to be overcome before this could be done. He said:

> "there is a philosophical agreement that XSEL is a good thing. But sales managers have not yet signed the necessary requisitions to get hardware and software

support for XSEL. Our goal is for the first three sales offices to have XSEL this quarter and for all sales offices to be using it this fiscal year."

This led to a consideration of the implementation plan. Three critical issues that must be addressed were training, support and synchronizing product releases. Training would be carried out in the sales offices and a training package would be developed by the XSEL team in collaboration with Sales Training. XSEL would initially be run on a central, corporate VAX. This had unexpectedly become available and could be used for a year, perhaps longer. This machine would enable the Santa Clara, Washington and Chicago sales offices to be running XSEL by September.

John McDermott said that he would deliver the latest version of XSEL to Bruce at the end of July. The data base now contained 2101 items—everything that was contained in Digital's April 1982, VAX systems and options summary list.

XSEL's progress appeared to be excellent, but Bruce felt that it would be wise to end on a note of caution. He told the User Design Group,

"It will work well, providing things proceed as scheduled. The scenario could be upset by unforseen problems with the software or with machine availability."

Despite this warning, the meeting ended on a note of excitement and optimism. There were plans to create a European design team so that XSEL could be implemented in European sales offices before the end of 1982.

Bruce's note of caution turned out to be justified. XSEL did not, in fact, run in the Washington and Chicago offices until 1985. It went into Santa Clara in March 1986. The reason for this delay was that the implementation plan was changed a number of times after this meeting and other offices acquired XSEL before these. But the story of XSEL's implementation in the United States is characterized by frequent change and delay. This was the result of a number of factors—the over-optimism of the development team; the inherent difficulty of automating the sales function; the newness of the technology; and the decentralized nature of Digital.

In July, 1982, the ownership and development of XSEL was transferred from Carnegie–Mellon University to Digital. The XSEL development team was now thinking hard about how XSEL could be integrated with other tools that were being developed within DEC. XSEL was the first interactive configuration tool to be designed for use by salespeople, but other tools and procedures had been, or were being, developed, that also had an impact on the work of a sales office. For example, AQS, an automated quote system that calculated the exact cost of a customer's order, would soon be in the sales offices.

The team recognised that XSEL's acceptability depended on it fitting with, and enhancing, these other support systems and began making plans to ensure that linkages were built between the new tools. Once this was done the linked programs would make it possible for a configuration to be generated correctly at the point of sale, quoted correctly and completely, and then be inserted into the order administration system without the data having to be keyed in again. XSEL was valuable as a stand-alone system but it would prove even more advantageous as a closely linked part of a total electronic order generation and handling system. It was decided that the target date for the completion of this linked system should be the middle of 1984.

As the date of XSEL implementation was approaching fast, the development team gave a great deal of thought to how hardware support could be provided. The plan was to make XSEL available on a cluster of VAX machines. Connections from this VAX cluster to a number of US sales offices would take place during 1983 and other VAX machines were scheduled to be located in sales offices during this period. These machine resources should enable XSEL to be distributed to all sales offices with access to a VAX by mid-1984.

Plans were also being made to introduce XSEL into Europe. Bruce held a number of meetings with the European Sales Productivity Manager in the United States, to discuss the best approach. He decided that sites should be chosen on the basis of machine availability and user interest. Munich and Cologne would be good sales offices to start with. It was important to introduce XSEL as a prototype for European use at an early stage, and to start up a European User Design Group so that its design could take account of the needs of the European user community. Bruce hoped to start a user design effort in Europe, supported by XSEL, by November, 1982.

The rest of the world was also being informed about XSEL. A demonstration of XSEL had been given to the Ottawa Sales office the previous November. Canada formed part of what Digital called its GIA group (General International Area). XCON was now being used there on a production basis to configure a number of VAX models. It operated from the Kanata plant via a telephone link to the US and it would not be difficult to incorporate XSEL into this link.

But, again, all this planning proved to be over-optimistic. XSEL's introduction into Canada would prove relatively easy but the move into Europe was to involve a long slow haul before it was accomplished.

AN UNEXPECTED CHALLENGE

In September, 1982, Bruce came under considerable and unexpected pressure. He, and the manager of US sales systems, had a meeting with the Vice-President, US Sales, and his staff and were challenged with the words, "why can't we have XSEL out by Christmas"?

This Vice-President had been a funder of XSEL from the start, and was the obvious candidate for the 'champion' role, but all along it had proved impossible to get more than money from him. He was so busy running the US

Sales function that regular communication was difficult. As a result he became a funder but not the champion that XSEL needed. Now, after months of apparent lack of interest, he jumped into the fray.

He expressed with some force the view that XSEL should be in the sales offices by Christmas. He wanted to know why this could not happen, saying with some vigour:

> "Look, I want to give the sales force a Christmas present, I want them to have these productivity tools we've been talking about for so long. What's preventing us?"

The US Sales Systems manager replied that the problem was mainly a lack of hardware. Bruce also referred to difficulties—saying that some software changes had to be made before XSEL could be put into production use. But Bruce's words could have been understood as meaning that these changes were relatively minor and the Vice-President did interpret them in this way.

The US Sales Systems manager, put on the spot, assured the Vice-President that he could get the hardware necessary to give all the US sales force access to XSEL by Christmas. Bruce then felt that he had little option but to say that the software could also be ready by that time.

Bruce felt caught in a trap at this point and, in retrospect, perhaps should have informed the Vice-President of XSEL's true state. This was that there were still too many problems for it to be implemented so widely and so quickly. Yet, other ISTG managers had told this Vice-President that rapid progress was being made and, in general, there was much 'hype' about expert systems, and specifically about XSEL and XCON. Managing the overly optimistic expectations of some executives had become a major problem. Now, here was the only potential champion of XSEL offering to solve the implementation problem at last. It seemed to Bruce that to tell him the software was not ready was to consign the project to instant death. Yet to accept the challenge seemed equally fatal. Bruce took a deep breath and decided that he would rather die trying than be killed on the spot.

Bruce left the meeting stunned and filled with apprehension. He had gone there to make a progress report. Instead he had made a commitment to implement XSEL and make it available to all US sales representatives by Christmas—which was less than four months away. He knew that this was not possible. He was convinced that the necessary hardware would not be available until April, 1983, and he believed that considerable work on the software was still required. This belief turned out to be correct as the software was not ready for another year. It was completed in September, 1983. Even then all problems had not been eliminated.

Despite his fears Bruce had no alternative but to begin planning for a fast implementation of XSEL. The development team decided to introduce XSEL on an area basis, and to provide all sales representatives with terminals. But it became increasingly clear that they were on a disaster course. The portable hard copy terminals that were available were too complex and heavy; the regional software teams who would have to provide space for XSEL on their machines were not committed to optimize its use and XSEL would have to run in parallel with other applications. This would slow it down, lead to poor performance and make users reluctant to use it.

John McDermott, the Carnegie–Mellon consultant, was also concerned. As he had been responsible for the early development of XSEL he was very aware of its present shortcomings. He questioned whether the XSEL development team would be able to respond to user problems; whether monthly release of updated information would be enough, and whether new product information could be obtained fast enough to fit with the sales force's requirements.

Nevertheless, despite all these anxieties the Vice-President's thrust did have the positive result of acting as a motivator and the XSEL team set out to meet his Christmas deadline. The first proper test of the system by the sales force members of the User Designer Group took place in October 1982 and, although in a rudimentary state, it proved acceptable. The rule base now contained around one thousand rules.

FIRST ATTEMPTS IN EUROPE

During this period of trauma an attempt was made to test XSEL out in Europe by running a pilot in the Cologne office. Bruce went to Cologne in November to set up the system so that the German sales staff could try it out and feed back their comments and criticisms to the development group. But he immediately encountered serious problems. XSEL in Cologne was being run on a machine located in Munich and users had to move through a number of switches to access this machine. Special software was required to enable users to access XSEL at all and the Cologne sales office did not have any terminals. Bruce felt that he had been caught unprepared. He should have anticipated these kinds of problems.

He had also underestimated the cultural and business practice differences between German and United States sales staff. He had intended that the participative design approach which had proved so successful in the US should also be used in Europe. He wanted the design of the European version of XSEL to be carried out by the European sales representatives. But he was not able to get this message across to the German sales staff. They assumed that the XSEL team were giving them finished software to test and did not understand that they were being asked to play a role in developing the software.

This misunderstanding, the poor performance of the prototype software, and the other problems led to criticism of XSEL and Bruce reluctantly decided that it was best to abandon the Cologne test.

Back in the US the search continued for machine capacity on which to run XSEL. The development team now realized that the file system of XSEL would have to be changed. The existing system required too much disk capacity and there was a need to create a data-base store system. If this was not done XSEL would overwhelm any disk capacity that could be provided by the sales offices.

By January 1983, all were aware that the Vice-President's Christmas date had been missed. The hardware was not yet available in the sales offices. From Bruce's point of view this was a good thing as the software was still far from ready. The XSEL team still had no defined test plan, they were rewriting major sections of the code and changing the way configurations were stored in the knowledge base. Everything was still very uncertain.

1982—PROBLEMS AND SUCCESSES

This was a period of testing and refinement as XSEL was turned into a viable product. At the start of 1982 the philosophy of user participation had to be firmly established and reinforced and the importance of integrating technical and organizational factors recognized by the members of the new User Design Group. They also had to accept that they were in a development role and understand what this involved. They were not there to criticize the embryonic XSEL but to improve it. XSEL's relevance and success depended on their inputs to the design process.

As might be expected there were both technical and human problems and successes during the year. Difficulties arose as a result of the development group's lack of knowledge of the technical problems that would be encountered and the time it would take to solve these. A shortage of terminals and machines in the sales offices held back implementation plans. This was unfortunate but at the same time it provided Bruce with a welcome breathing space as some of XSEL's software problems were not easy to overcome. The new BLISS compiler for XSEL proved a major technical breakthrough and greatly accelerated XSEL's speed of response.

The most difficult human problems were relations with senior sales management. These were caused by enthusiasm without knowledge and acceptance without action. Throughout the project Bruce had difficulty in finding a sponsor for XSEL at the top of the Sales hierarchy. When he did find a Vice-President who was enthusiastic about XSEL this individual had too high expectations of its progress. Not understanding the complexity of expert system design he demanded that XSEL should be implemented much sooner than was possible. The problems with senior field sales management were different. They were driven by short-term deadlines and were not greatly interested in long-term solutions. They had not been involved in XSEL's development, did not understand it and were reluctant to provide the machine resources necessary for its rapid implementation.

The lesson here is the importance of having a senior user manager as sponsor of a major project. He must feel the project is for him and his staff, be identified with it, understand what is involved in time and resources and take control of it. The existence of a top management steering committee that guides the User Design Group can facilitate this sense of ownership. Bruce had intended to form a steering committee for XSEL, but had continually put off the task as he addressed more tangible concerns. Through all these early years there was not true management steering committee to take ownership of the project, help steer it, and address the inevitable top management issues that arise during a large project such as XSEL.

Europe too produced difficulties for Bruce. The test of XSEL in the Cologne sales office was not a success and European senior management showed little interest in the new system and what it had to offer. Human problems were proving much more difficult to manage than technical ones.

The complexity of the design task was increasing rather than decreasing as XSEL grew. Bruce's major tasks were the protection of the development team and the User Design Group from external turbulence, the search for a senior sales manager as sponsor and the convincing of Field Sales management that XSEL was of value. In addition he had to ensure that XSEL was efficiently built and met the needs of the sales force users. This last was the least of his problems. Due to the influence of the User Design Group, the sales force were enthusiastic about XSEL and keen to have it implemented.

A continuing problem at this early stage of the project was the degree of over-optimism shown by everyone concerned with XSEL. Many of the objectives that were set were quite unrealistic—for example, the aim to have XSEL handling 10 per cent of all quotations by the end of March, 1982. No one really understood the difficulties of designing such a large, pioneering system.

Good Will: *An open door is set*
before thee and no
man can shut it.

Christian: *Now I begin to reap*
the benefits of my
hazards.

John Bunyan

Chapter 7

IMPROVEMENT AND IMPLEMENTATION

THE FOURTH USER DESIGN GROUP MEETING

The fourth meeting of the user design group took place on 13 and 14 January 1983. Bruce opened the proceedings by providing a general update of the status of XCON, XSEL and the other AI expert systems.

He told those present that the hardware situation was now improving. Sales management had ordered seven VAX machines for the sales offices, together with a large number of terminals. These machines were for XSEL and for DECmail—the electronic mail system. Two of the seven had now arrived together with some of the terminals. The goal was to have one VAX machine in each sales district.

Training was being given a lot of attention. The goal of XSEL was to free the salesperson from administrative drudgery and let him or her concentrate on what they were best at—'selling'. But access to XSEL would not take place until the users were sufficiently trained. The salesperson's first experience of the system must be a positive one.

The User Design Group considered these points and had a lively discussion on training. What exactly should be given to the first large group of XSEL users? How much training did they need and was video-tape a good way of reinforcing instruction? A Corporate salesperson stressed the importance of training as a means for avoiding problems. He pointed out that people needed to learn how to use XSEL effectively. Good hands on training could prevent many problems occurring. Another salesperson recounted his personal experience with XSEL.

> "I read the manual and had half a day's training. I then used the system for a while. I found I had only a few problems. One of these was getting access to XSEL via my terminal. In my view the people who need XSEL will be motivated to learn how to use it."

A third described how he had got some salespeople in his office to try out XSEL. Most had needed only a few hours of training before they could use it on their own with only occasional help from him. He stressed that the people who most needed the system were the ones most motivated to use it.

Bruce was delighted to hear this. The development team's goal had always been to produce a system that was largely self-teaching. This report bolstered his sense that they were approaching that goal.

Bruce reported that it was planned to give the trainers from each region a two-hour session on 21 January. This would concentrate on providing them with an understanding of XSEL and what it had to offer. Four weeks before XSEL was released to the sales offices they would have a two-day practical session. The aim of this would be to teach them how to use XSEL software and how to deal with user problems. They would then be asked to go away and use XSEL. A further in-depth training session would be provided once they were familiar with XSEL.

This proposal raised many questions in the Design Group. Should training start with one sales district only? Training for XSEL was still a relatively unknown task. Could computer-aided instruction be used as a training aid? How much information did users need to have about the terminal, computer and operating system before they could start using XSEL?

The Design Group moved on to the problems which they had encountered when testing XSEL. These were many and varied. For example, could XSEL provide a 'help' facility for commands? Could the flow of the program be improved? What effect would the existing problems have on the input of new product data?

It was decided that the XSEL development team should let the Design Group have a list of rarely used options so that they could see how XSEL handled these. The Design Group should also try and put a large amount of data through XSEL and test it to its limit.

Bruce stressed that once a large number of users were testing XSEL, feedback from this group to the development team was essential if the sytem was to be of a high quality. All salespersons in the larger pilot would be asked to use XSEL's 'COMMENT' facility so that the development team could learn of their problems and their successes. It was also psychologically important to have a feedback mechanism from the development team to the users. To facilitate this it was hoped to create 28 district coordinators of XSEL. They would report back to seven regional coordinators who would channel all comments to the development team and send results, answers and corrections back to the users.

Quality was another issue for discussion. A district sales manager pointed out that each regional sales team had its own set of goals and the XSEL development team must ensure that the system helped their achievement. He stressed that problems could occur because Digital was always evolving. This meant that new products and capabilities had constantly to be added to XSEL. Doing this was not easy and the new product data was not always comprehensive. He said, "let's work together to get this straightened out".

It was agreed that there must be a regional support function. The support group would be trained and maintained by the XSEL development team. It would handle user problems and pass all non-trivial problems, and design suggestions, to the development team. It was also decided that the first release of XSEL should not be too ambitious. It would concentrate on certain aspects of the configuring task—for example, component selection and how to create a limited room plan. Restricting XSEL in its early days would avoid arousing expectations in users which might later be disappointed. The general opinion of the User Design Group was that XSEL should not be released to the sales offices until it could provide 95 per cent accuracy in all configurations; it could handle all announced products, and a total configuration run took less than thirty minutes.

John McDermott was present at this meeting. He was now working on the 'sizing' facility that the sales force wanted as part of XSEL and described his approach in some detail.

At the end of the meeting Bruce asked the User Design Group to go away and do some work for XSEL. The development team needed to know all the problems they experienced and the queries that came up as they tried to operate it. It was also important to know the vocabulary which the sales force used in their day-to-day work so that XSEL could respond to their normal language.

Bruce went away from this meeting in high spirits. He felt that the User Design Group was showing great optimism and promise.

Waiting for the new VAXs to arrive in the sales offices provided him with a much needed breathing space. During February, 1983, he prepared budgets for sales, made operating cost analyses—which demonstrated that XSEL's costs were low when compared with the opportunities which it offered—and did some work on the 'sizing' function in XSEL. The Vice-President who had wanted XSEL 'ready by Christmas' had moved into marketing. This meant that XSEL no longer had a sponsor in the senior management group. Bruce was once more looking for a senior person in Sales who would accept 'owner-ship' of XSEL and responsibility for its resourcing, implementation and use. Although sales people in general were very interested and positive about XSEL, no senior manager was saying *"it is mine. I own it and will accept responsibility for it."*

DIGITAL REORGANIZES

XSEL's implementation had now been moved to July and Bruce was proposing to start the formal training for XSEL in the July to September period. A complicating factor was that major organizational changes were taking place within Digital. This reorganization meant that people at every level were far too busy with other things to worry about XSEL.

The reorganization was due to a recognition that the company was becoming too segmented and needed to reunify. This could be assisted by a reduction in product lines and a simpler organization structure. But the steps taken to change the company had a considerable impact and caused much stress during the summer and fall of 1983.

Bruce was not only seeking an owner for XSEL he was also looking for an enthusiastic group of sales staff in one of the sales offices who would really take XSEL on board and incorporate it into their day-to-day activities. He needed to provide these users with technical support and this was a problem. Fortunately he found an answer. He happened to encounter the Colorado Sales Support Manager at a meeting and a fruitful dialogue was begun. This manager was responsible for a technical support group which could provide assistance for sales staff using XSEL.

Work was still continuing at Carnegie–Mellon University on the incorporation of a sizing facility into XSEL. In May, John McDermott sent a memo to ISTG setting out what still needed to be done. John said that two man-years of work were still required on sizing—four people working full-time for six months—to develop a viable prototype. By the end of the 1983 financial year XSEL's sizing capability should have developed to a point where it could interrogate a user about his or her computing needs and propose plausible line items. The 'shell' sizing capability would be in place and the development task would be to extend and refine this in a variety of ways. In order to do this it would be necessary to focus on the following:

- extracting more realistic sizing knowledge from experts,
- making the component selector more sensitive to context,
- integrating the price constraint into the system,
- making the explanation capability an explanation expert.

The goals of the 'extracting sizing knowledge' task were to extend XSEL's knowledge of sizing to the point where it did the following,

- tailored the questions it asked to the users level of technical sophistication,
  asked essentially the same questions the expert salesman would ask,
  made inferences that an expert salesman would find plausible.

The goals of the 'component selector sensitivity task' were to ensure that XSEL:

- had knowledge of the relative importance of the various factors that determine which of a set of similar components should be selected,
  recognized situations in which an exception to one or more of the standard component selection rules must be made,
  understood how to take the uncertainty of various pieces of information into account in making its selection.

The goals of the 'integrating the price constraint task' were to ensure that XSEL could:

● understand as soon as it was given a price range and a description of a customer's computing needs whether an appropriate system could be found,
know how to determine what was only marginally useful to the customer's needs,
know how to take expected future growth into account when sizing a customer's needs.

The goals of the 'enhancing the explanation capability' task were to extend XSEL's explanation capability to the point that:

● it always focused on the critical criteria,
expressed itself succinctly,
allowed the user to probe for precisely the justification he or she wanted.

But the sizing task was to prove far harder than anyone anticipated. It would be a very long time before these goals were achieved.

XSEL AT LAST IS REAL

By June progress was good and Bruce was able to send out an 'XSEL Update' memo. This stated that the implementation of XSEL had begun for the US area. XSEL was being field-tested and would be released incrementally to the seven VAXs that had been placed in the regions. Training for XSEL would be by region as it was installed.

As there might still be people who did not know about XSEL, the memo explained that XSEL stood for EXPERT SELLER. It described XSEL's characteristics.

● It is an interactive tool that assists in developing clean orders for all VAX systems. It will be updated continuously to support new products for VAX configurations.
● It has a flexible user/software interface with some natural language capabilities. It has extensive help facilities that make self-teaching easy. It is user friendly.
● It contains XFL (THE EXPERT FLOOR LAYOUT ASSISTANT) which supplies environmental information. It can generate a generic diagram of a room and provide information to enable the correct cabling of components.
● It contains XCON (THE EXPERT CONFIGURER) which has been used daily since January 1980 to validate orders as configurable and supportable.

The memo also described the kinds of problems that XSEL addressed.

● Incomplete orders.
● Lack of consistent configuration knowledge in the sales offices.

- Customer/site specific configuration constraints.
- Unprepared sites.
- Unrealistic delivery estimates.
- The expense of providing accurate configurations.

And the memo drew attention to some of the risks that XSEL might encounter once it was implemented. These were overselling—making people believe that expert systems could provide a 100 per cent solution; difficulties in the configuration task that XSEL could not yet address; unknown and unending maintenance requirements, and the perception that expert systems technology eliminates jobs.

Planned future developments were for XSEL to show graphically a customer's room and how the hardware could be optimally sited there; for it to create customer specific configurations and provide delivery estimates, and for it to have an automated sizing facility and a link to AQS—the automated quotes system.

In June Bruce went to Europe to see if it was possible to overcome the Cologne failure and restart negotiations to implement XSEL. He met with the FMIC group in Ayr and with sales management in Geneva and discussed the Cologne experience. It was clear that progress in Europe was going to be slow. XSEL was not well understood and there were doubts about its value.

IS XSEL GOOD ENOUGH?

In July the fifth meeting of the XSEL User Design Group was held. This lasted three days and fifty people were present, drawn from a wide variety of groups and areas in the company. It was not a comfortable meeting for Bruce as some conflicts of interest were starting to emerge.

Bruce began the meeting by reviewing the user design philosophy, drawing a diagram (Figure 7.1) to show the composition of the design group.

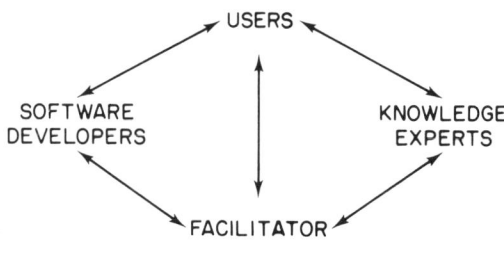

FIGURE 7.1

To help new members he explained that users were participating in the development of software for XSEL. He stressed that user involvement was essential to ensure that XSEL software did the job the users required; that it fitted with their job satisfaction needs and did not cause frustration or deprivation, and that it also fitted with the organization of work in the sales offices. User involvement was also essential to ensure that XSEL was implemented in the best possible way.

He drew another diagram (Figure 7.2) to show how the user design group had approached its task so far.

Here, he was trying to emphasize the dual aspect of the design process. It was not a consideration of technical needs and factors alone, but a careful analysis of technical and human needs so that both were taken account of in the design of XSEL.

He went on to explain other important aspects of participative design. As the design of XSEL progressed so an increasing number of other groups would need to be consulted and involved in the design task. For example, a management input was essential. The users developed the software but management must ensure that the software was properly related to the business needs of the corporation.

It was also necessary for the User Design Group to continually consult with the ISTG Management Steering Committee, the Software Development Group

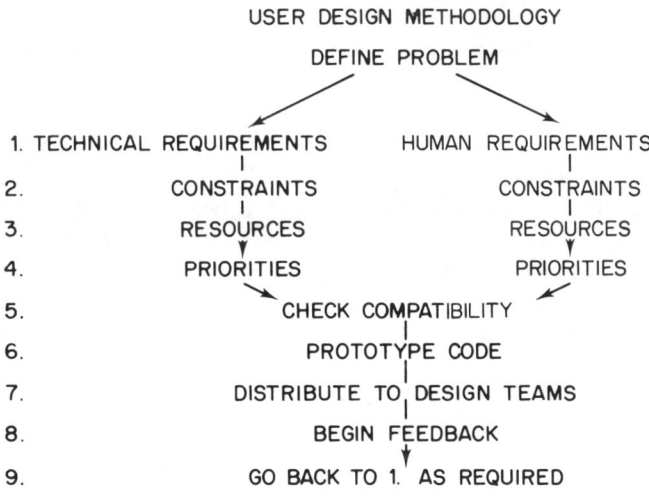

FIGURE 7.2

and the XCON Manufacturing Group. All of these had strong interests in the way the system was developed.

After this description of structure and policy the User Design Group started on its agenda. First, came a discussion of the changes made to the XSEL software since the January meeting of the group. These were described by one of the XSEL development team. This produced a number of comments from the sales representatives in the group concerning their experiences when testing XSEL—the additions and modifications which they would like to see incorporated into it.

As delivery dates were not always certain, they wanted an ability to choose between alternative pieces of equipment according to their date of delivery— they needed to be able to give commitments to customers. With the proposed XSEL–AQS link they wanted a single interface for the user so that the same information did not have to be inputted twice. They also said that they would like to have a data base which acted as an electronic catalogue so that they could look up information about components. And they wanted a faster update of the XSEL data base.

These last two points were difficult for the development team to respond to. In 1983, the data base was not constructed in a way that would easily provide information to a non-technical person. This was one of the problems of being a pioneer for today the provision of this facility would not be difficult. Bruce had to hand the problem back to the salesperson who had made the request. He said that the development team needed to understand how sales staff wanted to look up data. And that in order to use the existing data base the salespeople would have to learn its vocabulary.

The request for a faster update of XSEL also required an explanation. As is normal with new product announcements, Digital had a tendency to publicize these before the detailed configuration knowledge for the product was complete. The development team required information about new products, and their configuration rules, as soon as they were released if it was to meet the sales force's needs for an up-to-date database. A colleague in the ISTG team was trying to ensure that all information was fed into the XCON database as it was initiated, not after the event. If she was successful it would give the XSEL team time to get the information into XSEL and to analyse it. But this required a change in product announcement strategies that were common to the computer industry.

However, the situation was not so bad. The sales force actually had as much data, via XSEL, as anyone else in the company. XSEL might not know everything, but no one else did either. Every six weeks the latest update of XSEL would provide as much data in one place as it was possible to obtain with the present information system of 'sales update' announcements.

These kinds of problems were typical of those experienced by Bruce and his team as they tried to turn XSEL into a production system. As well as developing a product they also had to create new procedures for managing it. This added to the complexity of the design process.

A potential source of conflict was how XFL—the floor layout function in XSEL—should be developed and Bruce had decided to devote a morning to this topic. The problem was that site planning was now the responsibility of Field Service. They were called in by the sales force, usually after the selling process was completed, and charged the customer for their advice. They might not want part of this activity removed from them and located in XSEL where it would be provided free of charge. Yet some site planning information was necessary in XSEL—for example, the correct cables to use. Also, the ability to provide site planning information at an early stage in the selling cycle was seen by the sales force members of the User Design Group as a powerful feature that would provide Digital with an advantage over competitors.

Bruce hoped that the User Design group members, one of whom represented Field Service, could decide what planning features should remain in, or be developed for, XSEL; and which should remain with Field Service and be paid for by the customer.

There was a lot of uncertainty concerning what Field Service really wanted to do, and who should make the decision on what to include in XSEL. Bruce felt that the Group were trying to make a systems decision in the absence of a business decision. The delegate from Field Service was not able to clarify the situation, and the Sales members of the User Design Group argued strongly that the current floor layout facilities should remain in XSEL.

XFL could now do a great deal. For example,

A. Enter and modify information

   1. Create/delete and name room(s).
   2. Add a description of the room(s)—pillars, windows etc.

B. Show constraints

   1. The size of the floor area.
   2. The required cabling for terminals.
   3. The necessary positioning of certain items of hardware in relation to others.

C. Show how the floor area should be laid out

   1. Service areas.
   2. The placement/grouping of equipment.
   3. The links between hardware modules.

D. Provide graphics

1. Charts and environmental specifications for a room.
2. Product data.
3. Equipment grouping.
4. Constraints.

There were a large number of suggestions on how XFL should be developed. The User Design Group listed the features of XFL that were important to them and those that were not. This discussion did not resolve the potential conflict with Field Service on the ownership of the site planning activity. Field Service subsequently funded an XSITE expert system to assist the post-site layout program. But the project was eventually discontinued.

Other events at the meeting caused dismay and anxiety. For the first time a corporate sales manager was present. Bruce had invited him in the hope of making senior sales management more aware of XSEL. Bruce introduced this manager and explained that he was there to demonstrate the support of Corporate Sales for XSEL, and to provide input on the relationship of XSEL to other sales automation initiatives that were taking place. Unfortunately, this manager was believed by many of those present to have made some precipitous decisions on the implementation of other sales systems, without involving the users. His behaviour in the meeting was also regarded as unhelpful and unresponsive. At lunch Bruce received a large number of complaints about this. Bruce's objective in making the invitation had been to enable the manager to hear at first hand what the users were asking so that he could communicate this to top management. However the User Design Group members did not see his visit as helpful and Bruce was anxious in case he had lost some of their good will.

This illustrates one of the problems of participative design—how to involve management effectively in the discussions that are taking place. The existence of a steering group helps solve the problem and the invitation of senior managers to user design group meetings is also a good strategy. In this instance Bruce chose the wrong manager.

Another totally unexpected human problem also affected the morale of the User Design Group at this meeting. A member of ISTG has been working on the manufacturing configuring problem with a graduate student from the University of Massachusetts. Bruce's boss had asked if they could attend the meeting and give a demonstration of their work. He believed that their approach would produce a configurer that was faster and more accurate than the one being developed by the User Design Group. This was the latest in a series of alternative methodologies for XCON and XSEL that had been suggested by other members of ISTG since the project began.

The demonstration did not convince the User Design Group that another approach could prove more advantageous than the one they had adopted. But the fact that the demonstration took place aroused resentment. Both the sales force and the development team members of the User Design Group felt that they were being attacked and their work criticized. Bruce had allowed the demonstration because his boss had asked him to, and because he thought it would be useful for the User Design Group members to appreciate that there were a variety of ways to make XSEL faster and more accurate. He had again misjudged the situation. It was another example of the care that had to be taken to ensure that the User Design Group maintained its positive attitudes.

This kind of problem occurred from time to time throughout the XSEL design process and it is one that development groups are prone to experience. People become very committed to the route they are taking yet new inputs which question what they are doing may be very valuable. In pioneering projects there is a need to continually identify and examine alternatives and new directions.

There were also some criticisms of the relationships between the sales force members of the User Design Group and the development team members. A salesperson suggested that it was becoming more difficult to feel part of the XSEL project. He complained that the development team members were behaving like all the other development teams he had known. They had talked to the users and responded to them in the early stages of the project, but over time they had become more complacent and were now starting to ignore the sales force input. Specifically, there was not enough response to queries and comments when these were made using XSEL's 'COMMENTS' facility. Weeks went by before he could get a response from the COMMENTS administrator. Bruce had to admit that he was right and that the development team was relying too heavily on responding to users at the User Design Group meetings. They had ignored the basic need of people to get a quick response to a question or criticism.

Bruce recognized that this was another important problem. So many comments were coming in from the group testing XSEL that the development team had difficulty in providing the amount of response that was required. Also, they were spending so much time working on the software that they had very little time to do anything else. Nevertheless, the problem must be solved as good relations within the User Design Group were essential to the success of the project.

Other issues that came up during this meeting were related to fears and anxieties about XSEL and its impact on the sales force. Bruce had to handle these with tact and imagination although he regarded it as highly desirable that they surfaced and were openly discussed. An emotive question was the extent to which a sales person had to obey XSEL. Was it a tool of management to police the operation of the sales force, or was the salesperson allowed to override it and take a personal decision?

Bruce perceived that this was a very important and delicate question. He made a mental note to get it discussed by management so that he could give a definite reply at a future meeting. The sales force must know how they were to use XSEL. But it was also a question for the development team. Should their future efforts be directed at enabling XSEL to provide as much information as possible, in the most useful way? Or should they be trying to create a structure in XSEL which would handle the requirements of the sales force in a flexible manner, allowing them to do what they believed to be correct.

Bruce did not know the answer to this although he felt sure that it was important to develop a means for XSEL to accommodate different approaches and attitudes.

Finally the meeting discussed the key question of XSEL's implementation. Bruce asked the Group for a judgement on the quality and readiness of the XSEL software. He assumed that the User Design Group would agree to XSEL being released to a larger group of people for testing. To his astonishment they did not agree, saying that they needed more time to try out the latest version. After some debate it was eventually decided to discuss the matter further at DECWORLD, Digital's annual customer exhibition, which would be held in Boston six weeks later. This further meeting was held, and the User Design Group members then agreed that XSEL was ready for wider release.

Bruce was pleased that the User Design Group was strong enough in its ownership of XSEL to express this view. He was also disappointed that they did not think XSEL good enough for wider release. He was to experience this kind of user ambivalence in the future and it always caused a dilemma. If rigid criteria were applied to XSEL, for example, that it should include all announced products and that it should pass configurations with 95 per cent accuracy or better, then it might never be released. But if firm criteria were not used, its release would always be at the mercy of someone's subjective judgement. He was glad that the User Design Group existed to make this judgement.

Bruce was relieved when the meeting was over. It had generated both conflict and emotion. There had been adverse reactions to visitors who were seen as threatening and a number of issues had arisen related to fears and anxieties about XSEL and its impact on the sales force. Bruce had had to handle the proceedings with great care and tact. But he regarded it as highly desirable that problems had surfaced and been openly discussed.

By this time, July 1983, the Intelligent Systems Technologies Group had grown considerably in size. It now consisted of a marketing group, an XCON group, an XSEL group, applications development and administration, training, solutions marketing, organizational development, and knowledge-base systems development. In total ISTG had 33 projects underway at this time.

By September, 1983, XSEL's capability had considerably increased and it contained 1725 rules. Its use was starting to spread outside the original pilot group of User Design Group members. There were now users in the Mid-Atlantic region, D.C. District, and Bruce was treating these as a new pilot which would test how XSEL could help sales representatives who were not members of the User Design Group. During September he organized a training session for this new group.

The development team were thinking hard about the XSEL database and wondering if it could be used as an information resource for the sales force. They held a meeting to discuss this but decided not to proceed further at that moment in time. Too many problems would have to be overcome. They also considered whether there should be a software development freeze during the first part of 1984, so that all of XSEL's current problems could be fixed. They decided that this would be a good idea.

Bruce was still actively looking for a new senior management sponsor to replace the Vice-President, Sales, who had moved elsewhere. He wanted someone who would accept ownership of XSEL. Although Corporate Sales was pro XSEL, it did not see itself as owning it. Also, Corporate Sales had little influence over activities in the sales offices where XSEL would be located. He decided to approach the US Sales Management Committee for a sponsor.

THE SIXTH USER DESIGN GROUP MEETING

The User Design Group had its next meeting at the beginning of November.

First, there was discussion of a number of policy issues. Bruce told the meeting of his belief that there should be a freezing of XSEL software. He said that the XSEL software developers had suggested that the freeze should continue until 90 per cent of XSEL users were trained. There was considerable debate about this. A number of the User Design Group members asked for specific examples of what a freeze would involve. Eventually, it was agreed that there should be a freeze of software enhancements, but not a freeze on adding new products. A freeze would allow the software to stabilize and would provide time to bring documentation and training up to date.

The Design Group suggested putting a physical time limit on the freeze rather than using the criteria of 90 per cent trained XSEL users as the resumption point. It was eventually agreed that the freeze should take place from the beginning of February to the end of July. Bruce told the User Design Group that this would greatly assist the development team. He estimated that there would be between 500 and 700 new users of XSEL during that six-month period. Each of these could have a software enhancement request. The freeze would give the development team time to assimilate these requests and set appropriate priorities.

The discussion moved on to the means for giving XSEL to the future users as soon as possible. There was concern about the adequacy of support services for XSEL and the considerable dependency that users would have on those that did exist. It was agreed that implementation should not start until support was available and adequate.

There were also more questions about training. Should this be highly structured or based on a process of 'self discovery'? Was the present approach too conservative? No one would use XSEL effectively unless they were 'properly trained'. But what did 'properly trained' mean, both now and in the future?

Bruce emphasized that he was liaising with corporate sales management and with the area sales management committees on the issues of XSEL ownership, support and training in the sales offices. The Colorado region would provide user support and sales training had already begun in the North East Region.

The User Design Group then talked about the nature of its task and this stimulated a lively discussion on design and implementation problems, particularly those related to job satisfaction and the meeting of expectations. The User Design Group members still saw their role as an advisory and practical one—to make suggestions and to field test XSEL. But, one pointed out:

> "It is always a two-way street. The XSEL developers may or may not take our advice and use our comments, and we may or may not use the software."

Another did not want their role to be restrictive. He suggested that the software would be continually evolving and so the Group's approval would always be needed. However this did not mean that they had to sign off each software release before it could be used.

In addition to these policy issues there was considerable discussion of the structure and content of XSEL—overriding the system, sizing, the link with AQS, the HELP facility etc. These practical issues were tackled in small groups made up of a mix of sales representatives and members of the XSEL development team. The 'override' group discussed the different points at which the user should be able to tell the system not to do something which it was logically programmed to carry out. The 'sizer' group talked about the point in the configuring task when the 'sizer' should be used. The AQS group considered mechanisms for integrating XSEL and AQS. These small group meetings produced important inputs to assist the continuing development of XSEL. This ongoing discussion was a feature of most of the User Design Group meetings.

The meeting ended with one of the development team describing how properties for XSEL were decided. She showed how certain things affected others in XSEL and these dependencies influenced the order in which the development team approached problems. Priorities were also greatly influenced by the needs and goals of Manufacturing Engineering, Sales Management, and the User Design Group itself.

Bruce then gave the dates on which XSEL would be progessively released to groups of new users. These were 23 November, 11 January, 23 February and 11 April.

In December Bruce made another trip to Europe and gave a talk in London at a symposium on AI organized by the British Computer Society. His presentation increased the European AI community's interest in XSEL. This had already been aroused by references to XCON and XSEL in a number of popular AI books. On his way back to the States he called in at European Headquarters in Geneva and spoke to the manager in charge of European Sales Operations. The mood in Europe towards XSEL had apparently changed now that XSEL was actually being implemented in the US. Bruce found an enthusiastic audience for news of XSEL. He stayed for several hours with this manager. They discussed, and agreed on, a plan for implementing XSEL in Europe. The Geneva manager agreed to formalize and write up this plan but unfortunately this initiative failed as, soon after, he was moved to a new job.

1983—PROBLEMS AND PROGRESS

1983 was an exciting but difficult period. The User Design Group and the development team were getting used to managing the inevitable complexity and uncertainty of the design task. They were learning how to cope rapidly and effectively with unexpected events and to accept constraints—things which they would like to do but could not. But as XSEL progressed so new problems surfaced around it. It is interesting to consider whether the participative design philosophy increased or reduced the number and severity of these.

Bruce was as committed to user participation as ever, but was finding that the User Design Group had a stable core and a shifting periphery. A number of the sales force attended each meeting conscientiously, others attended sporadically and there was usually a group of new members at each meeting. These were sales people who had recently become interested in XSEL. They wanted to contribute to its development even though this was at an advanced stage. Bruce found that it was a good strategy to explain the philosophy and goals of participation at intervals. This reinforced the understanding and interest of the regular attenders and ensured that the occasional and new members understood what the User Design Group was trying to achieve.

Most user design groups go through a number of different emotional states *en route* to the successful building of their system. These include confusion and uncertainty when the task starts, enthusiasm as it gets underway and they realize what participation can offer them, frustration and conflict as unexpected difficulties are encountered and progress is slowed or hurdles have to be surmounted. When these are overcome and the last stage of systems building is reached, excitement and enthusiasm returns as the group prepares to launch its new product.

One source of difficulty can be the User Design Group's changing perception of its role and responsibilities as the project progresses. By the time the mid-stage is reached the group is usually working confidently and has clear ideas of the tasks it should be doing and the decisions it should be taking. It becomes unwilling to have these usurped by other individuals or groups.

This kind of reaction caused a problem for Bruce when there was a reluctance to say that XSEL could be released to other groups. The sales force members of the User Design Group wanted to continue testing and improving it. Bruce believed that it was ready for release. This highlights one of the dilemmas of participation for a project manager. If a user design group has been given responsibility for decision taking, then the project manager cannot arbitrarily remove this if the decision is not to his or her liking. Advice and recommendations from the manager are acceptable but in the end it will be the group members who take the final decision. This fits in with the notion of 'user ownership'. Bruce believed strongly that for XSEL to be acceptable it must belong to the sales force. Once this belief that 'it is our system' was established the sales force naturally wanted the right to take major decisions.

A number of conflicts were experienced at this time. A potential source of conflict in all user design groups is the different interests contained within them. A group made up of members of the same department will still represent different grades and functions and not necessarily agree. Similarly, when users and technologists are collaborating, relationships will not always progress smoothly. In the Digital User Design Group, tension developed between the sales force and the development team members. The development team were viewed as not responding as they should to the sales force criticisms of XSEL. Bruce had to take steps to speed up the feedback process.

Many of the problems that cause conflict and confusion for a user design group originate with other groups who feel threatened by what they are doing or do not fully understand it. This was the case with the dispute with Field Service over what XSEL should or should not contain. This kind of disagreement is typical of the disputes that arise over technology when new systems impinge on different functions and roles. Solutions have to be negotiated between the different groups and this is not always easy to accomplish.

A different kind of problem arises when groups who should be involved in a project are reluctant to associate themselves with it. Bruce always had difficulty in getting senior sales management committed to XSEL. Frequently he experienced the problem of the 'vanishing sponsor'. As soon as a senior sales manager expressed his commitment to XSEL and agreed to give practical proof of this, he moved to another job. In 1983 Bruce was still searching for a senior manager in Sales who would be XSEL's sponsor and accept ownership of the system. The Vice-President, Sales, who had wanted XSEL to be operational by Christmas, 1982, had now left Digital and no other senior sales manager was showing a positive and active interest in the project. Yet XSEL's future depended on it being acceptable to senior and junior sales staff. Salespeople would use it, but senior managers would have to pay for it. They therefore had to be completely convinced of XSEL's value and be willing to take responsibility for its introduction and operation.

The creation of the User Design Group had solved the problem of getting the interest and commitment of the sales force in the field. But it had not, as yet, contributed to obtaining a similar response from senior sales management. The invitation to a corporate sales manager to attend a meeting had not proved successful. This was to continue to be one of Bruce's most pressing and difficult problems.

New suggestions and ideas could also, on occasion, threaten the User Design Group. The configuring demonstration by the University of Massachusetts at the fifth User Design Group meeting caused a hostile reaction. The User Design Group had become committed to XSEL and did not want to know about rival contenders or approaches. Bruce had a dilemma here. He wanted the Group to be aware or relevant developments that were taking place in other parts of Digital, or outside the firm. At the same time he did not want to introduce people or ideas that were viewed as disturbing and threatening.

Cyberneticians believe that complexity and variety can only be handled if the methods and tools which are used to address them contain an equal amount of variety. Bruce was now convinced that he had done the right thing in setting up the User Design Group. By giving its responsibility for testing XSEL and contributing to its design, he had created the means for managing effectively a mass of human and technical problems. These could have proved impossible to solve without a participative structure.

Participation does not prevent problems occurring, but it does enable them to be brought out into the open and rationally discussed. When users are not involved in systems design they know little about what is taking place, learn about attitudes and events through rumour, and become alienated because of their lack of information. But successful participation does require a facilitator who can help users arrive at acceptable solutions and ensure that morale remains high.

*Here they were in sight
of the city they were
going to . . . they met
with abundance of what
they had sought for in
all their pilgrimage.*

John Bunyan

Chapter 8

US ACCEPTANCE AND SUCCESS

At the beginning of January, 1984, Bruce knew that he had to face up to the enormous problems of introducing XSEL into all Digital sales offices. It was now a greatly improved system, both in what it offered and in the speed at which it processed data. This last advantage was due to the use of the BLISS compiler which enabled XSEL to respond twice as fast as before. Software development was now frozen for six months but the development team had many other things to do. One of the most immediate was training the Colorado support team which had agreed to provide a user support service for XSEL. Another was setting up a problem reporting procedure.

During this period one member of the development team was working on a new flexible data structure for XSEL. This was called the 'bus network'. It was a set of rules to make sure that when a set of components was on an order there was a clear and efficient pathway to the central processing unit. The objective of the project was to create in XSEL a data structure based on the electrical pathways from a component to the central processing unit. This structure could form the basis of many XSEL functions, making them easier to maintain and add to. Applications which would be associated with this new structure included tests of configuration completeness, the explanation facility and the default intelligence.

The bus network would not solve all configuration problems but it would provide a good foundation on which further developments of XSEL could be built. It was another example of the technical improvement of XSEL.

In April, Bruce had a meeting with the GIA (General International Areas) MIS group to begin planning for the release of XSEL in countries outside the United States and Europe. He anticipated that it would be another two years before XSEL began to be generally used in these countries. He also began to organize a survey of user opinion on XSEL and asked a member of staff at the Harvard Business School if she would do this. And he talked with sales management about the possibility of legislating the use of XSEL so that it became compulsory for sales offices to use it. But he wondered if this was a wise strategy, and who would support such a proposal. He decided not to take the idea any further.

There was still a great deal of work to be done on implementation issues. Sales had now managed to install VAX machines in each of the sales regions. But the management of these varied greatly. There were differences in machine performance and in what the machines were allowed to be used for. Bruce had hoped that the new VAXs would be used only for XSEL, but the fact that they were in place before the software was ready meant that they were used for other tasks such as DECmail—the electronic mail system. It proved difficult to turn them into dedicated XSEL machines.

Things were also happening in Europe. The sales executive who looked after the Shell account in the Utrecht office was using XSEL and providing a great deal of useful feedback. He was running XSEL on a development machine located in Hudson, Massachusetts. In May, Bruce and Enid met at Digital's offices in Geneva and talks began about restarting a European pilot. The Shell account salesperson was also in Geneva at this time and Bruce asked him if Utrecht would act as the first European pilot site. He reacted favourably to the idea.

XSEL was still encountering unexpected problems. A review of company business policy at this time led to a very significant challenge to its legitimacy. In 1984 senior management were moving towards a strategy of selling more standard systems. In the past Digital had been proud of its ability to tailor-make systems to meet individual customer requirements, although this was an expensive policy and one that was not followed by other computer manufacturers. But the more standardized products became, the less configuring was a problem and the less need there was for XSEL. Bruce was worried at these developments. They could place a question mark over the project.

This worry was partly tactical; if Digital marketed only standard configurations then there would be no need for XSEL. But it was also strategic. Bruce, and most of the User Design Group, believed that if Digital moved sharply towards a standard configuration marketing approach, much of the company's appeal for its customers would be lost. In the end Digital opted for a very limited number of standard configurations. The vast majority sold were still customized systems designed to meet specific customer needs. Hence XSEL and XCON were needed as much as ever.

Still, a minor problem for Bruce was that these new standard systems had to be incorporated into the XSEL database. There was also the continuing problem of keeping XSEL up to date and the development team decided that they must provide a quarterly release of new product data. At the same time Bruce was travelling round the States trying to get the district sales managers excited about XSEL and willing to give it their support. Life was full of challenge and hard work for the XSEL development team.

In July there was another meeting of the User Design Group. The big issue raised at the meeting was whether US Sales management really wanted to go ahead with a full-scale XSEL implementation. The User Design Group members sensed an ambivalence in some of the regions and they stressed the need to get the commitment, or recommitment, of the US Sales Management Committee. The view of the meeting was '*we must ask them whether or not they want to go ahead and risk their saying no*'.

There was considerable discussion on who should go and talk to the USSMC and recommend that the full-scale implementation of XSEL should go ahead. Several members of the group volunteered and it was eventually agreed that one of the sales representatives should make the case. This was a sales unit manager who had originally been sceptical about XSEL but had now become convinced of its importance and value.

Bruce was anxious about what might take place at the meeting with the USSMC and wondered if he should risk leaving the fate of XSEL in another person's hands. If the USSMC did not say '*go ahead*' then the progress of XSEL would be greatly slowed down. But he felt that he must trust the representative of the User Design Group. It was right that it was one of them who went to sales management to ask for commitment and the provision of more funds for XSEL. The difficulty was that this person now became the only link between sales management and the User Design Group. The future of XSEL could rest on what he said at the meeting.

The strategy decided on by the delegate was to be positive but honest. He told the USSMC that XSEL should now be released for all sales staff to use. He stressed, "it's not great, but it's the best thing we have. We should go ahead with it".

The USSMC was impressed, accepted everything he said and gave its blessing to the company-wide implementation of XSEL in the United States. Bruce was relieved and delighted. This was a key event in the history of XSEL. There was now agreement from sales management for XSEL's general introduction.

A number of US OEMs (Other Equipment Manufacturers) now became interested in XSEL. These were firms which produced their own products but had Digital equipment as part of these. Because they were using Digital hardware and software in this way they too had serious configuring problems. They were anxious to find out what XSEL could contribute to their needs.

There were other events that were not to XSEL's advantage. Bruce discovered that a sales group in the Western Region were worried about the number of errors in the orders they sent to Manufacturing. They had built a pilot program based on a paper checklist of configuring relationships. They claimed that this program solved their problem. The development team were astounded at this. The Western Region group had not consulted them, did not appear to know about XSEL, or understand what it had to offer, and were producing rival solutions to the configuring problem. It was a major challenge. Like the move to standardization it was an example of how long projects can be unexpectedly affected by events taking place in their environment. In compensation, the results of the survey carried out by the Harvard researcher showed that most of the sales staff using XSEL were happy with what it had to offer and found it an improvement on manual configuring.

Meanwhile XSEL was becoming more versatile and sophisticated. The development team began receiving strong suggestions that they should start incorporating a facility to configure machine clusters and networks. They began talking about the development of a network configurer and made plans to tackle machine clusters in six months time—around April, 1985.

A new version of XSEL was released in October, 1984, but Sales was not happy with it. The program contained many bugs and it seemed that it had not been tested adequately. This led the development team to think about, and review, the testing procedures. It was apparent that the testing of a large interactive system, with many paths through it, was an extremely difficult process. They decided on a good manual testing process to help solve this problem. Bruce was pleased with this, because he knew the December release would show even more improvements to XSEL as it was going to be built on a new OPS compiler. This would speed-up the development of software, an improvement for which the development team had been waiting a long time.

The US Sales Management Committee was now fully committed to the implementation of XSEL and had become the senior management sponsoring group that Bruce had been looking for for so long. The Field Operations Management Committee (FOMC) had approved the allocation of additional VAXs to the sales offices so that XSEL could operate on stand-alone machines. Bruce was spreading awareness of XSEL by setting up a new pilot site in the New York/New Jersey Region to demonstrate the benefits of XSEL to the salespeople located in that area. He visited New York early in November to discuss this and to carry out some user training. He was also working on yet another implementation plan—one that he hoped would this time be used.

The sales force were now responding very favourably to XSEL. They saw it as having many benefits for them.

The sales offices using XSEL were providing technically accurate configurations for quotations to customers; they were able to match specific products more precisely to customer needs; individual salesperson productivity had increased, and Digital was presenting an even better professional image to its customers than before. By January, 1985, 25 per cent of the sales force were trained in its use and XSEL had increased in size to 2330 rules.

Other developments now began reinforcing XSEL's value. In January, Bruce became involved with a group called the Front End Transaction Process Committee (FETP). This was examining the order processing procedures to see how these could be improved. Its work eventually led to a major corporate initiative called the Order Transaction Process (OTP) programme. This committee was a possible vehicle for getting XSEL more widely implemented. The development team attended its meetings and persuaded the members to think about the need for automated configuration capabilities as part of the order transaction process.

The development team also continued to introduce more information about standard systems into XSEL. Digital was split over the wisdom of this move into standard systems. Some parts of the company saw this as the route to take—all the other large manufacturers were selling standard products. Others believed that it was an unwise move. The company's reputation stemmed from its ability to meet a wide variety of user needs. If it ceased to do this it might lose a market advantage. Bruce was inclined to the second view. He believed that the future of the company lay in selling à la carte computer systems. But he recognized that if standard systems were being produced then they needed to be sold, and XSEL facilitated the ease of the selling process.

THE EIGHTH MEETING OF THE USER DESIGN GROUP

At the end of January, the eighth meeting of the user design group was held. Again there was a large attendance. Thirty-six people came—twelve of these from the sales offices. For the benefit of new members Bruce once again opened the meeting by talking about the participative design process. He described how the group set its priorities and how it was influenced by the views of field services, corporate sales and ISTG. The task of the group was to decide what the XSEL software should do; how this software could be built; how the system should be implemented and the technology requirement for successful implementation, and how the system fitted with the job satisfaction needs of the sales force.

Bruce pointed out that sales offices did not all work in the same way and each office tended to have its own individual requirements. For example, the New York/New Jersey Region wanted to provide its sales force with the tools to work at home.

The User Design Group were then asked their present reactions to XSEL. Was it accessible and available? Was it useful and effective? Was it productive? Had it got better? The answer to these questions was 'yes' although there were still some problems in using XSEL effectively. There was criticism of the amount of hardware available in the sales offices on which to run XSEL. This was too small for the number of people who wanted to use it. It seemed that XSEL had improved and made good progress but its increasing popularity had reduced its accessibility. There was a suggestion that the number of people having access to XSEL should be restricted. If access to the system continued to deteriorate the enthusiasm of staff would start to wane.

These comments stimulated a general discussion of the problems now associated with XSEL. They could be summarized as *'access to XSEL'*, *'persuading people to use it'*, *'increasing management's commitment'*, *'improving communication between policy makers and implementers'* and *'getting sufficient hardware'*.

Bruce was not too worried by the reported access problem. He knew that a decision had been taken to separate XSEL from DECmail so that XSEL could operate on a dedicated machine. This would enable it to give a faster response to users. This had been decided at a July, 1984, meeting of the Regional MIS Management. But the User Design Group's response showed that this information had not yet reached the sales offices. Clearly, communication needed to be improved—policy decisions were being taken at high levels but they were not always communicated to the grass roots level.

The Sales representatives also said that there was still a problem of management acceptance. Sales management was not giving XSEL its whole-hearted support. Too little hardware was available in the sales offices and management there appeared to be sceptical about XSEL's benefits. They could not see any immediate payback. The attitude of some managers was 'no improvements, no XSEL'. Clearly acceptance depended on results and it was still too early for the benefits of using XSEL to show up clearly.

But the salespeople present at the meeting were very positive about XSEL as a tool. They saw XSEL as a really good tool which produced satisfactory results. The challenge was to pass this message to members of the sales force who had not yet got close to XSEL.

The group now talked about a strategy for making XSEL more visible. There were many suggestions, for example:

- Making a video of XSEL showing what it could do.
- Demonstrating XSEL to management on a good machine;
- Giving presentations in all the sales regions.
- Publicizing XSEL's successes.
- Placing an article in *DECSELL*, one of Digital's magazines;
- Putting a number of machines in a motorhome on the back of a trailer truck and driving it around as a mobile trainer.

This last suggestion raised the issue of equipment availability again. Perhaps increasing XSEL training was not a good idea. If all sales staff were trained to use XSEL and then there were not enough machines for them to access the system, there would be a great deal of frustration.

Another point made was that the marketing and training of XSEL were different activities and should not be confused. They probably should not be carried out at the same time.

These problems of XSEL's visibility, the availability of machines on which to run XSEL, and management's attitudes to it were left unresolved. Bruce recognized that he must pay a great deal of attention to all of them in the weeks ahead.

The rest of the meeting was devoted to discussing XSEL developments and improvements. John McDermott gave a report of the work he was still doing on the 'sizing' tool. He asked for confirmation that the sales force really wanted this tool.

The view of the meeting was that while the sales force would not need to use it very often, it would make a useful front-end to XSEL. Automated tools of this kind gave customers a good impression—they had public relations value in addition to their practical value.

Suggestions for developments after XSEL were also made. There could be a need for a new expert system to handle networks. This would not be an easy system to develop for although networks started small, they could grow to a very large size. It would be a tool for software services rather than for sales.

Bruce said that this was a good problem to consider for an expert system. In the future Digital could be doing so much networking for customers that there would not be enough human experts to go round.

This led to a discussion of the problems of developing a network configuration tool. The question was asked 'would an expert system of this kind have a high pay back?' The answer was a resounding 'yes'. The configuring of networks was not easy and without an expert system errors could be considerable. It was pointed out that the field service group now spent 90 hours a week configuring networks, checking them and drawing them out. It would be a great improvement if they could have a picture output from an expert system.

Bruce agreed that the development team should consider building an expert system for networks. This would take two or three years to complete and should address both the configuration and the design of networks.

The User Design Group next went on to discuss a number of other items. One was a proposal to give XSEL the capability to configure clusters of machines. Another was how XSEL should handle standard systems. These were not usually sold alone but with additional components and so there was still a configuring problem.

After the User Design Group meeting the rewrite of XSEL continued. Feedback from the sales force had shown that parts of the system were not performing as well as they should and some of these were cut out. The sections removed included part of the floor layout capability, checking for restrictions and bundling, and the 'show' command.

ACCEPTANCE INCREASES

In February, Bruce prepared a detailed plan for the implementation of XSEL throughout the US. He noted the status of XSEL in each sales region—the hardware available, the number of XSEL users, the amount of training that had been carried out, and the name of the manager responsible for XSEL. He also noted the date when new, XSEL dedicated, hardware, would be installed in the sales office. In many offices the comprehensive use of XSEL depended on the installation of these dedicated machines.

He found that the use of XSEL was already quite extensive. All the sales regions were using it with the exception of the Western Region which was waiting for the necessary hardware. Several hundreds of sales people had now been through the XSEL training programme, and 80 per cent of those trained were using XSEL regularly. This did not mean that use was totally related to training for a number of regular users had not yet received it.

XSEL was now beginning to make a major contribution to increasing the efficiency and reducing the costs of the sales offices. Configurations were taking less time to complete and were much more accurate. This gave the sales force more time for selling and reduced the administrative costs associated with errors in orders and quotes. A sales manager reported with delight that he could now sell systems to customers with confidence, knowing that they contained all the necessary parts.

As the year progressed the acceptance of XSEL in the sales offices continued to grow. On 1 June the Great Lakes sales office decreed that XSEL must be used for all system quotes. At the same time, one of Digital's largest customers insisted that all the quotes it received should be accompanied by an XSEL print-out showing the details of the configuration for which the quote was being made. This customer then asked if it could use XSEL itself. Digital's OEM customers were also becoming aware of how XSEL could be of benefit to them.

The interest of GIA (General International Areas)—countries outside the United States and Europe—was also increasing and Bruce began planning an implementation programme for the sales offices there.

Meanwhile the development of XSEL and related systems continued. Bruce spent a lot of time planning how to commence building a network configuration tool. The development of a link between AQS and XSEL was also well underway. And a pilot project was starting up to enable the OEM customers to use XSEL on a Digital machine. The 'sizer' project was also proceeding, although slowly.

By the Winter of 1985 the cost of running the XSEL development team was more than paid for by the financial pay-off of XSEL. This was saving around $25 million a year. XCON was now universally in place in Manufacturing; XSEL was working well in Sales; the OEM pilot was underway, and the European pilot was being organized to start at the beginning of January, 1986. Sales had reorganized itself and created an organizational structure that was much better for the development and building of sales support tools.

Everyone was now getting ready for the big DECWORLD exhibition that Digital held once a year to display its products. Many of Digital's largest customers would be there and XSEL could be shown to them and to the rest of the world.

1984 AND 1985. FRUITION AND SUCCESS

In 1984 and 1985 XSEL reached maturity. A good, usable tool had been built. This had been tested in the sales offices and proved itself useful and acceptable to sales staff. It increased their efficiency and paid off financially. Sales offices outside the US were keen to try it and in Europe the Utrecht sales office was already using it with some success.

Technical progress had been made through the development of the new 'bus network' and the release of a new, improved version of XSEL which included a module for use by expert configurers. They were now able to use the system more efficiently than novices.

The US sales management committee had given its approval for the general use of XSEL in sales offices, and Bruce's anxiety that this might not be forthcoming had proved unfounded. He now had the challenge of planning for the full-scale implementation of XSEL—ensuring that it was successfully introduced into all of the US sales offices.

Progress had not been completely straightforward during the year. Some doubts had been thrown on XSEL's future by a pressure for more product standardization which came from a number of senior managers. A large amount of standardization would simplify the configuring problem and diminish XSEL's value. Bruce's team discussed this possibility but decided that even if policy changed non-standard applications would be sold for many years ahead. The need for a configuring aid would continue to be present.

A major challenge was how to make XSEL more visible. There had to be excellent strategies for diffusing knowledge about XSEL and telling all the sales force what it had to offer. Sales staff also had to be trained to use it. XSEL's implementation placed Digital in another pioneering role. It would be the first company to introduce a major expert system on both a national and an international scale. An external market for XSEL was also appearing and becoming increasingly important. OEMs and large customers were recognizing its value in enabling them to configure their own systems.

The sales force members of the User Design Group now had an important new role. They had to become the ambassadors for XSEL. Their identification with XSEL and recognition of its value carried great weight with other sales staff because, as one said—"they are part of us and we are part of them". Their development role was to continue into the future. Regular meetings of the User Design Group are still held so that XSEL's progress can be discussed and potential new problems avoided. Participative design has now become participative evaluation and improvement.

Bruce was left with two major problems. The first was to decide what direction to take next in the US. Was the way forward the development of an expert system to configure networks or were other problems more important and likely to have a larger pay-off? The second problem was how to move ahead with the implementation of XSEL into the European sales offices. The story of how XSEL was introduced into Europe is told in the third part of this book.

Part 3
MOVING XSEL INTO EUROPE

*Atheist. I laugh to see what ignorant
persons you are to take upon
you so tedious a journey; and
yet are like to have nothing
but your travel for your pains.*

*Christian. Why man? Do you think we shall
not be received?*

John Bunyan

Chapter 9

XSEL IN EUROPE: PLANNING FOR CHANGE

EFFECTIVE PLANNING

Effective planning requires the setting of clear objectives, the mustering of required resources and the recognition that change is a volatile and complex affair that may take years to achieve. Planning is itself a process of creative innovation which requires those responsible to be excellent observers and interpreters of attitudes, emotions, relationships and events, and able to respond to these in a flexible and imaginative way.

Planning also requires understanding, in particular an understanding of the situation where the change is to be introduced. Understanding, in turn, requires breadth of vision and a recognition that most situations are complex, unpredictable and peopled by individuals and groups with diverse interests.

Planning for international change is even more difficult. There is a requirement for an understanding of national as well as local cultures; for communication across country and company boundaries, and for the reconciliation of vested interests. Planning must now be even more intelligent and responsive with a willingness to change plans as knowledge and insight increases. Plans conceived at the start of a project usually need to be modified as time passes. If they are not then they become obsolete and out of touch with the reality of the situation that exists at a later date.

Good planning is essential for successful implementation and many excellent systems have failed to be introduced because of a lack of it. But it is never easy. Democratic companies will bring together representatives from interested or affected groups to contribute to the planning process and this will assist eventual success. But this kind of participation will also bring differences of opinion and conflicts of interest out in the open where they have to be discussed and resolved. This can be a painful and time-consuming process.

Digital handled its planning for the European introduction of XSEL with care, taking account of different views and holding frequent meetings at which these could be aired. But, despite its attention to processes, it did not escape problems. Different groups had different objectives and XSEL was not always seen as assisting these. To make matters more difficult, powerful groups with strong views were located in different countries.

The lesson here is that if a company as experienced in the management of change as Digital has difficulty in 'changing', then less experienced companies must proceed with great caution. They must recognize that major change is complex and requires excellent planning. This, in turn, requires thought, flexibility and foresight. If matters are left to chance, or management is over-optimistic about the ease of changing, then they may never successfully implement their new system.

THE AYR PLANNING MEETING

The first major moves to secure European acceptance of XSEL began in 1985. In February, Bruce visited Digital's manufacturing plant in Ayr, Scotland, and met with the senior European Sales Manager—who was based in European Headquarters in Geneva, and with Field Management Information Centre staff. FMIC was located at Ayr and contained a technical edit group which was responsible for checking orders were correct before manufacturing and assembly began. FMIC was already testing XCON's ability to assist configuring at the manufacturing stage. Bruce's task was to tell the meeting about XSEL and what it had to offer and bring them up to date on the state of its US implementation. He also proposed to provide a demonstration of XSEL, discuss its future development and raise the question of the planning requirements for a European pilot.

He began his talk by stating that Digital had a great need for a high level of professional productivity. XSEL could contribute to this for sales staff and for technical support groups such as FMIC. He pointed out that, on average, every customer order required three quotes before the order was finally closed. Preparing these quotes took up a great deal of a sales executives time. The US salespeople liked the time-saving aspect of the system very much. Two hundred and forty-eight were now using it, although the potential user population was around 1200.

In his demonstration he showed how a typical order could be handled with XSEL. His salesperson wanted to configure a 240 volt, 50 hertz on-line VAX system with 16 megabytes. This system would require 3 disks, 2 tapes, 15 terminals, and a console. All of this had to be fitted into an existing room of 18 feet by 14 feet. When Bruce fed this information into XSEL, it produced a detailed list of the on-line components that were required—their names, descriptions and the quantity of each required. A list of equipment for the computer room was also produced, together with a diagram showing the room, the optimal layout of hardware and the floor load that had to be supported.

This demonstration aroused great interest and a good deal of discussion. Bruce was delighted to hear that the Ayr group were keen to carry out pilot tests on XSEL to check its level of accuracy and its fit with European configuring needs.

Bruce, who had learnt a great deal from his US experience of implementing XSEL, pointed out that a considerable amount of thought and work was required in planning a European pilot. There had to be agreement on what the pilot was trying to achieve, and a clear statement of this. There had to be top management support and user interest; and the machine capacity and equipment required to run XSEL had to be available. In addition, the role of FMIC in the pilot had to be thought through. ISTG in Hudson had to be prepared to commit resources to a European initiative. And a plan for the pilot had to be formulated and agreed.

However there were likely to be very real benefits to the European sales function, particularly through a reduction in existing costs. He listed some of these costs, giving examples from the United States.

- The estimated annual allowances for misquotes were $10,500,000. (These were financial allowances to customers because an order had not been correctly costed.)
- The estimated annual reduction in time for direct selling because problem orders containing errors had to be dealt with cost $6,300,000 (the argument here was that if the sales staff did not have to deal with these errors, they would have time to sell more hardware).
- The additional time spent configuring manually as opposed to using XSEL cost $5,250,000.

There were also other cost saving aspects of XSEL which were only just beginning to be recognized.

In addition there was evidence that the sales staff found XSEL of great value. A telephone survey of top salesmen in the US had found that 81 per cent were active XSEL users and 87 per cent of this group rated XSEL as 'very effective'.

The meeting concluded with the proposal and acceptance of plans for the setting up of a UK pilot for XSEL. The final decisions were:

- To carry out parallel trials in the Basingstoke, Birmingham and Utrecht sales offices. It was hoped that these would start on 1 July with a review in September.
- To introduce a new role into sales offices—that of Configuration Technical Specialist (CTS). The person in this role would be an expert in configuring. He or she would use XSEL to check the configuring process and ensure that orders were error free. It was proposed to have one CTS for every twenty sales staff. Altogether here would be 70 CTSs in Europe.
- XSEL would be located in Ayr and the pilot project would be managed by the Technical Edit Group there (FMIC). Basingstoke and Birmingham would use this machine. Utrecht would have XSEL on its own VAX machine.

- FMIC would be the UK centre of knowledge on configuring. They would monitor and evaluate the use and success of XSEL and report to Bruce's group in Hudson.
- Information and test use data would go from the pilot sites to Ayr and from Ayr to Hudson.

The goals of the pilot study were:

1. to check that XSEL could configure correctly and efficiently,
2. to examine the roles and relationships of sales people and the new Configuration Technical Specialists.

   The CTS was seen as a job for a young dynamic person who would be in it for two years, and then move into Sales.

The idea of having Configuration Technical Specialists as the principal users of XSEL came from European Sales Management in Geneva. They had created this new role to help solve the configuring problem before they were aware of the existence of XSEL. Bruce had some doubts about restricting the use of XSEL to the CTS. In his view the major benefit of XSEL was to the sales force. XSEL could help them reduce the amount of time they spent configuring orders and increase their selling productivity. If someone else used XSEL, there would be fewer benefits for salespeople.

Certainly, a smaller number of orders would be returned by Ayr for correction as the CTS would check that orders were correct before sending them off. But this would mainly help Ayr's objective of 'clean orders' for the Technical Edit group who would then have fewer problem orders to handle. The CTS role would not relieve the sales staff of configuring. They would still have to do this manually. There was also the possibility that the CTS role could become a bottleneck with sales staff unable to send their orders to Ayr until the CTS had time to check these.

The week after the Ayr meeting Bruce and Enid met another member of ISTG in London. They discussed the decisions that had been taken at Ayr and Enid's future research role. This would be to monitor and record the experiences of the three pilot groups—watching particularly for problems of trust, acceptance and organization. Very little research had as yet been carried out anywhere into how expert systems affected work organization and the jobs of individual users.

Bruce was anxious to establish the extent to which the parts data base in XSEL was correct for Europe, as Europe had some parts which were not used in the US. He also wanted to find out if the configuration rules were right for Europe and if there were any errors in these. Much of this information would come from Ayr.

He also wondered if UK sales staff were similar to or different from their American colleagues. Did they work in the same way and want the same kinds of information? It would be interesting to find out how well XSEL interfaced with the British users. What did British sales staff want from the system?

Lastly, he felt strongly that there was a need for a European 'user design' process. XSEL had been participatively designed by the US salesmen. Would it be possible to involve Europe Sales staff in redesigning the system to meet their needs. If this could not be done there was a risk that they would see XSEL as something developed by the US sales force for its own use, and not relevant to the needs of other countries.

THINGS START TO HAPPEN

In the spring of 1985 FMIC produced the first draft of a plan for setting up the European pilot. But, despite this initiative, progress towards implementing XSEL started slowing down after the first Ayr meeting. FMIC was still hoping to start the pilot project in Basingstoke and Birmingham on 1 June, but this date began to seem over-optimistic and unlikely to happen. It depended on Ayr getting XSEL up and running on a machine with enough capacity to handle communications from the two sales offices in Basingstoke and Birmingham. Utrecht was proposing to run XSEL on its own VAX machine and so there was no problem there. It had been decided that, initially, there would be three CTS—one for each pilot site. Their training would begin in Ayr in June.

As yet there was no project plan for the wider introduction of XSEL into Europe. Bruce was hoping to visit Ayr in June and work on this with the Ayr FMIC group and with one of the Geneva sales managers. UK sales management had now accepted the Geneva policy and decided definitely that CTS should be the sole users of XSEL.

Bruce was still not happy about this decision. XSEL had been designed for the sales force and it seemed unlikely that a single CTS, even using XSEL, could take over the configuring task entirely. This would mean that UK salespeople would still be left with the time consuming task of manually configuring orders. The proposal to introduce CTSs would clearly help the FMIC group at Ayr. Orders received from sales offices would now be correct because they had been checked by the CTS before transmission to Ayr. This would help sales staff as orders containing errors would not be returned to them for correction. But it would not save them a great deal of time. Letting the sales people use XSEL to do the initial configuring might produce a much greater saving.

This difference of opinion between Bruce, the FMIC group in Ayr and European sales management in Geneva seemed to have a number of causes.

Ayr was less concerned about saving sales force time than about receiving correct orders in the manufacturing plants. They therefore focused on their own priority problem. European sales management in Geneva had conceived the notion of CTSs some time before they became aware of XSEL. In their view the existence of a configuration specialist would reduce errors, whether or not he or she used XSEL. They were also unsure what XSEL had to offer—how good was it? What would it cost to run? What resources would it require? For Geneva the solution to the configuring problem was the CTS rather than XSEL, although they were prepared to let the CTS test XSEL out as an aid to productivity.

Here was an example of a problem that is often experienced when new systems are being designed and implemented. A number of different groups had an interest in XSEL and saw it as either helping or hindering their particular objectives. Somehow these differences would have to be resolved and XSEL introduced and organized in a way that enabled them to be met.

The plan now was to commence training the CTSs in Ayr in June. Once they were trained Bruce hoped that some of the sales force could also be given training so that they could be 'back-up' users of XSEL. He was very reluctant to have a situation in which only one person in a sales office, the CTS, had access to, and knew how to use XSEL. This seemed to be contrary to the purpose for which XSEL was created—to be a tool for the sales force.

He also thought that some experimentation would be a good idea. Why not let two pilot sites go along with the 'CTS as XSEL users' policy, but try a different approach in a third sales office by training the sales force there to be the principal users? This approach would provide flexibility and a learning situation. If the CTS strategy was not successful then it would be simple to change over to a 'sales staff as users' strategy.

Bruce recognized that there were problems in giving the sales force immediate access to XSEL. At present there were insufficient resources—for example, terminals and machine capacity—and salespeople might have too high expectations of what XSEL had to offer. The best policy would be to start training them slowly once the CTSs were trained. But he was anxious that giving the CTSs the sole use of XSEL might turn the sales staff against it. In the US the sales force saw itself as the owner of XSEL; if this was not going to be the case in the UK then XSEL had to be introduced with great care, and sales staff needed to have some control over any changes that occurred. Bruce was keen that the sales force should be directly and participatively involved in modifying XSEL. They needed to reorganize their work to fit with it and maximize its use, and they must agree the new roles and relationships that would be required.

SOME QUESTIONS FOR RESEARCH

In May, 1985, Enid went to Digital's UK Head Office in Reading to see the Sales Organization Development Manager. The visit was primarily to discuss how her research could be arranged so as to help Bruce and his team in Hudson. The Reading manager suggested that she should also do some work on sales office problems. This seemed to be an excellent idea. It would enable her to gain an understanding of how the two UK sales offices in the XSEL pilot functioned and this, in turn, would help her to appreciate the factors assisting or inhibiting an easy assimilation of XSEL. In 1983, when it was believed that XSEL would cross the Atlantic faster than it did, she had made a study of the organization of the Warrington sales office. Further studies would enable her to spend time in the pilot offices and become familiar with their needs and problems, while at the same time observing how XSEL was being used.

She agreed to try and identify and assess those factors that were assisting sales offices to maintain and increase their effectiveness and those factors which were reducing effectiveness.

The policy of European sales management in 1985 was to try and release the sales force from administrative activities so that they could concentrate on 'selling'. In order for this to happen a number of new administrative groups had been created to service the sales staff. These included Customer Administration Services (CAS), a group whose role was to relieve the sales force of many of its non-selling activities, for example such things as processing orders, chasing up overdue products, discussing delivery dates with customers. Another new service which formed part of CAS was the Customer Advisory Desk, a telephone answering facility whose staff could handle customer queries or ensure that these were routed to the person in the office best able to deal with them.

The Reading manager said that the CTS would be located in the CAS group and this new role fitted into the servicing model. The decision to give XSEL to the CTS was influenced by the policy of removing non-selling activities from the sales force. Selling activities were defined as face-to-face relationships with customers.

It was decided that the research should try and answer the following questions.

- Is the hypothesis correct that removing non-selling activities increases a sales person's effectiveness?
- What are the organizational difficulties associated with implementing this model?
- What are the principal factors in the sales office environment that contribute to the effectiveness of sales staff?

- What are the problems and constraints that reduce effectiveness?
- To what extent can XSEL contribute to effectiveness?
- Should it be given to sales staff?
- How significant are the configuring errors in UK sales offices?
- To what extent can UK sales staff trust XSEL?
- To what extent does XSEL need designing by, or for, UK salespeople?

The principal research output was to be a report on how the effectiveness of sales staff could be maintained and increased. A detailed record would also be made of the UK experience in using and introducing XSEL.

At this meeting Enid learned that the decision to test XSEL in the Basingstoke and Birmingham sales offices had now been altered, and the Leeds sales office had been substituted for Birmingham. She wrote to the Sales Administration managers at Basingstoke and Leeds, asking if she could visit them to discuss the research.

SETTING UP THE PILOT

The next meeting to discuss the XSEL UK pilot was held in Ayr in June. Representatives of four different groups were present. The FMIC technical edit group, European sales management, Geneva, UK Sales and ISTG. One of the UK sales managers at the meeting had been designated XSEL project manager and Bruce was looking after the interests of ISTG. Each group was likely to regard XSEL from its own particular perspective.

The FMIC group said that they had been involved for some time in testing XCON, but had had, as yet, no contact with XSEL. They believed that their experience with XCON would have some relevance for the XSEL pilot. When XCON was first tried out in Ayr they judged that its accuracy with European systems was about 50 per cent. They believed that this had now considerably improved.

It must be noted that disputes between Ayr and Hudson over the accuracy of XCON had arisen immediately testing began and could not be resolved for a considerable period of time. They were caused by disagreements over evaluation criteria and testing procedures. How, for example, should a missing part which turned up in 500 orders be treated? Ayr took the view that all these were wrongly configured, and in a test of a 1000 orders would rate XCON as only 50 per cent accurate as a result. Hudson argued for the view that repeated errors like these could be the result of quick manual revisions and should be treated less stringently. By the June meeting a better understanding had been reached, and both organizations agreed that XCON was more than 90 per cent correct. The XCON pilot was now over. XCON's knowledge base would become operational for the next product release and should then have 95 per cent accuracy. This meant that XCON would be properly integrated into the work of FMIC. At present orders were checked manually for Manufacturing.

The meeting now discussed FMIC's role in relation to XSEL. FMIC had agreed to provide the computer and human resources to support an XSEL pilot in the UK. Their role, as they saw it, was to assist the assimilation of XCON and XSEL into Europe; to be responsible for European knowledge acquisition and for monitoring the XCON/XSEL knowledge base. They were also prepared to take responsibility for advising Manufacturing and Sales about XCON/XSEL deficiencies, for dealing with problems coming from Manufacturing and Sales, and for acting as the European interface to the XSEL/XCON development team in Hudson.

This led once again to a lively debate on the accuracy of XCON and XSEL, particularly in relation to new product information. The Ayr group stressed the difference between Europe and the United States. They pointed out that although XSEL was intended to be a corporate tool its development had been influenced by its use to the United States. It therefore included features which would not be used in Europe.

Bruce accepted that this was a problem but said that XSEL's knowledge base could be changed. He went on to explain the knowledge acquisition process.

> "Twenty-eight people support XCON and XSEL. Of these, about fifteen are the rule writers. There are five teams—each with five or six members—and each team has total responsibility for a product. We spend a lot of time on knowledge acquisition but it is hard to get data, and even harder to get it in advance of product announcements."

The meeting agreed that there must be a group in Ayr to give Bruce advice on how the knowledge base should be changed to meet European needs.

Bruce made another point about XSEL's capability.

> "Although FMIC has been evaluating the accuracy of XCON, XSEL contains 2400 rules of a different kind. Whereas XCON is intended to help Manufacturing to configure and assemble systems accurately, XSEL is to help the salesperson produce a correct list of items for a customer's system, which can be submitted to XCON. This list of items has not yet been evaluated to check its fit for the European user. This needs to be done."

This raised some questions on the differences between XCON and XSEL. Was XSEL just a checking tool or could it also configure—give advice to the salesman on how the different components in a system needed to relate to each other?

Bruce explained that there was a terminology problem with XSEL and XCON. XCON was the principal configuring tool and told Manufacturing how the hardware components must relate to each other. XSEL specified the required hardware components. It could show the customer what he needed to purchase and the salesperson what he or she needed to order.

Discussion now turned to the pilot and how XSEL's performance could be evaluated. What should be measured? Was it increased customer satisfaction; a reduction in the time sales staff needed to configure orders, or the accuracy of XSEL in checking quotes for customer orders?

The divergent interests of those present now became apparent, as they had at the previous meeting. XSEL was being considered from very different points of view, and by people with very different opinions and objectives.

One of the UK sales representatives who was manager of a CAS group said that he regarded XSEL as part of a productivity drive to reduce the cost of order booking. He explained:

> "Sales is trying to get more business out of fewer sales staff. They are interested in the organizational effectiveness of salespeople. There is a need to make the salesperson efficient first, then effective. We don't want sales to do tasks that others can do, for example, quote preparation and configuring."

In reply to this Bruce pointed out that XSEL had been designed to help salespeople with the configuring task. A US survey had shown that 25 per cent of a salesperson's time was spent on problem orders.

The new UK XSEL project manager, supported his colleague, saying:

> "The introduction of a Configuration Technical Specialist into the Basingstoke sales office has resulted in a spectacular improvement of quality and raised questions about the need for XSEL. We think the CTS role is very important. We could be wrong. The US may be right in giving XSEL to sales staff."

It was clear that there were two very strong views in the meeting. The Geneva and UK sales groups who wanted, if possible, to remove configuring from the sales force so as to give them more time for selling; and Bruce's US view that XSEL had been designed for the sales force and they should have it. The Ayr FMIC group's principal concern was that orders should not be sent from sales offices to Manufacturing unless they were correct. They therefore supported the use of XSEL by the CTS as a way of ensuring that order checking was accurate.

Bruce saw a number of weaknesses in the proposal to make the CTS the principal XSEL user. In his view this would not be popular with the sales force. They would be reluctant to hand this activity over to someone else because it affected their relationships with customers. Incorrect orders damaged Digital's image and the sales person's credibility. It was bad when the sales person made a configuring mistake—it would be far worse if someone else made the mistake yet the sales executive was held responsible by the customer. Also, he believed that it would be impossible for a CTS to handle all configuring. If he or she tried to do so a tremendous bottleneck would be created which would slow down order processing and frustrate the sales staff. But if the CTS was only given the task of checking the correctness of orders, with XSEL as an aid, then the sales force would still have to do the early configuring for quotations and orders. If they had to continue doing this manually little of their time would be saved.

Bruce felt that the problem of how XSEL could be most effectively fitted into a sales office was not being systematically thought through. European sales were trying to fit a sophisticated tool into a new organizational structure, CAS, which had been devised without any knowledge of XSEL's possibilities. He tried to get the meeting to address this problem but it was not easy to do so. It seemed they had already taken the strategic decision to introduce the CTS role and to remove non-selling activities from sales staff. They were not to be shifted away from this model. XSEL had to fit into it.

The argument continued for the rest of the day, moving later into a debate on exactly how many configuring errors now occurred. On this issue there was also a considerable difference of opinion.

Later, Bruce again raised the question of measurement, suggesting some results that were required from the use of XSEL. For example,

clean system orders
clean system quotes
greater sales staff efficiency
reduced customer allowances
reduced number of change orders
increased customer satisfaction
more expert system sales

He also raised again the issue of the goals of the XSEL project. Were these:

1. To prove that XSEL produces clean, error-free, orders?
2. To prove the effectiveness of XSEL in handling a number of quotes?
3. To assess the ability of XSEL to increase sales force productivity through assisting sales executives to configure accurately?

But it proved difficult to get the meeting to address these issues. Attention and discussion focused on the new CTS role and on sales force efficiency. There appeared to be little interest in XSEL and little understanding of what it had to offer. There was also some anxiety about how much XSEL would cost to introduce and run. Europe had to be sure that there would be a return on investment.

DIFFERENT INTERESTS AND CONFLICTING VIEWS

There seemed to be conflicting views on the seriousness of the configuring problem. Some of those present thought that little of a sales executive's time was spent configuring, others believed that configuring errors lost Digital large sums of money.

The European and UK sales management representatives were strongly committed to the new CTS role, saw no problems in its introduction and believed that sales staff would welcome it. But they did not necessarily believe that the CTS needed to use XSEL to be effective.

Enid wondered if this CTS role would be a viable one. It was an interface role between FMIC in Ayr and the sales force, and boundary roles of this kind are notoriously difficult to manage. FMIC appeared to see the CTS as an extension of themselves in the sales offices. Instead of sales staff having to telephone Ayr if they had configuring problems, they would, in the future, go to the CTS for assistance. But would the sales staff welcome and accept the role? Would they see it as eroding one of their important responsibilities? And, how would it affect the role of FMIC? They would be losing some of their present tasks and responsibilities.

Another question was, 'Are XSEL and the CTS role complementary, overlapping or conflicting? If XSEL was in use was the CTS necessary and vice versa'? The view of the meeting appeared to be that the CTS was more important than XSEL. The sales management present appeared to have little understanding of XSEL and of what it could do.

The FMIC view was that XSEL was required. It would be difficult for the CTS to keep up with new products, and not all CTS would be expert configurers. They saw the CTS as having the dual role of checking quotes and orders and giving advice on configuring problems.

They saw the goal of the XSEL pilot as 'assessing the value of XSEL as a tool to assist in ensuring clean quotes and orders'. Clean orders meant that there would be fewer change orders, reduced customer allowances, greater sales office efficiency, more customer satisfaction and greater potential sales effectiveness.

They also believed that although the pilot would be carried out by FMIC it was essential that it should be run as a partnership between FMIC, ISTG and Sales. There should be monthly review meetings, with the venue rotated around the pilot sites. The target for the presentation of the pilot results would be the end of October, 1985.

The minutes of the June meetings were sent to the Senior European Sales Manager in Geneva. On receiving them he sent a note to the FMIC Manager, with a copy to all those who attended the meeting. He made his position very clear by saying:

"I would like to confirm the following points:

1. We are definitely going ahead with the CTS program and it is essential that

we continue getting your support to make this happen. Our first CTS in the Basingstoke sales office has enabled errors in configuration to drop from 144 in April to two in May.

   If we simply focus on some major mistakes the quality rapidly improves. In addition the CTS is of use to our OEMs to help them configure.

2. The XSEL pilot is to test what XSEL will add to the CTS specialist. At present, as you know, I am still not at all convinced by XSEL, but the final decision will take place after the pilot."

Bruce, now back in Hudson, was not happy with the outcome of the Ayr meeting. He had not succeeded in getting the participants to define their goals for XSEL or the success criteria they wished to measure. He also recognized that some conflict of goals was emerging. European Sales were committed to the new CTS role and were only prepared to accept XSEL if it was used by the CTS. Bruce's experience with XSEL in the US had persuaded him that XSEL might make the CTS role unnecessary, but Europe was apparently not prepared to examine this possibility.

   The Ayr and European groups saw the objective of the pilot as measuring XSEL's accuracy. In Bruce's opinion a more important objective was to find out how XSEL could best fit in with sales office processes and procedures.

   He felt that those present at the Ayr meeting had not really thought through the management of the pilot and it was important that the pilot should not be started until this was done.

   Two major questions were now associated with the use of XSEL in Europe. First, the practical one of was XSEL accurate? Did it configure as well as a human expert? It would be an undesirable and expensive innovation if it did not. Second, how should it fit into the organization of sales offices? ISTG had designed it for sales staff but Europe wanted to relieve its sales force of non-selling tasks and had introduced the new role of CTS to assist this policy. The CTS was to be an expert configurer. Did sales offices want both a human and an automated expert?

DOUBTS ABOUT XSEL

At the end of July Bruce was still worried about the progress of the XSEL project in Europe. He had heard from the FMIC manager in Ayr that the senior European Sales Manager had withdrawn his support from XSEL and was now saying that he was not prepared to commit any funds to it. Bruce pointed out with some amazement that he had not yet been asked for any funds. To confuse matters further, the American manager responsible for Digital Europe had recently appeared in a videofilm saying how much he welcomed and supported XSEL. But he was also known to support the move towards more standardized systems and Bruce suspected that this strategy was causing some ambivalence in attitudes to XSEL. One of XSEL's principal virtues was that it could configure a wide variety of systems without any difficulty. If Digital reduced its product variety too much XSEL could be seen as less valuable.

It seemed that strategic decisions which had still to be taken would greatly influence XSEL's value to the company.

Bruce felt that these changes in top management strategies were affecting attitudes to XSEL. When he had talked to the European Sales Manager the previous December it had been agreed then that if the XSEL trials went well an implementation plan would be drawn up and XSEL would be introduced into Europe. This now seemed to be increasingly uncertain.

Views in Ayr also seemed to be altering, but in a pro-XSEL direction. Management there had begun to think that the plan to introduce CTS into all sales offices might prove unworkable because it was too expensive. This made the introduction of XSEL all the more necessary. The FMIC manager suggested that they should get out the costs of using XSEL and show how little it cost in comparison with employing CTS experts. The proposed CTS role could be carried out, as it was now, by FMIC. It seemed that FMIC were beginning to suspect that the new CTS role could threaten their own activities in a variety of possible ways.

Bruce's personal view was that there was a need both for XSEL and for some product standardization. Even if the number of standard systems increased by 50 per cent the non-standard part of the business would still be substantial.

In August the problems continued. FMIC became increasingly convinced that the European sales group in Geneva were enthusiastic about the value of the new CTS role, but lukewarm, if not disinterested, in XSEL. The manager at Ayr responsible for XCON and XSEL came to the conclusion that he might be asked to stop the pilot which was now underway in the Basingstoke and Leads sales offices. Bruce appealed to him not to do so.

These doubts about XSEL in Geneva caused increasing anxiety in Ayr. Ayr had agreed to bear the costs of the pilot, but Manufacturing management there, which had responsibility for FMIC, became more and more concerned that European Sales might decide not to implement XSEL. The senior manufacturing manager in Ayr finally decided that Geneva must provide evidence of their commitment. He went to see the European sales manager, and told him that Geneva Sales must pay half the costs of the XSEL pilot. These amounted to $50,000. Geneva refused to do this. Ayr then cut off the communication lines between the sales offices and Ayr. Leeds and Basingstoke could no longer use XSEL.

This was not seen as helpful by UK sales management and at the end of August the UK Sales Organization Development Manager, wrote to Geneva asking why this had been done and protesting that things were happening without the 'field'—Leeds and Basingstoke Sales Offices—being consulted. Geneva responded by calling a meeting of European and UK sales management. At this meeting the European sales manager stressed his total commitment to the CTS role. He said that he was still interested in XSEL but only as a tool for the CTS. He did not see it as a tool for the sales force.

These problems seemed to have arisen for the two reasons already referred to. First, the development of XSEL in the States meant that there was little knowledge of it in Europe. People were unaware of what it had to offer; they were also unaware of what expert systems generally had to offer. Second, at the time the pilot for XSEL was being discussed Geneva had already formulated a new policy for improving the effectiveness of sales offices. This was directed at reducing the non-selling activities of the sales force and introducing the Configuration Technical Specialist role. Geneva did not see how XSEL could enhance this strategy and European sales management were also worried at what it would cost. These perceptions and decisions made European top management very ambivalent about XSEL. A third reason was that, despite Bruce's early endeavours, no European sales managers or salespeople had played any role in its development. There was no sense of ownership.

ISTG in Hudson, in contrast, was anxious to diffuse an excellent example of Digital's lead in artificial intelligence throughout the company. They knew XSEL worked and saved money, but it was difficult for them to communicate these facts to Europe. The XSEL pilot sales offices in the UK were also keen to continue testing XSEL and appreciative of its potential value. Their reaction was quite different from that of European Sales and they were very indignant when the XSEL pilot was suddenly terminated.

ARGUMENTS FOR AND AGAINST XSEL

The arguments in favour of XSEL from a European perspective were that, given the CTS role now existed, a CTS would make fewer errors with XSEL than without it. Also, many future occupants of the CTS role would not have a comprehensive knowledge of Digital products. XSEL could help them acquire this. XSEL would also be an excellent training tool for people in the CTS role. It could provide a new recruit with a prop and a guide when learning the job. It could also act as a continuing trainer as new products and options were added to the Digital range. And, should Digital wish to abandon or change the CTS role in the future, XSEL would enable the sales staff, or any other group, to assume the configuring task without difficulty.

But there was another, even more important, set of arguments from a wider company perspective. These related to Digital's image, credibility and AI marketing strategy. The European AI community were now well aware of XCON and XSEL. Descriptions of these systems had been given in many of the most influential AI books. In addition a senior member of the ISTG had recently made a videofilm for the Alvey Directorate—the British Government body sponsoring AI research—on how XCON and XSEL had been designed and the benefits which Digital was deriving from these systems. This would have a wide circulation throughout Europe. If XSEL was then not introduced into Europe, this could be interpreted by the outside world as Digital showing a lack of confidence in its own products, and abandoning its leadership role in AI. This could put in jeopardy a major marketing advantage in the AI product area.

Towards the end of September Bruce was very relieved to hear that the XSEL pilot was restarting. It was now proposed that the pilot should run for an eight to twelve week period from October to December, with a management review in January. FMIC was still favourably disposed towards XSEL although they wanted its accuracy improving. They believed that it would become increasingly accurate as new products were added to its knowledge base.

Unfortunately this proposal to restart the pilot was not implemented immediately because Ayr now did not have a VAX machine available on which to run the pilot. The machine which they had proposed to use for this purpose was being used for work viewed by management as more important than XSEL. The pilot would have to wait until the end of November when Ayr would receive a new VAX.

The continuing delays and problems meant that the FMIC group at Ayr were showing an understandable, but increasing irritation with their XSEL commitments. Even though the new VAX did arrive in November, they began suggesting that European Sales in Geneva should provide a machine and take responsibility for designing the pilot. After all, they said, Sales were the intended users of XSEL.

Bruce became apprehensive that FMIC would refuse to accept responsibility for running XSEL on a long-term basis once the pilot was over. Anticipating further machine availability problems he started preparing XSEL to run on Digitals new MicroVax 11—a small machine which had just come on the market.

Bruce now felt that there was a need for an intervention on his part which would make the Geneva group's attitudes towards XSEL more positive. He wrote two papers: the first setting out the worth of XSEL to European Sales if used in addition to the CTS programme; the second showing the value of XSEL to European Sales if used without, or instead of, the CTS programme.

In these papers he considered three basic activities of the order preparation process. These were:

1. The time it takes for sales representatives to manually prepare systems configurations for quotation, compared to the time it will take with XSEL plus the CTS in place.
2. The time it takes sales representatives to administer the change order process. (Altering an order to correct errors or omissions.)

3. The amount of allowances that are made to customers because of configuration errors.

Bruce had to base the figures in these papers on a number of assumptions. He predicted that over a five-year period Digital would be employing 1200 European sales staff; that XSEL would be implemented in time to affect 12 per cent of orders in the 1986 financial year, and that XSEL would only be used on 75 per cent of configurations.

If these assumptions were correct Bruce estimated that the use of a CTS plus XSEL would produce annual savings of $4,533,000 by 1990. This model included the costs of the CTS salary and training as well as the costs of running and developing XSEL. It did not include the savings to Manufacturing from receiving orders that were always correct.

If XSEL was used without a CTS then the savings were even greater and were estimated at $12,706,000. This suggested that XSEL was a more cost effective way of checking orders than a CTS. It must be remembered, however, that the CTS was being introduced with a dual role—to check orders, but also to act as a technical expert who gave advice to sales staff on configuring problems.

These figures were based on US experience of the factors that created costs and benefits. Bruce was unable to produce a breakdown of the savings provided by a CTS working without XSEL—the original European strategy, as the role of CTS did not exist in the United States.

Bruce had clearly now made a powerful financial case for XSEL, although it was apparent that European Sales were totally committed to the CTS role and would not abandon it. But at the beginning of December the XSEL pilot had still not restarted and the Leeds and Basingstoke sales offices were becoming increasingly frustrated.

HUDSON INTERVENES

During December Enid went over to Hudson to see Bruce. She found considerable anxiety in ISTG over what was happening in Europe. They could not understand why there was so much reluctance to go ahead with the XSEL pilot. Dennis O'Connor, the manager of ISTG, was concerned about the problems which were affecting the attempt to introduce XSEL into Europe. He believed that a rejection of XSEL by European Sales might have an adverse effect on Digital's reputation as a world leader in the design and use of expert systems, and on its ability to sell these systems to its customers.

Dennis decided to discuss the XSEL problem with his boss, Bill Hanson, who was Vice-President Manufacturing Operations and very senior in the management structure. He then sent a memo to Pier-Carlo Falotti, the Managing

Director of Digital, Europe, headed *Leadership in The European Marketplace*. In his memo Dennis emphasized Digital's lead in the use of large expert system technology applications, and the expanding marketing opportunities in this field. He then expressed anxiety at Europe's slowness in accepting XSEL. He concluded by asking Pier-Carlo for help in speeding up XSEL's introduction into Europe.

Dennis sent a copy of his note to Bill Hanson, his own boss, to Bruce and to a number of other senior managers.

A new factor in XSEL's favour was that a group of senior US managers were now engaged in an 'order improvement exercise'. They saw XSEL as playing an integral part in the order processing procedures and making a major contribution to the efficiency of these. But while a strategic debate on AI and experts systems was taking place amongst senior management, at the grass roots level of the UK sales offices expert systems were still little known and understood. A member of the Basingstoke sales office commented to Enid at this time:

> "You keep coming here and saying how advanced XSEL is and how Digital is leading the world in AI. But we know nothing about XSEL. We've hardly heard of it."

1985. ATTITUDES AND ACTIVITIES IN EUROPE

During 1985 the planning, setting up and progress of the XSEL pilot was influenced by the differing reactions to XSEL in the various groups with an interest in the functioning of sales offices.

Bruce, as he had always done, saw the European sales force as the principal users of XSEL. XSEL had been developed by US salespeople for use by salespeople. He was concerned that there was opposition to this policy in Europe. In his view the route to the future lay in providing more and better tools for the sales force, not in adding support organizations which would tend to become bureaucracies. His vision was of an XSEL that was so easy to use that one had only to specify a few salient high-level characteristics of a proposed system, and XSEL would do the rest. But, he thought, we will never get there if we keep assigning these tools to support people.

FMIC in Ayr were broadly in favour of XSEL but somewhat ambivalent about the CTS role which they suspected might threaten their future existence by removing responsibility for checking orders from their technical edit function. They were also not convinced that the configuring knowledge of the new CTS was sufficient to prevent incorrect orders being sent to Ayr from the sales offices. They saw XSEL as a means for helping the CTS to avoid errors. In their view it should be used by the CTS and not by the sales force.

The ISTG group took yet another position. Senior management there were dedicated to ensuring that Digital was a world leader in the development of artificial intelligence and the building of expert systems. This required a public demonstration that the company had these systems and was using them. XSEL was important to AI marketing.

The end of 1985 saw Digital faced with managing a complex European situation in which the various groups had different, often conflicting, attitudes and expectations. These had to be resolved.

It must be stressed that any international company introducing a revolutionary new technical system into another part of the world would face similar problems of communication, support generation and the creation of interest and confidence in those receiving the innovation. None of these would be susceptible to rapid solution and great political skill would be required in their resolution.

Some interesting lessons can be learnt from the Digital experience of trying to introduce XSEL into Europe. First, that an innovation developed in one country and culture is not easy to transfer to another. Resistance to change was shown less in outright rejection of XSEL than in a refusal to alter organizational arrangements to accommodate it. Innovation had to fit into the existing organization of the European sales office and this was quite different from the US structure.

Second, it is often argued that innovation is acceptable when a problem is recognized as painful and serious. This is undoubtedly true but in the Digital situation European management believed that they had solved the configuring problem by introducing a human configuring expert. They did not perceive the need for an automated solution as well.

Third, innovation is viewed as desirable or undesirable to the extent that it assists or threatens the interests of the groups affected by it. When a group is both powerful and strongly in favour its voice is likely to have a strong influence on how the innovation is implemented. This strategy will not necessarily be viewed as the best one by other groups.

Fourth, acceptance of an innovation is assisted by the participation of future users in planning for its introduction and use. In Europe there was disagreement over who the future users should be. European Sales wanted the CTS to operate XSEL, if it was to be introduced at all. Bruce believed that it should be a tool for the sales force. In the event, neither the CTS nor the sales force had any say in the matter. The decision was taken by Sales Administration in Geneva and FMIC in Ayr.

Lastly, good communication plays a vital role in stimulating interest and acceptance of innovation. There was very little information about XSEL in Europe. Few people in the sales offices had heard of it. There was no appreciation of its potential and value.

*Well the time drew on that
the pilgrims must go on
their way, wherefore they
prepared for their journey.
They sent for their friends,
they conferred with them.*

John Bunyan

Chapter 10

XSEL IN EUROPE: PLANNING CONTINUES

XSEL's use by salespeople in the United States had demonstrated its accuracy in an American context, but the European group wished to check its accuracy in their own situation. They had to be absolutely sure that their first expert system did not make mistakes. XSEL had three potential sources of error. First, some of Digital's European products were not sold in the States or were given different names and numbers there. XSEL would not recognize these products and therefore needed to be amended to fit the European scene. This was not a very serious problem provided that, in the short term, the European users knew which these products were and did not ask XSEL to deal with them. A second more serious difficulty was XSEL's need for constant updating. Digital was continually launching new products and these had to be entered into XSEL's database as quickly as possible once they were being sold to customers. Bruce's ISTG group was responsible for updating in the States, but there was no comparable group to do this in Europe.

The XSEL/XCON technical group had been entering the European variants of Digital's products into the data base from the beginning. However, until there was active European use of XSEL, there had been no systematic testing of the completeness of this process. Also, in Europe, certain components were bundled together and sold as a single product, which caused problems both for XCON and for XSEL. All of these issues would now have to be effectively addressed by ISTG in Hudson if Europe were going to put the system into production use.

A third problem is that expert systems can never be totally accurate. Because expert systems are always in a state of development with the knowledge base being added to as new knowledge is acquired or old revised, they can never reach a final state of complete accuracy. There will always be knowledge gaps or items of knowledge which are ambiguous or imprecise.

The European sales group were concerned about these problems, particularly the first—the number of items of information in XSEL that were correct in the United States but incorrect in Europe. They also wanted to test XSEL's ease of use, cost-effectiveness and resource requirements. They needed to ensure that the pilot provided data on all these things.

THE PILOT RESTARTS

On Monday, 7 January 1986, Enid heard from the Leeds sales office that the XSEL pilot was to restart in the following week. Both Leeds and Basingstoke were waiting for Ayr to send them some evaluation criteria against which they could judge XSEL. At the same time, in Ayr, FMIC was finalizing a second version of the XSEL pilot process document.

In this document the goals of the pilot were described as:

> to gather information which will help assess the value of XSEL as a tool to assist Configuration Technical Specialists in ensuring that system 'orders' are technically complete before quote generation and/or order entry.

It also clarified what would happen in the pilot.

> The CTS will have remote access to the XSEL/XCON software running on a 11/ 785 VAX machine located in Ayr. For the duration of the pilot they will be required to process all system proposals and orders through XSEL/XCON, as they receive these from the sales staff. This will be done in parallel with their normal quote/order completeness check.

During the pilot the following measurements will be made.

> XSEL reliability
> • The percentage of XSEL recommended configurations that are clear of errors.
> • The percentage of CTS approved configurations that are clear of errors.
>
> Computer resource
> • XSEL/XCON machine utilization.
> • Throughput of orders.

In addition assessments will be made of the following:

> • the ease of using XSEL/XCON,
> • the responsiveness of XSEL/XCON,
> • the configuration expertise required to use XSEL/XCON
> • the level of support required from FMIC,
> • the level of support required from ISTG.

On 10 January 1986, FMIC sent out the following note to all those concerned with the XSEL pilot.

> The European pilot will commence on Monday, 15th January, and will run until the end of March. To achieve its required objectives the pilot has been designed to:
>
> Measure
> • The reliability of XSEL's configuration recommendations.
> • Machine utilization.

Assess
- The ease of using XSEL.
- The configuration experience required to use XSEL.

Pilot findings will be published weekly and monthly. Review meetings involving FMIC and Field and Area Sales Operations will be held to monitor progress and process.

On completion of the pilot, Sales Operations will draw up a proposal for future action.

When the pilot did restart the objective was principally, although not solely, to judge XSEL's accuracy. The Leeds and Basingstoke CTS were asked to keep records of XSEL errors and omissions and make sure that Ayr was notified of these. Bruce was not at all happy about this. He recognized that it was important to know what modifications needed to be made in XSEL to fit the European sales situation. But he believed that XSEL's general accuracy had been thoroughly tested in the United States and also by the Ayr XCON pilot study. Because both XCON and XSEL used the same data, if one was accurate then the other would also be accurate. In Bruce's view, what was needed in Europe was a pilot which would test different ways of using XSEL in sales offices and come to some conclusions on how each sales office could use it most effectively.

Bruce would have preferred a much broader evaluation of XSEL's capability than the one proposed. He wanted answers to questions such as:

What are the benefits that sales offices can derive from XSEL?
Which of these can be measured?
What are the most useful measures?

He believed that sales offices would say that they were seeking the same benefits from XSEL as they would require from any other tool or technique—improved selling performance, better customer relationships and loyalty, more effective use of sales staff's time, no major increase in costs without commensurate benefits.

He wanted XSEL to be measured in terms of its *effectiveness* in helping a sales office to achieve these objectives; in terms of its *efficiency* as a viable operational tool; in terms of its *acceptability* to the sales force, other sales office staff, and customers, and in terms of its general *usability* as shown by its diffusion to a large number of sales offices and customers.

Useful measures of effectiveness would be:

- The improved quality of the order processing task. (A higher percentage of correct quotes and orders.)
- The reduced time spent on configuring. (This would relate to all staff who did configuring whether salespersons or CTS.)

Measures of efficiency would be,

- Ease of use. (Time required to access XSEL, clarity of instructions and options.)
- Ease of learning. (Time required to learn how to use XSEL.) XSEL's value as a configuring training tool also needed to be assessed.
- Comprehensiveness. (The percentage of orders that XSEL can deal with satisfactorily; the nature of the orders with which it cannot cope.)
- Accuracy. (The number of rules and amount of data that do not fit the European situation.)
- Special instructions. (Sales staff often send special instructions to Manufacturing. The extent to which XSEL can cope with these.)

Acceptability could be measured by 'amount of use', 'generality of use' and 'satisfaction with use'. *Diffusion* by noting how quickly a knowledge of XSEL and a desire to use it diffused to other sales offices and customers.

Bruce also believed that the optimal use of XSEL required some experimentation with different ways of fitting it into sales office organization, and an evaluation of these in terms of the needs of each situation. Organizational options were:

- Orders were configured by sales staff without using XSEL, and passed to the CTS who checked these with XSEL before sending them through to Ayr.
- The sales force did a generic configuration without using XSEL. The CTS completed these using XSEL and sent them through to Ayr.
- The sales force did their own configuring, using XSEL, and consulted the CTS over difficult problems.
- The sales force did not configure. All configuring was done by the CTS, using XSEL.

One problem that was of concern to the group at Ayr, to European Headquarters and to the Sales Offices was the amount of hardware that would be required to support the use of XSEL throughout Europe. This would be a major element in XSEL costs. Discussion was also commencing on the nature of this hardware. Should a number of large VAX machines be located in different parts of the UK and dedicated to the use of XSEL or would it be preferable for each sales office to have a small MicroVAX and run XSEL on this.

The major cost factors were telecommunications costs, user support costs, the cost of operator training, and terminal and printer costs.

Telecommunications costs were hard to determine as they would differ significantly between countries. User support costs fell into two categories— hardware costs and the costs of installing and maintaining the software on the systems. Hardware costs could be worked out without difficulty on the basis of machines and maintenance. Software maintenance costs were more complex. There would be a cost in loading XSEL software into the system but a more significant cost would be the XSEL updates which would be required every quarter.

During the pilot, software was being supported by Hudson in the US. But if Europe installed XSEL on a large number of sites then some kind of European support organization would be required. This would involve decisions on who was to be responsible for support and where this group was to be located. The cost of operator training would depend on the number of users of the system. Training would need to be an ongoing activity. Terminal and printer costs would again be influenced by the number of users.

A problem with estimating these costs was knowing how XSEL would be used in the different sales offices and different countries. For example, each district office might have a small MicroVAX machine; or each country might install a large VAX for use by its district offices; or a number of large VAXs might form part of a geographic network which any sales office could access.

Whereas in 1985 the principal question was 'shall we use XSEL in Europe'? In 1986 serious consideration was being given to *how* XSEL should be used, and to the various options that needed to be examined.

A REVIEW OF THE PILOT

The first meeting to review the progress of the XSEL pilot was held at Digital's UK office in Reading, in February. Those present wanted answers to two questions. These were:

1. At what point do we decide if the accuracy of XSEL is good enough?
2. How do we implement XSEL in the sales offices?

The view of the meeting was that the pilot results so far showed XSEL to have a high degree of accuracy. It was decided that the pilot should continue until the end of April. If at the end of April the results continued to be good, then firm plans should be made for XSEL's implementation.

The minutes of this meeting, written by one of the Geneva managers, listed the expected benefits of XSEL for different sales office groups. These were:

XSEL—EXPECTED BENEFITS FOR SALES OFFICES

1. FOR THE CUSTOMER
   —Accurate quotes and orders.
   —Better documentation of quotes: diagrams, layouts, unused machine capacity.
   —XSEL will help ensure there is a complete, installable system which arrives on time.
   —Enhanced customer satisfaction and Digital image.

2. FOR THE SALES FORCE
   —Orders without errors.
   —Time saved in: configuring and checking quotes and orders; time saved in chasing problem orders.
   —Better documentation for presentation to potential customers.
   —A marketing message: Digital is using AI/Expert systems in its own business.

All of these should produce improved productivity and a better image. Increased business should result from increased selling time.

3. CTS SPECIALIST
   —Time saved in providing configuring support to Sales and in quote and order checking.
   —Greater accuracy
   —Updated information and support
   —XSEL can act as a replacement in sales offices where the sales volume is too low to warrant a CTS.

The advantages should lead to higher productivity and accuracy for the customer and better sales consultancy, training, etc.

4. COST SAVINGS
   —Fewer cash allowances will be made to customers for missing items of equipment.
   —Orders will be altered less frequently, thereby reducing administrative and selling costs.

5. FMIC—AYR
   —Fewer problems with incorrect orders.

This will mean there is more time available to support the CTS in the sales offices.

6. CUSTOMER ADMINISTRATION SERVICE GROUP
   —Correct orders
   —Faster throughput of order processing

By the end of February, the tide was slowly, but increasingly, turning in favour of XSEL. In the US Manufacturing had become very interested in the contribution XSEL could make to improved efficiency and lower costs. In the UK some interesting figures were coming out of the XSEL pilot. These showed that while the accuracy of a CTS in ensuring correct orders was greater than that of a salesperson, the accuracy of XSEL was considerably greater than that of a CTS. The fact that the CTS in Leeds, Basingstoke and Utrecht had been checking orders without XSEL during the period when the line with Ayr was cut, enabled these comparisons to be made.

Countries other than the United States and those in Europe were planning to implement XSEL and they too had been testing it out. Geneva sales management contacted the manager in charge of GIA (General International Areas—Canada, Australia, the Far East, India, etc.) to find out what he had been doing. They asked:

- Does GIA plan to move the technical edit function to the sales offices. If so, is XSEL part of this plan?
- During the GIA test of XSEL were quotations configured and checked with XSEL or was it just orders?
- Who will actually use the system in the GIA sales areas—will it be the sales force, sales administrators or the tech edit staff? (The GIA countries did not have the CTS role.)
- What procedures will be established to handle the various activities involved in processing an order—from first quote to final checking of the order?

The GIA manager replied that he had been working on a support plan for XSEL in the GIA regions. All the regions were in the process of ordering large VAX machines and the MicroVAX II machine had been tested to see if that could be used in smaller areas. It was hoped to begin implementation in Canada at the end of 1986. Other regions would go on the system in 1987. He was preparing an implementation plan and working out the support requirements of using XSEL and XCON.

He told Geneva that he saw everyone—sales representatives, administrative support staff, tech edit staff—using the system. But he saw administrative support becoming increasingly involved once they had become used to XSEL. He said:

> "Why tie the rep up doing a new configuration if it is a look alike with that of another customer. With XSEL we can call up the old configuration, modify it, and check it for validity. One of the support staff can do this, and more, once learning curves are overcome."

He continued,

> "We know the system works—it is getting people to use and understand it that is difficult."

MORE MEETINGS

On Tuesday, 1 April, Bruce and Enid met in Geneva for talks with the European Sales Group. After these were over they planned to meet some of the Ayr managers in London and to continue on to an implementation planning meeting at the Basingstoke Sales Office.

In Geneva, they talked with one of the sales managers about the new CTS role in sales offices. He was pleased with the success of this and said that sales offices were finding quite a few technically competent and experienced people who wanted the job. These tended to come from Field Service. The expectation was that they would move into Sales after spending some time as a CTS. Bruce had some doubts about the long-term viability of the CTS role. He thought the job might attract two very different kinds of people—the technical expert who was rather introverted but liked the technical consultant role, and the more extroverted person who wanted to move on to a selling job.

He was also worried that no one in Europe seemed to have clearly thought through how XSEL fitted into the CTS role. It seemed likely that the CTS would want to use XSEL for problem configurations, whereas the sales staff, or their secretaries, would use it for simple ones.

Geneva were still looking for evidence of XSEL's financial benefits. Bruce was asked if these were qualitative or could they be quantified? He replied that in the US there had been time savings, dollar savings, an impact on sales and an increase in customer satisfaction. Many of these could be measured. For example, if it took three hours to manually configure a system, this could be done in thirty minutes on XSEL. The amount of time sales representatives spent chasing bad orders and making 'change' orders could also be measured.

Dollar savings from XSEL were: (1) reduced allowances—10 per cent of the allowances now made to customers were due to problems with orders. If XSEL could reduce this to 1 per cent there would be a 28 million dollar saving. (2) Reduced returns—unnecessary equipment which a customer returns and has to be given credit for. These caused administrative costs of 5.4 million dollars and could be avoided with XSEL.

Bruce also made the point that even if Digital increased the amount of standard systems which it sold to 50 per cent, this would still leave 50 per cent of business which could benefit from the use of XSEL. His objective was to double the use of XSEL each year. This had already happened in the United States, although one or two factors were still delaying progress. These included access to terminals and training. There were only three XSEL trainers in the US and use of XSEL was not allowed without training. Also, XSEL could be on machines with other applications, this slowed down its response time. The Geneva sales managers were impressed by these arguments but suggested that the saving would be less in the UK because the CTS role had some of the same functions as XSEL.

Bruce and Enid also met with the senior European Sales Manager who had always been very ambivalent about XSEL. At this meeting Bruce hoped to discuss a number of important matters. These included funding for XSEL—there was as yet no implementation budget; how area support could be provided in Europe, and implementation policy.

This manager now seemed very positive. He said that Digital had been reviewing its long-term future and saw advanced systems as assisting this. He saw XSEL eventually being used by customers as well as sales offices. He was prepared to support its implementation. But he seemed more concerned with strategic issues than with implementation detail and Bruce did not get answers to his questions.

It looked as if the tide had now turned for XSEL at the top of the company as well as lower down. Instead of XSEL conflicting with the move towards product standardization its use now complemented the recognition by top management that advanced systems must be used in the future by both Digital and its customers.

After leaving Geneva, Bruce and Enid travelled to the UK for the next formal meeting to review the XSEL pilot. This was to be held at the Basingstoke sales office on Tuesday, 8 April. On the way they stopped at the Excelsior Hotel, Heathrow Airport, where Bruce had arranged to meet two senior managers who had an interest in XSEL. These were the manager of Manufacturing—Field Relations and the manager, MIS Manufacturing. They were already at the Excelsior participating in a planning meeting, although their normal base was Geneva.

Both were interested in staking a claim in the ownership of XSEL as they saw the system as a means for actively assisting the manufacturing–sales relationship. They told Bruce that, in their view, Digital's business strategy had recently altered and was now focused on the long-term future of the company with a horizon of five years ahead. They saw XSEL as contributing to this long-term strategy in a number of ways, but primarily through the provision of clean orders to Manufacturing. It was essential for Manufacturing to work closely with Sales to secure this improvement. They were willing to act as XSEL sponsors in Manufacturing although, they pointed out, there was still a need for a committed sponsor in the sales function.

They stressed that XSEL needed to become a European project, with consent from Geneva but 'management' from the countries using it. They asked Bruce if he could release a technical expert from ISTG to work on XSEL with the European AI group in Valbonne. Bruce mentioned his fear that FMIC might decide it could no longer provide machine support for XSEL and this would jeopardize its continued testing by the sales offices. They promised to see that the Ayr link with the pilot sites was not broken.

Bruce was delighted to receive this support from Manufacturing although he was concerned that each Digital function sill seemed to have different interests and questions. In April, 1986, Geneva Sales were asking 'Can we trust XSEL?' and the senior European Sales Manager was also asking 'What will it cost?'. Manufacturing were now asking 'will it enable us to get clean orders from Sales?', and the pilot sales offices were asking a question that was not yet receiving an answer, 'Will it save our salespeople's time and free them to do more selling?'

Bruce believed that Manufacturing's new interest came from a recognition that they must play a stronger role in preventing errors in orders. This could not be left entirely to Sales. At present each function tended to blame the other. Sales said of Manufacturing, 'You don't understand our orders, you return them as wrong when they are correct'. Manufacturing said of Sales,

'You don't know what you are doing, all these wrong orders cause us serious problems.' Manufacturing was now convinced that Sales would make fewer errors if it used XSEL.

Bruce was trying to integrate the two sets of interests—Manufacturing and Sales. In the past he had worked hard to make Sales feel that XSEL belonged to them.

Manufacturing's interest in XSEL was helpful but also added a new interest group to those that already existed. Manufacturing would add to the complexity of the communication process and to the discussion of the most effective way of using XSEL. Also the sponsorship problem that had caused so many headaches in the States now existed in Europe. XSEL did not have a European sponsor. There was no senior sales manager who would say 'XSEL is mine and I am going to ensure that it is implemented as soon as possible'.

EVALUATING XSEL

The agenda of the meeting held at the Basingstoke Sales Office on 8 April was to evaluate the XSEL pilot results to date and to decide on future action. Those present included representatives from FMIC, from European Sales in Geneva and from the AI group in Valbonne, France. The two CAS managers from Leeds and Basingstoke were there, also the Leeds CTS and Bruce and Enid.

The meeting began with a discussion of the XSEL pilot results. It was reported that 67 orders had been processed correctly from a group of 96; XSEL had experienced some problems in handling the rest. These problem were primarily due to difficulties in keeping the XSEL data base completely up to date. Bruce said that the ISTG did quarterly and interim updates, but it was not possible for them to update every week. It was agreed that for XSEL to meet European needs there should be an update facility in Europe. There were some differences between Digital products in Europe and the States and US updating would miss these.

Bruce explained how the existence of a user design group could help the solution of problems. He said:

> "In the US we have a user design group. This now meets twice a year and includes the AI group, task experts, programme managers etc. This group produces a set of priorities for future work. It is a democratic process. We list ten top priority issues which are agreed. This works for everything except new product announcements. These keep coming all the time. The fundamental request from US users is for XSEL to be up to date. Europe needs to have a user design group of this kind. What we are doing here is not unlike the design meetings in the US."

A question was asked '*What do you do when a salesperson says "How do I do this"? How do you train salespeople?*'

Bruce replied,

> "In the US sales staff are trained to use XSEL. We train the trainers. We also have a group at Colorado that answers technical queries. Ayr could have a similar role in Europe."

The Basingstoke meeting went well but the basic difference of view on how XSEL should be used, and by whom, that had dogged XSEL in Europe from the start was still present. The Leeds sales office, represented by the CAS manager and the CTS, was happy with the Geneva Sales HQ formulated strategy of only a CTS using XSEL. Basingstoke, in contrast, believed that the sales staff should be the users and had encouraged a number of salespeople to try it.

It was agreed that the pilot should now be terminated. The accuracy of XSEL has been proved. The next step was to prepare an implementation plan, work out the costs of this and present it to top management for their approval. Developing an implementation plan would be a major exercise and the group would need to meet several times in the future to complete it.

But there was still a divergence of views on how XSEL could best be fitted into sales offices. The FMIC representative said emphatically:

> "the old battle between the CTS and XSEL is over. XSEL must be used as a tool by the CTS."

But the Basingstoke CAS manager hastily intervened,

> "and used by the salespeople also."

The Geneva manager said that he would now go back to European Sales and make a case for XSEL. This case would go to top management. If they agreed this would lead to a European XSEL programme.

The meeting now had to deal with an urgent practical problem—how to enable the sales offices using XSEL to continue to do this in the short term?

This was an unanticipated problem triggered by a remark from the FMIC representative that Ayr could not provide machine support for XSEL after the end of April. He expressed doubts on Ayr's ability to continue providing machine support. The meeting was astonished and taken aback at this statement and recognized that they were faced with a major issue. But it was one that no one there could resolve. The Geneva manager said that he would make a formal request to the European Sales Manager that the Ayr machine link should not be severed.

The meeting concluded with agreement that there was a need for a summary of the pilot results to be prepared for top management. A further meeting would be held in May in Ayr.

Bruce believed that the Basingstoke meeting had accomplished a number of important things. First, the value of XSEL now seemed to be recognized. The view that the CTS role made XSEL superfluous and unnecessary was no longer held by Sales in Geneva. Second, the meeting had accepted that XSEL could be used by different people and groups in different ways and had recognized that this variety of use could be of value. The policy of freeing the sales force from configuring was still a priority but there was a doubt in the Basingstoke sales office whether making the CTS the sole user of XSEL was the best way of doing this. Some organizational experimentation was required to identify the best approach for each sales office.

There were still a number of important decisions that had to be taken. The most urgent was 'who is going to pay for XSEL?'. Bruce required a contribution to ISTG development costs from Europe, and the AI group at Valbonne, or another similar group, would have to accept some responsibility for XSEL's development and up-dating in Europe.

Another decision that had to be taken was the nature of the machine support to be provided for XSEL. What was to happen when Ayr ceased to provide this?

Bruce was also concerned that there should be a mechanism for user feedback from Europe to the States. He believed strongly that the high level of US user involvement in the design of XSEL had greatly contributed to its relevance and success. He wished to have a similar level of user involvement in Europe to assist the future development of XSEL.

PLANNING FOR IMPLEMENTATION

Later in April, the European Sales and CAS managers met with a group from FMIC, Ayr, to review the CTS programme and the XSEL pilot results.

They all agreed that the introduction of the new CTS role into sales offices had greatly improved the quality of orders sent to Manufacturing. Most of the European sales offices had now acquired CTS, although Germany had still to recruit theirs. XSEL too was proving successful and there was a need for planning for general implementation to begin. This would involve the setting up of an implementation team which should include management science personnel. It would also require a statement on the implementation of XSEL within Europe to be made at the European Sales Meeting in October 1987.

The XSEL meeting scheduled for 2 May in Ayr was cancelled as it proved difficult for a number of members of the committee to attend. The next meeting was held on 20 May in Geneva. This time there were few people from the UK. Those present were five Geneva representatives—one from European Sales, two from Management Science and two from Information Services, a representative from FMIC, one from Valbonne, and Bruce.

The purpose of this meeting was to agree a European implementation plan for XSEL. This would be presented to top management at a meeting of the System Business Core Management Group on 6 October 1986. The agenda for the day was to decide what should be included in the plan, to determine who was to take responsibility for different aspects and activities, and to agree a method of working and a time scale.

A number of important decisions were taken at the meeting. First it was agreed that the plan to be presented to top management should have the following structure.

1. How to use XSEL in the field, and who should use it.
2. How to support XSEL in Europe.
3. What the benefits of XSEL were to the selling process—i.e. productivity etc.
4. An analysis of XSEL costs and return on investment

It was also decided that the investigation of how XSEL should be used, and by whom, should focus on:

1. Customer Administration Services, and the CTS, as the managers and key users of the system.
2. Determining the impact XSEL had on the throughput of the CTS by (a) checking the numbers of orders and quotes that were processed (this had already been done in the pilot) and (b) establishing how XSEL assisted the configuring and consulting activities of the CTS.
3. Developing a process and work-flow model and examining viable options.
4. Evaluating the use of XSEL by others, especially salespersons.

The meeting agreed that the proposal to implement XSEL should focus on the value which its use added to the CTS role. XSEL's productivity and other benefits for sales persons should also be examined, but it was recognized that it would be more difficult to assess how XSEL reduced selling costs and increased sales productivity than to estimate how it assisted the CTS. User evaluation and broad productivity data would have to be used to do this.

Bruce again had some anxieties after this meeting. He was concerned that the Geneva group were apparently deciding on an implementation plan without consulting anyone in the sales offices—no one from a UK sales office had been present. Geneva management did not seem to appreciate the need for sales force consultation and involvement.

But the debate on who should use XSEL was not yet over. In May, the European manager of the CAS function joined the debate on who should use XSEL. He wrote to the European Sales Manager saying that in his view the critical issue was not how much XSEL contributed to the CTS role, but how much XSEL contributed to Digital. Therefore the total situation should be examined to see how improved sales quality, productivity and customer impact could best be achieved. FMIC and Manufacturing productivity should also be examined in relation to XSEL.

PREPARING THE PROPOSAL

There was now an XSEL Proposal Team whose brief was to prepare a case for XSEL to be put to the European Managing Director. The task of this group was to agree on the actions, structure, timetable, etc. of the work required to complete the proposal. This would include an examination of the hardware and network options available for running XSEL.

By July, planning for XSEL's implementation was progressing for the whole of Europe. All European sales offices were to be encouraged to use XSEL and Europe would provide the necessary support team and back-up. As yet, no decision had been taken on whether XSEL was to be used by the sales force for no concrete data was available on whether this would be a worthwhile strategy. In the first instance it would be used by the CTS, helped by an administrative assistant who did the routine checking of orders with XSEL. This would free the CTS to spend more time on difficult configurations.

There seemed now to be recognition that a major advantage of XSEL was its ability to provide the CTS with a training and an up-dating system. Without XSEL the CTS would be permanently struggling to keep up with product changes. XSEL could provide him or her with an easy and reliable way of doing this. This approach would enable major savings to be made, particularly in training costs.

Once XSEL was in use then studies could be carried out to see if it should be made available to the sales force. But there was a problem. If salespeople did use XSEL then there would be a need for ten times more hardware and telecommunications support than required by the CTS.

The XSEL Proposal Team met in Geneva in July to discuss the implementation plan. If European top management approved the plan then there would be a central fund to support XSEL and AI would be in the forefront of Digital developments.

The principal issues discussed at this meeting were:

> Who will be responsible for XSEL's implementation and ongoing management after the proposal is approved?
>
> How do we set up an implementation team and what are its responsibilities?
>
> What are the support responsibilities of Valbonne and ISTG for XSEL and how are these to be divided between the two groups?

Although plans for the implementation of XSEL were making progress, Bruce was not entirely happy. He felt that there was still uncertainty over the ownership of XSEL. He saw warning signs of a possible power battle ahead. This time between FMIC and the AI group in Valbonne, both of which seemed to be making claims for ownership. In Bruce's view neither of these would be an appropriate owner. Ayr was primarily interested in XSEL as a means for providing Manufacturing with clean orders, it had little interest in it as an aid for sales staff. The AI group at Valbonne would like to take XSEL under its wing as an excellent example of an operational expert system, but it was not interested in it as an aid to the sales force.

Bruce still held the view that Sales should be the owner of XSEL. The system had been designed to assist the sales force. But there was a problem here also. The Sales function primarily interested in XSEL was the Customer Administration Services support group. CAS provided a back-up service for the sales force but had no responsibility for them. Bruce wanted the sales force themselves to be the owners of XSEL but it was difficult to make this happen. Few salespeople in the UK had, as yet, even heard of it.

The XSEL Proposal Team met again in Geneva in August. Before the meeting all participants were sent an outline of the proposal which would be presented to European Corporate Management. They were asked for feedback in advance of the meeting.

Bruce could not attend this meeting and Enid went in his place. With the exception of one person from FMIC, all the participants were Geneva-based staff—two were from Management Science and one was from Information Systems. Once again those present represented some, but not all, of the groups with an interest in XSEL.

The European Sales Manager opened the meeting by announcing a number of critical dates. The case for XSEL had to be presented to the European Managing Director and the senior Sales Manager on 23 October. This meant that the proposal must be ready by the end of September. There would be a meeting on 1 October to discuss the implementation of XSEL; how the CTS users were to be supported; the amount of support that FMIC could provide, and the interface of XSEL with Marketing.

There was a discussion of the resources which XSEL would require. Digital had sales offices in four large countries—UK, France, Germany and Italy—and twelve smaller countries. XSEL would be introduced at District level in the major countries. This coverage would require a total of 39 installations of XSEL.

This again raised the question of the amount and kind of hardware needed to support such a major effort. Should there be a number of large, central machines or should each district have its own machine, or access to one? If each sales district or office had its own machine could these be networked to communicate with each other? These issues had to be decided. It was agreed that a specific recommendation should not be made on whether a sales office should have its own small machine or link into a larger system. The FMIC representative suggested that the decision should be left to the sales districts. They were going to have to pay for the hardware.

He stressed that the machines must be networked. The network traffic would be small, but it was needed for back-up solutions if anything went wrong.

Anxiety was expressed that some sales offices might choose to use one of Digital's new machines—a microVAX—for running XSEL. Bruce was known to have tested XSEL on this in the States, but there was no European experience of running XSEL on this machine. There was a need to get facts and figures from Bruce.

Before the meeting ended there was a statement of how FMIC could support the proposed strategy for XSEL in Europe. In FMIC's view, software development should be carried out by the ISTG group in Hudson; and also by Valbonne, where the European AI group were located. The distribution of software should be handled by a 'release management' group. Training for XSEL would be provided by FMIC and system maintenance—ensuring that XSEL was correct and up to date—would be monitored jointly by FMIC and Valbonne. Pre-release testing of new versions of XSEL would be carried out by either FMIC or the ISTG group in Hudson.

It was stressed that there was an urgent need for a European manager of XSEL to implement and coordinate all these things. There was also a need to clarify the roles of FMIC, ISTG, and AI in Valbonne.

The meeting concluded by agreeing a timetable which would enable the final proposal to be presented to the European Managing Director on 23 October. The presentation date had now been moved forward from the original 6 October.

There was to be a final meeting of the XSEL Proposal Team in September in Geneva. This would review the proposal and its presentation. On 1 October the proposal would be presented to FMIC management and selling operations staff at a technical quality meeting. On 6 October the final proposal would be submitted to the European Managing Director and the Selling Core Management team. On 23 October the final presentation would be made to this group.

After this meeting Enid gave Bruce her impressions of the meeting. She pointed out that there were still three unresolved issues. These were:

1. How is responsibility to be allocated between Ayr and Valbonne?
2. Who is going to be the project manager—responsible for seeing the system works.
3. Who is going to be the programme manager—responsible for seeing the system is implemented successfully?

She expressed her dismay that no representative of the sales force had been present at the meeting. Clearly they were an important group in the introduction and use of XSEL, yet no one seemed to be looking after their interests.

On 23 October 1986, Bruce attended the final presentation. All went well, Geneva top management was at last convinced of the value of XSEL. Approval was given for the implementation of XSEL in sales offices throughout Europe. The decision was based on the positive financial analysis which was presented, on FMIC support, and on support from top management who were eager to implement AI solutions.

1986. EUROPEAN TOP MANAGEMENT APPROVES XSEL

But despite this 'go-ahead' many of the issues that had been debated over the years were still unresolved. 'Who should use XSEL?', 'who should own it?' and, most important, 'who should pay for it?' European Sales had a budget to pay for XSEL's introduction but once this was spent the cost would probably fall on the individual sales offices.

Different groups were still seeking different benefits from XSEL although all were now agreed that it was a valuable tool and that the pilot tests had demonstrated its worth.

The second half of the year was devoted to preparing the case that would be presented to top management. Thought was also given to the back-up and support services that XSEL would require—telecommunications, software, updating facilities. An implementation manager would be required. Someone who could help XSEL to be accepted and used. Bruce hoped that this person would be committed to participative design and would set up a user design group similar to the one that was operating with great success in the US.

There was also a recognition that XSEL would cause reorganization outside as well as inside the sales offices. FMIC's role would be altered as the CTS, using XSEL, took over many of its order checking functions. The AI group at Valbonne would also have to reorganize so that they could meet XSEL's software and updating needs.

The challenge of introducing a pioneering front edge system throughout Europe was about to begin.

European behaviour in 1986 continued to demonstrate the importance of national culture and feeling in the acceptance of innovation. XSEL had been thoroughly tested in the United States and found to be accurate. It was working successfully there and saving Digital considerable sums of money. But this carried little weight in Europe where Geneva Headquarters sales management insisted that XSEL must be tested again to confirm its accuracy and cost-benefits.

XSEL had been developed by and for the US sales force, and sales people were the group using it for configuring in the United States. This strategy was seen as unacceptable in Europe where the new CTS role was believed to be the solution to the configuring problem. XSEL must therefore be used by the CTS. Europe was not necessarily wrong in this strategy, but there was little interest in experimenting with different user groups and finding the most effective way of exploiting XSEL.

There was also a group missing from the planning process. This was the sales force. Geneva Headquarters had a strategic planning responsibility for Digital Europe and handled this very well in operational terms. The Customer Administration Group, in which the new CTS role was located, supported the use of XSEL. The Geneva management responsible for CAS took great care to review every aspect of XSEL's performance that was known or could be ascertained, so that a convincing case for its acceptance could be made to senior sales management. In order to prepare this case they held a number of meetings with groups interested in XSEL. Those present included FMIC in Ayr and Geneva managers associated with the CAS function.

Unfortunately, a critical interest group—the sales force and their managers—was not involved. Throughout the very careful planning process for XSEL's implementation, the group whose efficiency XSEL was intended to enhance did not have a voice. Yet the sales force would still have a major interest in XSEL's performance even if they were not its principal users. The mission of the sales offices was to 'sell'. The role of support service such as CAS or XSEL was to help them do this more effectively. Participation at the strategic planning level suffered from the absence of this important group.

Honest: *He was a very zealous man.*
Difficulties, lions or
Vanity-Fair he feared not
at all.

John Bunyan

Chapter 11

THE UK SALES OFFICES

While Geneva is making a case for the introduction of XSEL into Europe let us go back a few years and look at the operation of the European sales offices at the time XSEL was being developed in the United States.

On 18 May 1984, Ken Olsen, the Digital Chairman, sent out a message to his Strategy Committee. This was headed 'Goal for 1985—Sales Automation'. In his note Ken congratulated his colleagues on introducing automation so effectively into the office and factory, saying:

> "we have changed the jobs, changed the red tape, changed how we do things, and the results have been very good. We have removed much of the frustration and drudgery in these jobs. People are more efficient and have time for more important things."

The punch came in the next sentence.

> "I would like to make the goal for 1985 to introduce automation into Sales. Every part of the company is getting more efficient by significant amounts and we are doing a lot more with fewer people almost everywhere except Sales. The main reason, I think, is that we are interested in doing things the way we used to."

He also set out suggestions for improving sales efficiency.

> "Salespeople, or an approved customer, should be able to order from a terminal and immediately have serial numbers of the product assigned for straightforward products. Salespeople should have a portable terminal that can be plugged into any telephone. For orders of simple equipment no paper should ever be produced."

Ken Olsen was therefore asking the sales force, world wide, for a major increase in productivity. Although XSEL was not specifically referred to in the memo, it was clear that it fitted very neatly into the Board's plans for the future.

THE SALESPERSON'S ROLE

In the summer of 1984, Enid decided that she must obtain some knowledge of how Digital sales offices operated. This would give her a better understanding of the impact of XSEL when it was introduced. She therefore approached the Warrington Sales Office, which was close to her home, and asked if she could make a study of its policies, practices and problems.

Bruce was interested in obtaining answers to a number of questions which related to the use of XSEL, and the Warrington project also provided an opportunity for asking these. Bruce's questions were:

- Would an expert system designed by American sales staff to meet their own needs be of value to the European sales force?
- Were selling strategies and problems the same throughout Europe or were there differences between British, French, German and other national sales offices?
- Would European sales staff accept a system designed by a group in another country, even though this group were sales staff like themselves? Would they not also want to be involved in the participative design and decision processes that were inputs to the XSEL project?

Bruce and his group were also asking:

- In which direction should XSEL be developed so that it can become an even more valuable tool for the sales force in all countries?

Permission to carry out the project was willingly given by the Warrington District Sales Manager and in October, 1984, Enid interviewed and had discussions with the sales people in the Warrington office. This sales office was organized into three sections—public sector customers, manufacturing industry customers, and a third section dealing with both OEMs and finance and distribution.

Because the salespeople's spheres of interest were industry, not product based, all except one sold every item of hardware or software that the customer wanted. The exception was a salesperson responsible for selling personal computers to the public sector. He concentrated on strategic accounts—that is, very large organizations such as universities.

All of these salespeople had regular contact with other departments. In particular marketing, sales administration, order administration, credit control, software services and field service. The role of order administration was to chase deliveries; credit control checked customers for credit worthiness; software services provided Digital's latest software products and information about these; field service handled technical problems.

The salespeople were asked to describe the content of their jobs in the following way. (1) By identifying their regular day-to-day tasks—the activities that were stimulated by requests from customers and from within Digital and the work initiatives they themselves took. (2) By describing the principal problems they had to deal with if they were to provide an excellent customer service. (3) The different activities that had to be coordinated if they were to work efficiently and effectively. (4) The development aspects of their work and

(5) the system of controls that enabled them to check that they were achieving their sales objectives. This is the work description framework provided by the ETHICS method.

They described the majority of their day-to-day activities as looking after customers, providing advice and assistance, giving information and finding new customer contacts. They saw all of these tasks as part of their 'selling' role.

Problem solving activities included helping customers with technical questions but were dominated by a major problem, common to almost all the sales force. This was the difficulty of getting accurate hardware delivery dates from the manufacturing plant at Ayr. This led to coordination difficulties with customers who could not be given precise dates on when equipment they had ordered would arrive. The result was that the salespeople felt that they were unable to provide their customers with an optimal service.

Development activities were concerned with finding new customers and creating new sales strategies. But they also related to personal development. All the salespeople were keen to increase their knowledge of new Digital products and of new computer developments generally. The older sales staff also accepted that they had a responsibility for the development of their junior colleagues.

Controls were based on targets mutually agreed once a year between a salesperson and his immediate supervisor. This discussion produced a budget which the salesperson had to achieve during the year. Although at the time of this project the sales force was paid a straight salary and not a commission on sales, an inability to achieve this budget could affect a salesperson's salary the following year. In addition to achieving the agreed budget the Digital 'goals' also required the salesperson to obtain a number of new customer accounts. Many of the salespeople also had personal goals such as acquiring a particular firm as a customer.

The sales force were asked which of their activities they regarded as (1) most important to Digital, (2) most important to their customers and (3) most enjoyable and interesting.

The activities regarded as most important to Digital were obtaining and maintaining customer satisfaction. This was described as developing good personal relationships with customers and the existence of good administrative systems so that salespeople could keep the promises they made to customers. There were references to getting 'good' business and getting 'clean' business. The first referring to selling a product which the salesperson could deliver accompanied by software that worked, while at the same time preventing the occurrence of customer problems that were disproportionate to the cost of the machine. The second meaning that business must not be got at any price. The salesperson making this point spoke about the company's very ethical approach to business.

The activities seen as most important to customers were not very different. They included 'keeping problems from the customer, making things appear easy', 'keeping customers abreast of product developments so they can work out realistic strategies for the future', identifying which of the products would best meet a customer's needs and providing customers with general support.

The answers to the question on which aspects of their work the salespeople found most enjoyable and interesting showed them as a highly motivated group. They enjoyed all of their activities, particularly selling to customers, working with customers on projects and helping customers to solve their business problems. They also got great satisfaction from finding new customers or new opportunities in the firms of existing customers. The principal factor marring their enjoyment of work was the equipment delivery problem.

The sales force were all agreed on the nature of their work mission—the key objective or objectives that they were trying to achieve. They all saw this as getting more business and making Digital the preferred supplier. Here again they stressed that this was not to be done at any price. They emphasized the ethical nature of their employer's business practices and suggested that many sales people worked for Digital because of the company's strong ethical values.

The key tasks that had to be undertaken to achieve this mission were of three kinds. One, gaining an understanding of the client company, learning who were the major decision makers and establishing the right relationships with these. Two, making Digital an easy firm to do business with and ensuring that once equipment was delivered the customer had few problems with it. This required good information about customers and their needs and also good configuring ability on the part of sales staff. Three, providing reliable information to customers so that they knew what products were available, how much they cost, what they could do and how they would fit into existing systems.

In order to be efficient and effective the sales staff required certain resources. The most important of these was information. They required accurate and timely information about equipment delivery dates, Digital products, competitor's products and customer requirements. Information from the manufacturing plants on delivery dates was the salesperson's most critical unmet need. The absence of this information led to the creation of an internal 'black market'. Spare and demonstration stock were borrowed and wheeling and dealing took place in order to avoid letting customers down.

They saw this absence of accurate delivery information as the factor most affecting their personal efficiency and their relationships with customers. Long deliveries and late deliveries caused difficulties but these could be coped with if only the salesperson knew when the customer would receive the product.

Configuring computer applications to provide customers with quotations and Manufacturing with orders also caused problems. Digital had so many products that it was not easy for the salesperson to remember what was related to what. When machines did arrive from Manufacturing there could be cables missing or of the wrong length. Similar problems were experienced with quotations.

Items of equipment could be missed out from these and the customer given an incorrect costing.

WHAT ABOUT XSEL?

The raising of configuring as a problem by the Warrington sales force led to a discussion of XSEL. When asked if salespersons should do configuring, or if another group in the sales office could take it over, they were adamant that it must be their responsibility. Their view was that 'no one else has the knowledge to do it'. But they did recognize that an automated configuring aid such as XSEL could be useful. Only two of the Warrington sales force had heard of XSEL, one because he had met Bruce, the other because he had attended a sales symposium in Boston.

When XSEL was described to them their reactions were extremely positive.

'It would be a great advantage. Configuring and quotations by an expert system would be excellent.'

'It would be very good as an *aide-mémoire*. To check that the salesperson is right. But he or she must be certain that there are no errors in XSEL'.

'I see it as helpful. It would keep the costs of Sales low and help us avoid mistakes'.

Bruce had hoped that the discussions with the Warrington group would provide him with answers to four questions.

Would an expert system, designed by US salespeople to meet their own needs be of value to European salespeople?

Are selling strategies and problems in Digital the same throughout Europe or are there differences between British, French, German and other European salespeople? Would European salespeople accept a system designed by a group in another country?

In which direction should XSEL be developed?

The answer to the first question was clearly 'yes'. The Warrington salespeople were enthusiastic about the idea of XSEL and keen to test it out. They were not certain how to answer the second question. They believed that UK sales offices did not all sell in exactly the same way, therefore it was likely that there were considerable differences between the European countries. In answer to question three they said that they would certainly not be inhibited in using XSEL because it had been designed by the American sales force. But they suggested that American salespeople and sales practices were rather different from those of Europe. Therefore XSEL might have to be modified to match European practice. They could not suggest how XSEL might be developed until they had some experience of using it themselves.

Enid had a further meeting with the Warrington sales force in March, 1985. She was now able to give them more specific information about XSEL and told them that the two pilot sites had now been selected. These were Basingstoke and Birmingham, (Birmingham was later changed to Leeds). There would also be a pilot project in Utrecht. XSEL would be run on the Ayr machine and FMIC in Ayr would monitor and evaluate the use of XSEL in the pilot sites. Digital US saw Ayr as the centre of UK knowledge on configuring. It was hoped that field trials would commence on 1 July with a review in September.

The new role of CTS (Configuration Technical Specialist) would be introduced into each sales office with one CTS for every twenty sales staff.

She explained that the goals of the pilot study were,

1. To check that XSEL could configure correctly and efficiently.
2. To examine the roles and relationships of the new CTS and the sales staff.

It was hoped that the pilot would answer the following questions.

1. Is the parts data base correct for Europe?
2. Are the configuration rules right for Europe?
3. How well does XSEL interface with the user. What are the European user interface requirements?
4. Will European sales groups need to modify XSEL to fit their needs?
5. How can XSEL best fit into European sales offices?

The Warrington sales force were very interested in these developments. They expressed the hope that they could be the next pilot site after the two initial ones. But they had some reservations after the new role of CTS. Would this additional member of staff add to their overheads? If the CTS was to be the user of XSEL would it not take the sales force as long to tell him or her what was wanted as to use XSEL themselves? Their view was that they would prefer to have a terminal on their desks and access XSEL directly.

One said:

> "Salespeople always do their own quotes and like to be in control of their own situations. The buck stops with the sales rep."

These visits to Warrington and talks with the sales force gave Enid a feel for the Digital sales function and what it was trying to achieve. The sales staff were clearly dedicated and enthusiastic. They were also keen to use XSEL as it would help solve their problems with configuring. It would not, however, solve their most critical problem which was late and unpredictable deliveries of hardware.

Contrite. You may be sure we are full of hurry in fair time. 'Tis hard keeping our hearts and spirits in any good order, when we are in a cumbered condition.

John Bunyan

Chapter 12

THE XSEL PILOT IN EUROPE

POTENTIAL PROBLEMS

Introducing technology is never easy. It is well known that the best designed and most friendly system may founder on implementation. People may object to having their cosy work system disturbed by someone else's unwanted innovation; they may fear that its impact will be alien, even threatening—for example, they could lose their skills or even their jobs. They may not want the bother and trouble of learning something new, particularly something that falls into the threatening 'new technology' category. Implementing XSEL was not easy, but before describing the events that occurred when it moved across the Atlantic to Europe let us consider some of the factors that can and do cause problems when any new technology is being introduced.

The group with the most direct interest in the new system are, of course, the future users. If their management is skilled in introducing major change, or even just lucky, they will be looking forward to using the new system. They will expect it to work well, be useful, and help them to become more personally effective in their jobs. They will be highly motivated to make it a success.

Unfortunately, attitudes of this kind do not always exist. There may be a group of potential users who are fearful of, or sceptical about, the new system, do not particularly want it, and are in no sense dedicated to making it a success. Other users may be guardedly neutral—reserving judgement until the system demonstrates that it is to their advantage to use it.

What are the factors that create negative attitudes? The primary, and most powerful fear in many situations is loss of job. This is a particular fear in the UK where unemployment is more than two million and there is, as yet, little evidence that new technology creates jobs. Although computer systems are now being sold by vendors to 'help you make money', instead of 'to help you save money'—the sales pitch of a few years ago which was usually accompanied by promises of staff reductions—many staff do not believe that their jobs are secure.

Senior staff are usually powerful enough to have computer systems only on their own terms—and no computer can yet replace a senior manager. But middle and lower grade staff are more vulnerable. The reality is that office automation has been used in many firms to reduce clerical staff numbers. The expectation is that expert systems will do the same. This may be a too pessimistic conclusion but it is probable that some expert systems will replace middle level specialist staff who have been experts in a narrow area of knowledge. Resistance to change based on a fear of job loss is not the result of a foolish phantasy, but a belief based on past experience.

Older staff, who have not had contact with computers at school or in their homes, may be unsure of their own ability to master these machines. Again this fear may be well founded as many computers and word processors are still user unfriendly—difficult to use, difficult to learn to use and difficult to remember how to use if not used regularly. Expert systems are likely to be more user friendly, as most are designed to communicate easily with the user, but the very words 'artificial intelligence' and 'expert' may strike fear into a naive user heart.

Users who are not threatened with job or skill loss and are using an expert system to enhance an existing skill may still be unenthusiastic and mistrustful. They may regard the new system as an indication of top management's lack of confidence in their knowledge and expertise. They may mistrust the new system and believe that no machine can compete in expertise with a human being. They may not appreciate what an expert system has to offer, and perhaps be unwilling to disturb an existing comfortable work situation.

When the new system is developed and designed by a head office or specialist group situated in another town or, with a multinational company—country, local top management may also have its doubts. Senior managers will ask questions such as, 'is this system going to be cost effective, or is it yet another expensive white elephant forced upon us by corporate management?' and 'how is the system going to fit in with the long-term strategies which we have been carefully developing for our part of the company?'

It can be seen that in many situations the dice are heavily stacked against easy and successful implementation. By the time the new system arrives, attitudes have hardened, fears have been reinforced and the forces against charge are marshalled in battle order. The system may now go in grudgingly, be badly used, and, in that event, take the role of scapegoat for many work problems which have nothing to do with it.

Fears may be at their worst before the system arrives, but the first experiences of using the system may add extreme frustration to anxiety. The system is likely to have teething problems. It may break down, or be slow and inaccurate. Worst still it may be seen as irrelevant—doing nothing to meet the real, critical needs of the users. It is at this time that even groups with positive attitudes to new technology may become disillusioned and feel that their favourable expectations have been disappointed. The new system fits uneasily into the existing organization structure and initially does not produce the anticipated improvements in decision taking, information management and costs. This last factor may make top management as nervous as the user group about the benefits of the system.

Other groups who are not direct users of the system, may also voice complaints at this time. Customers may find that the personal service which they value highly has now been reduced. Other departments may find that their work procedures have to be altered to fit the new system, although it is of no real advantage to them to take this change.

These points have been made to show that implementation is a difficult and complex process. Many problems can be experienced at this time that affect the reception and use of what may be an excellent system. Implementation is particularly difficult when a group in one country is designing a system for a group in another part of the world which has no opportunity to participate in the design processes.

THE REASONS FOR US SUCCESS

Computer manufacturers are likely to be better at introducing change than other firms. Developing and marketing technology is their business and they are experts in it. Nevertheless their staff are still likely to have anxieties and to feel insecure from time to time—attitudes which are a result of the fast pace of the technological world in which they are working.

Despite the potential problems of implementation, XSEL was introduced successfully into sales offices in the United States. This was due to a number of factors. First, sales staff had been actively involved in its development and their ideas were incorporated into its design. Many had attended the participative design meetings run by Bruce. Others, who had not been able to be present had received requests for suggestions and comments via Digital's comprehensive electronic mail system. They had sent their ideas back electronically and, in this way, had made an important contribution to the design of the new system.

Second, XSEL was a really helpful and non-threatening tool. Everyone gained something from its use. The salespeople were able to complete the complex and time consuming configuring task more quickly and without the risk of making errors. They were saved from the embarrassment of having to admit to customers that certain components had been missed out from an order form. Customers gained because the order costings which they recieved were accurate—nothing was incorrect or forgotten. And machines could be delivered to them more speedily because orders did not have to pass backwards and forwards between sales and manufacturing until all errors were corrected.

In addition the group that supplied the configuring knowledge for XSEL, the engineers, were not threatened by the system. They had limited contact with customers and their jobs and skills were not jeopardized by the transfer of information to the sales staff. Digital as a company gained financially from the use of XSEL. Customers did not have to be given allowances to compensate for mistakes, and salespeople could sell tighter systems because XSEL reminded them of the components that particular applications required.

XSEL, in the US was therefore a 'win win' system—helping everyone and threatening nobody. It was an example of the ideal expert system. The question was 'could it be implemented easily and successfully in Europe?' Europe consisted of many different cultures. Would the cohesiveness of the Digital culture be strong enough to offset any factors in the local culture that could cause resistance to change? Also, the US sales force were clearly the 'owners' of XSEL. They had moulded it to fit their own needs and welcomed it as a useful helpmate to ameliorate the rigours of the selling role. XSEL was relatively unknown in Europe. European sales staff had not contributed to its design and were not aware of what it had to offer.

Unless Digital was careful in its strategy it was likely that the implementation of XSEL in Europe would prove much more difficult than its introduction into the United States. There was a need for careful diagnosis, good management and an understanding of the differences between Europe and the United States.

THE BASINGSTOKE AND LEEDS SALES OFFICES

In July, 1985, Enid made her first visits to the Basingstoke and Leeds sales offices where the XSEL pilot was to be carried out. Basingstoke was a new office; it had only been in existence as a separate entity for two years. It had been created as a result of a 'small is beautiful' policy which stated that no district sales office should employ more than 400 people or have a budget larger than $100,000,000. The reorganization which followed the introduction of this principle had caused Basingstoke and the south and south-west districts to split off from the London districts.

Basingstoke had a staff of 68, over half of whom were the sales force. The selling function was split into five groups—the Public and Technical OEM unit which sold to government bodies and other computer manufacturers, the New Business unit which dealt with new customers, the Large Account unit which looked after national or international customers, the Manufacturing and Commercial unit and the Customer Services unit, which handled small accounts. In addition there was the Customer Administration Services unit which provided a service to the others.

Each group was supervised by a sales unit manager who reported to the District Sales Manager. He, in turn, reported to a regional manager and there were four of these in the UK. Regional managers were responsible to the UK Sales Director. European sales strategy, formulated in Geneva, was translated into national strategy through this hierarchy. The principal measure of success was 'selling yield'—the revenue returned to the Company per salesperson. Top management's philosophy was to say what must be achieved but to leave the individual sales offices with the freedom to decide how it was achieved.

At the time of the reorganization Basingstoke acquired an entirely new management team which was dynamic and forward thinking, ready to change and enthusiastic about change. The District Sales Manager was keen to secure as many of the benefits of automation as possible and he welcomed new systems such as XSEL.

The sales function was also in the process of change. Salespeople, who had previously been technically knowledgeable, were now becoming increasingly business oriented. It was more important for them to be experts in their customer's business and to understand his or her needs and problems than to be technical experts. This was a recent and dramatic change in the salesperson's role.

Basingstoke, in common with other sales offices, already had a number of potentially useful automated systems. It was testing out AQS—an automated quotes system. This contained the current prices of equipment and would logically fit well with XSEL if the two systems could be brought together. There were other systems, including a system that monitored the performance of individual salespersons, and a sales forecasting system. All of these systems could contribute to the productivity of the sales force but they needed integrating, and some needed redesigning. Basingstoke was planning to do this.

A recent internal study had shown that the sales force spent only 19 per cent of its time face-to-face with customers. If this could be increased through more use of automated systems this would greatly assist the productivity of the Basingstoke office. For example, if XSEL and AQS could each reduce the time a salesperson required to configure and do quotes by 2 per cent, then this would provide the sales force with an additional 4 per cent selling time—or a further 20 per cent selling capacity.

Leeds was a much smaller office. It was divided up into four groups— Manufacturing and Education, Finance and Services, a new 'Installed Base Systems group' which handled the orders of customers who already had Digital equipment, and Customer Administration Services. It employed a sales force of 22, many of them newly recruited.

The attitudes of the two sales forces were similar to those of the Warrington group. They saw their business missions as concerned with increasing Digital's market penetration, providing a high quality and ethical customer service and ensuring that customers were satisfied with Digital products and developing a loyalty towards Digital. The problems which they encountered in achieving these objectives were associated with a lack of information, particularly on deliveries and prices, and a need for more effective administrative systems. Digital was in the process of introducing a number of these and XSEL would be an important addition.

XSEL, in the United States, had been developed as a tool for the sales force. In Europe, Geneva sales management had decided that the Configuration Technical Specialist should be the principal user and the CTS role was located in the CAS group. The tasks of CAS covered checking the credit worthiness of customers, establishing the correctness of quotes and orders, monitoring delivery dates and answering customer enquiries. Once the XSEL pilot was underway the sales force would pass their orders to CAS where they would be checked by the CTS before being sent to Manufacturing in Ayr. This process would ensure that the orders were technically correct, although it could not establish if they were also commercially correct—the right system for the customer's needs.

When the pilot started at the end of July, the Basingstoke CAS manager was not certain that this was the right approach. He accepted that XSEL must be tested out to make sure it was technically accurate, but he believed that the sales force was the right group to use it. He was worried that the combining together of the new CTS role and the testing of XSEL would make it difficult to distinguish clearly the advantages of each. It might not be possible to tell if improvements in quote and order accuracy were due to the CTS or to XSEL.

He could see other disadvantages. His CTS was a technical expert and might rapidly become bored with checking quotes and orders with XSEL. And he wondered if the sales staff would trust someone else's configuring. He was convinced that the crucial question that needed to be answered was, 'does XSEL provide sales staff with more "selling time" because it reduces the time they take to configure systems for quotes and orders?'. If the sales force did not have access to XSEL and continued to do their configuring manually there would be very little time saved.

Although the CAS manager was not happy with the CTS as sole user of XSEL, he was enthusiastic about the technical consultant aspect of the CTS role. This was proving to be extremely useful. It seemed that its value was being generally recognized, for many other UK sales offices were now asking for a CTS.

The Basingstoke CTS held similar views to his CAS manager. He was enjoying his technical adviser role but did not want to be the principal XSEL user. He was a configuring expert and had little interest in checking the sales peoples configurations, either with or without XSEL. This was not a challenging activity. He wanted to be consulted on difficult configuring problems.

The Leeds CAS manager and CTS did not share the Basingstoke view. They were willing to accept the CTS as sole user of XSEL, but unsure what would happen if he was away ill or on holiday. The Leeds CTS was not so technically expert as the CTS at Basingstoke and more prepared to regard XSEL as a useful aid in checking orders and providing configuring information. He was anxious to assist FMIC in Ayr to achieve a 90 per cent accuracy for XSEL in Europe.

But as the pilot got underway both CTSs began experiencing problems in trying to use XSEL. The lines between the two sales offices and Ayr were subject to a great deal of noise and interference. This meant that orders had to be continually re-entered and this took up a great deal of time. When contact was established XSEL's response was very slow because the VAX machine at Ayr was being used for other work. Also the CTS were using XSEL in different ways and this made it difficult to control the testing process. The procedure of the Basingstoke CTS was to keep XSEL totally separate from his own activity. He received an order from a salesperson, identified any errors, and returned it to the salesperson for correction. He sent the salesperson's original, incorrect, order through to Ayr using XSEL and let Ayr check if XSEL had picked up the errors. The Leeds CTS, in contrast, was using XSEL to check orders and identify errors. He then corrected these before transmitting the order to Ayr.

Both CTSs were finding some conflicts in the joint CTS/XSEL role. The Basingstoke CTS did not think he needed any assistance from XSEL. He could check the accuracy of configurations by merely looking at them. He wondered if other CTS who had good technical knowledge would have any use for XSEL. He supported his CAS manager's view that the sales force should be the principal users of XSEL with the CTS acting as configuring consultant. He was also suffering some work overload. The CTS role was proving so useful and popular that he was inundated with queries from sales staff who previously would have telephoned Ayr for help. He proposed to hand XSEL over to a clerical assistant once he knew it was accurate—managing two jobs was not possible.

The Basingstoke sales force seemed to have mixed views on the configuring task. Experienced salespersons enjoyed it, although they pointed out that they could not remember everything. One said:

> "You get very good at tech editing new products, but as time goes on you forget a lot of information about the old products. XSEL would enable you to remember this."

Newer sales people were more ambivalent about configuring, claiming that it was difficult and time consuming and they had to look up a great many things.

The sales force at Leeds, like those at Basingstoke, had little information about XSEL. A majority of the Leeds sales staff had recently joined Digital and had not yet become experienced configurers. Some indicated that they would prefer not to have to acquire this skill—they would be happy for the CTS to have the responsibility. Two of the Leeds Sales Unit managers who had heard of XSEL expressed strong opinions that it should be available to the sales force. If only the CTS used XSEL then a major bottleneck could be created in the work of the office. They were not sure whether or not salespeople wanted to configure but were convinced that they would not want anyone else to do it.

In August, disagreement over who should pay for XSEL—Ayr or Geneva—caused the pilot to be halted. This created a great deal of frustration and annoyance in both the Basingstoke and Leeds sales offices, although no one there understood why it had happened. The Basingstoke District Sales Manager and the CAS group thought that the reason might be the amount of expensive computer power which running XSEL required. They were afraid that if this hypothesis was correct XSEL would prove too expensive to give to the sales force. The CTS was concerned that the pilot was by no means complete. XSEL still needed a further three-month test to determine its accuracy. Only then should a decision be taken on how best to fit it into the sales offices.

Reactions in Leeds were similar. The CAS manager and the CTS were puzzled and surprised but assumed that the problem was something to do with costs. Perhaps the cost of updating XSEL was proving too high.

CONFUSION AND UNCERTAINTY

In October, XSEL was still disconnected and no one knew when it would be available. The Basingstoke District Manager and the CAS manager went to Ayr to talk with FMIC but did not receive any definite information. They were unhappy that Geneva was so lacking in enthusiasm for XSEL. It seemed that Geneva management were not prepared to take responsibility for XSEL. Despite this uncertainty, thought was being given to how best to organize the pilot once XSEL restarted. Basingstoke decided that XSEL should first be tested by the CTS and then by the sales force. Leeds, in contrast, decided to continue with the Geneva approved policy of the CTS alone testing XSEL. The two pilot sites were therefore proposing to test, and use, XSEL in different ways.

FMIC was now examining whether the testing of XSEL by the CTS was the best strategy. Would it produce a fair judgement of XSEL? XSEL had been designed to be used by sales people. Its principal benefit was in helping someone with limited configuration knowledge to produce reliable configurations. It might be seen as unnecessary, or even as a threat, by experienced CTS. Because of their expertise they might be convinced that they did not need the assistance of a machine. The purpose of the XSEL pilot was to provide senior management with information which would enable them to decide whether or not to implement XSEL in Europe. An objective assessment of XSEL was essential and the CTS might not provide this.

As a result of these doubts, the group organizing the XSEL pilot agreed that is was important to test and compare the different approaches of the Leeds and Basingstoke sales offices. They recognized that there were three possible ways of using XSEL: as a configurer for salespeople; with the salesperson and the CTS working together using XSEL; with the CTS using XSEL to check configurations. The early pilot had been answering the question '*can we trust XSEL, is it accurate?*'. Now there was a need to answer the question, '*how do we use XSEL?*'.

The two CAS managers were happy with this proposal. The Leeds CAS manager knew that his CTS was keen to use XSEL, whereas the Basingstoke

CTS was not. He believed that the inevitable teething problems were best handled by one person. There would also be organizational problems if twenty sales people were trying to use XSEL at the same time.

The proposed strategy meant that when the pilot restarted it would be testing different things in each office. Basingstoke would be testing the amount of a salesperson's time that XSEL saved—the sales force there would use XSEL for straightforward orders but consult the CTS when there were problems. Leeds would be testing the ability of their CTS, using XSEL, to reduce errors and increase the number of clean orders reaching Ayr.

During November and December the CTS in both sales offices were frustrated at not having access to XSEL, but there were compensations. Both were suffering from too much work. As well as receiving many requests for configuring advice from the sales force they were constantly talking to customers on the telephone. Technical queries were transferred to them if the customer's own salesperson was out of the office. It seemed likely that work overload would be a continuing problem with the CTS role whether or not the individual in it was using XSEL.

THE PILOT RESTARTS

The sales offices were reconnected to XSEL in January, 1986, and the pilot resumed. In February, the Basingstoke CTS left Digital and went to work for another company. A member of the CAS group who did not have a technical background now took responsibility for XSEL. She began to use it herself and agreed to organize the pilot and the sales staff who would be involved in this.

Because the Ayr VAX was not used solely for running XSEL she found that the response time was still slow. XSEL also needed Europeanizing—it did not always fit the European configurations. And Basingstoke needed to understand the nature of its costs and benefits more clearly. Both she, and the CAS manager, had a number of new questions about XSEL. How effective would it be as a training tool? Could new sales people learn to configure using XSEL? How could this be tested? They decided to find out how long it took a new person to learn to configure. This could then be compared with the time it took when XSEL was used as the teacher.

The value of XSEL as a configuration problem solver was another interesting issue. Could it give advice as well as check configurations? Basingstoke had not yet tried to use it in this way. They thought that XSEL would be particularly useful when new systems were being configured, and for add-ons—new hardware to add to an existing system. With these, either a record of the original configuration could be kept, or this could be ghosted when the add-on system was being worked out. There must be many spin-off benefits from XSEL which were not yet known to European users.

They also wanted to find out exactly how XSEL fitted into US sales offices. How was it used in the US? How much was it used? How accurate was it? And they wondered if Europe would follow the American pattern of salespersons working from home. At some time in the future this was a decision that the Basingstoke sales office would have to take. XSEL could greatly assist staff working from home, although a good electronic mail service and other electronic aids would also be necessary.

By the end of April five of the Basingstoke sales staff had become enthusiastic XSEL users and their progress was being carefully monitored. These five were located in three different sales groups and so a knowledge of XSEL was being communicated to fifteen sales staff. The salespeople liked XSEL although they wanted it to be anglicized and to communicate with them in simple English. They had learnt to use the system quickly and without difficulty. New sales people had found that XSEL helped them to learn configuring.

The procedure was for the salesperson to use XSEL to help him or her set out the customer's configuration and XSEL produced a print-out of this. The sales secretary then put the order through AQS—the automated quote system—and obtained a quote. XSEL was then used by the CAS administrator to check the configuration before the order was sent to Manufacturing. If there were problems FMIC was asked for advice. This way of using XSEL seemed to make sense. Had Basingstoke had a CTS at this time, he or she would only have been responsible for the final order check. This would have freed the CTS to provide configuring advice when the sales force required this.

All the salespeople using XSEL were very positive about it and believed that it was saving them a great deal of time. This amount of time varied between 10 and 60 per cent depending on three factors—the technical knowledge and experience of the salesperson; the complexity of the configuration; the newness of the system being configured. A relatively new salesperson with little technical knowledge, who was attempting to configure a complex system experienced a 60 per cent saving in the time required to configure the system manually. A technically knowledgeable salesperson configuring the same system achieved a 25 per cent saving. XSEL always saved time for the new salesperson with the amount depending on the complexity and novelty of the system being configured. The experienced, technically trained, salesperson only saved time using XSEL when the system was either very complex or very new, or both of these.

An additional benefit for new salespeople was XSEL's ability to act as an instructor on configuring. The sales people said that the standard system menus on XSEL were easier to follow than the information in the Digital price book, and the general rules of configuring could be effectively learnt from XSEL. New sales people said that they would use XSEL for all configurations. Experienced salespeople said they they would use XSEL only for new products and complex systems.

All five of the salespeople testing XSEL for the pilot saw its ability to increase their confidence as an important advantage. From their point of view 'getting the system right' was more important than saving time. If a system was 'right' Digital did not have to make financial allowances to customers to compensate for errors; quotes were always correct, and customer satisfaction was increased. An experienced salesperson described his experience using XSEL.

"XSEL is great. My technical background means that I can understand XSEL's logic. But I do have one or two criticisms. The first is that XSEL does not have an 'expert' mode, it is a Noddy guide which makes the user follow a particular logical route. It is difficult to take short cuts and it locks the user into things he is not interested in. The way the system is set up means that you can't jump back or jump around."

This criticism was not quite fair as XSEL could be used in both 'novice' and 'expert' mode. Also, its flexibility would increase as it was developed.

The salesperson added:

"XSEL is a great checking tool. It removes routine work, for example the routine of adding up voltages. But I don't think it enables me to configure more quickly because my experience means that I am very fast doing this manually. However it offers me security. It is a great 'insurance'. It also provides evidence if there are queries at a later date. If I am dealing with a standard system then I do this manually. If, however, the system is complex, with many items, then I XSEL it. XSEL will also save a salesperson's time in unexpected areas. For example, with deliveries. Once systems are delivered sales people can spend a great deal of time 'cable chasing', because certain cables have been omitted from the order. XSEL can ensure that this does not happen."

A new salesperson who did not have technical knowledge was equally enthusiastic saying that *"any tool that helps with options and prices is of value"*. He too had a few criticisms. He pointed out:

"XSEL does not always pick the best starting point. If you want a particular system with a certain tape drive, it starts asking questions about the tape drive. It also asks me technical questions when all I, and my customer, want is information about functions. Neither of us want technical detail. XSEL also asks me questions which I can't answer. I want XSEL to tell me, not question me."

But XSEL's advantages outweighed its disadvantages.

"It does save me time. It removes a lot of routine from my work. Manual configuring requires me to look several times into three or four books. XSEL also helps me to learn configuring. It speeds up the learning process. And I like XSEL's diagrams. I hope that eventually a graphics package will be added to XSEL. I can then draw a picture of equipment and XSEL will interpret this."

THE SITUATION AT LEEDS

Basingstoke's plan to let the sales force test out XSEL provided valuable information. In contrast, the Leeds CTS had been the sole user of XSEL and the Leeds sales people had continued to configure manually. Because many were new they found this difficult and frequently asked the CTS for help. He became so occupied with giving advice that he did not have the time to use XSEL regularly as the system was still slow. He believed that he now had enough knowledge to check most configurations without it, although he found it an excellent aid for large, complicated systems.

Interestingly, he had now decided that the CTS role should be kept separate from XSEL and the CTS should not be the only user of XSEL. Once XSEL's accuracy had been established for Europe it should be given to the sales secretaries for them to use with AQS—the automated quotes system. The Leeds approach of the salesperson doing the configuration and then passing it to the CTS for checking was causing the sales staff to spend too much time configuring. XSEL was a much more efficient configurer than the individual salesperson. The Leeds CTS hoped that he would soon have a line dedicated to XSEL which would be open all the time. He would then encourage the sales force to use this for their configurations. He saw his own role as technical consultant.

Experience with using XSEL had now caused both sales offices to believe that XSEL should be available to the sales force as well as the CTS. The CTS, because they were technical experts, did not think that they needed to use XSEL for checking configurations. They could tell if they were correct by looking at them. FMIC, which had to cope with the problems of incorrect orders arriving at the Ayr manufacturing plant, never agreed with this view. They claimed that the CTS overestimated their skill and this manual checking led to many wrong orders slipping through. XSEL was far more accurate.

In May the pilot was terminated. The accuracy of XSEL had been proved. The next step was for representatives from Geneva, Ayr and the CAS function to prepare a general implementation plan, work out the costs of implementation, and present these to senior management in Geneva. XSEL developments in the sales offices now died away as the Geneva Proposal Team prepared its strategy for making XSEL's case to the European Managing Director and the European Sales Manager. Basingstoke acquired a new CTS and the salespeople there had to stop using XSEL. FMIC was suffering from a shortage of machine capacity. It had to reduce the number of lines available to the sales office and the use of XSEL had to be restricted to the CTS.

1985/86 IN THE SALES OFFICES

This was a time for testing XSEL's accuracy and seeing how XSEL fitted into the work of European sales offices. Bruce argued that XSEL's accuracy had been fully tested in the United States but the Europeans wanted to secure their own evidence. They particularly wanted to check how XSEL handled the Digital products which were not identical in the two parts of the world.

Fitting XSEL easily into the work of the sales offices proved to be a more difficult problem than had been anticipated. Because Geneva had created the new CTS role while still being unaware of what XSEL had to offer, management there believed that they already had a good solution to the configuring problem. Could XSEL add anything to this? They did not want to reject XSEL and it seemed logical to give it to the CTS to test and eventually use as a production tool.

This caused problems. The CTS and XSEL did not always work harmoniously together because the CTS were technical experts already and did not want automated advice. Putting the two together made it difficult to assess what XSEL had to offer, and the restriction of XSEL's use to the CTS did not provide the sales force with any more selling time. They still had to configure manually before passing an order to the CTS for checking. XSEL could advise on configuring as well as check the accuracy of quotes and orders. It had been designed for sales people and the help it gave had proved to be of enormous value to them in the United States where the CTS role did not exist.

The XSEL pilot experience illustrates the difficulty of fitting new tools into an existing situation. Roles and relationships have to be carefully considered and organizational changes made. If possible, these changes have to be advantageous to the user environment as a whole, not merely to parts of it. The CTS role was an excellent idea. If anything it was too popular as the occupants soon became overloaded with work and had to place restrictions on what they would do. But it did not fit easily with XSEL. The CTS felt that they did not need the assistance of XSEL except for very difficult configuring problems. They tended to see it as a rival rather than a helpmate.

FMIC, the technical edit group at the Ayr manufacturing plant, had a strong interest in orders being checked with XSEL before they received them. Inaccurate errors caused them serious problems and they believed that XSEL was much better at identifying errors than the most expert CTS. It had the potential to provide an order accuracy of 95 per cent.

In both sales offices the sales force were keen to use XSEL. It was difficult for them to do so for two reasons. First, the organizational solution of giving XSEL to the CTS prevented its use by the salespeople. Second, for all salespeople in an office to use XSEL would have required many more lines and terminals than were available. Basingstoke did incorporate five salespeople into the pilot and they became enthusiastic users of XSEL. It became apparent that XSEL could be used in many different ways. The experienced salesperson wanted to use it in one way, the inexperienced new recruit in another.

The end of the pilot left Digital with a major implementation task—how to ensure the successful introduction of XSEL into all European sales offices. It also left the implementation team with an unresolved question. Given the Basingstoke experience, should XSEL's use be restricted to the CTS or should it be made available to the sales force?

There were also a number of broader questions about the impact of expert systems and automated tools generally. How would XSEL affect the configuring knowledge of the different groups in a sales office? Most sales people now knew how to configure, although some were more expert than others. What would happen if this knowledge died away as staff became dependent on XSEL? How would the organization of sales offices change as more of these automated tools arrived? These were very large, important questions which no one could yet answer.

The sales offices experience with XSEL demonstrates the difficulty of introducing technology into different environments. Digital did not always take account of this fact. First, the pilot was used only to test XSEL's accuracy, it could also have been used to try out different organizational arrangements and systematically evaluate these. This could have provided the 'best fit' between the needs of each sales office and the use of XSEL. The Basingstoke sales office did experiment with the salespeople as users but this strategy was not approved by Geneva management. They were convinced that the XSEL should be used primarily by the CTS.

Second, there was no evidence that making the CTS the principal or sole user of XSEL in all sales offices was an optimal strategy. The sales offices were organized in very different ways in each country and had different needs. A flexible strategy where each made its own decision on how to use XSEL might have produced better results. Geneva's argument for not encouraging this was that a uniform strategy for implementation would be easier to manage and control. Sales offices could later choose a different solution if they wished to do so. This argument had validity but it discouraged experimentation.

The message here is that technical innovation also requires organizational innovation if it is to be effective. Experiments need to be carried out to find the best technical/organizational combination for a particular situation. General solutions may not cater well for unusual needs. This was particularly true in the European sales offices. These operated in very different market environments and were organized in very different ways.

Part 4
LESSONS FROM THE JOURNEY

*Not that the heart can
be good without knowledge;
for without that the heart
is naught.*

John Bunyan

Chapter 13

DESIGNING AND MANAGING IN A TURBULENT ENVIRONMENT

The purpose of these final chapters is to identify and discuss what managers can learn from Digital's experience in designing and implementing XSEL.

A number of distinguished researchers have criticized studies of change for concentrating too much on the narrow range of activities that are associated directly with the change (Pettigrew, 1985). They have argued that this approach ignores the influence of history and environment and can make change appear to be a straightforward, sequential set of events. For example, the change process is often split into a number of steps to which terms such as 'diagnosis', 'design', 'implementation' are attached.

This can make change appear structured and simple because the unexpected obstacles and pushes that slow it down or accelerate it are omitted from the analysis. These are frequently due to factors occurring in the environment and can only be explained if this environment is understood. They may be due to company culture, to business policy, to new senior managers arriving and old ones quitting, or to the reactions of powerful groups who either want or do not want the proposed change. Major change cannot be fully understood unless these contextual factors are taken account of and this book has tried to do this.

The authors have described what happened as XSEL was built and they have noted the environmental issues that explain 'why' unexpected occurrences took place. They have also examined 'how' things happened—the processes that assisted the design of XSEL and enabled the project to reach a successful conclusion. These processes included philosophies, attitudes and relationships within and outside the activities of the design team and those responsible for XSEL's implementation. These processes were often assisted by structures—groups created to assist the fulfilment of the design task, and by methods—tools for identifying and solving different kinds of design problems.

This chapter will analyse the creation of XSEL from two broad perspectives. These are the factors in the design environment that influenced the route the change took and produced challenges and obstacles that had to be met and overcome, and the nature of the design task itself. These two streams of activities and attitudes will be called the 'task environment' and the 'core task'. They will be considered in terms of the processes that influenced them—what people did, said and thought; and in terms of the structures that existed, or were constructed, to facilitate these processes.

The core task—the building and implementation of XSEL—will be examined using four broad headings which describe the major activities that took place. These were 'designing', 'involving', 'managing', and 'implementing'. In the section on designing we shall again use the headings suggested in the first chapter—problem identification, decision to build, resource creation, experiment and learning. The design of XSEL was never a neatly bounded task in which these activities followed one after the other, but all were important and did take place. Design was always complex with some or all of the activities frequently having to be managed simultaneously. It was often iterative with the design task moving round in a circle as options were reviewed and altered and new, unexpected, opportunities appeared. The diagrams in Figure 13.1 set out the analytical framework for this chapter in a simple form.

Designing was the direct route to the core objective of a working system; involving was an important means for realizing this objective; managing was critical to the facilitation and control of the task. Managing was primarily concerned with motivating and influencing people. It was also concerned with handling the complexity of human, technical and organizational factors which were in a state of constant interaction and change. It required very special skills. Implementing proved to be the most difficult process. Users in both the United States and the rest of the world had to be convinced of the system's value before they would accept it.

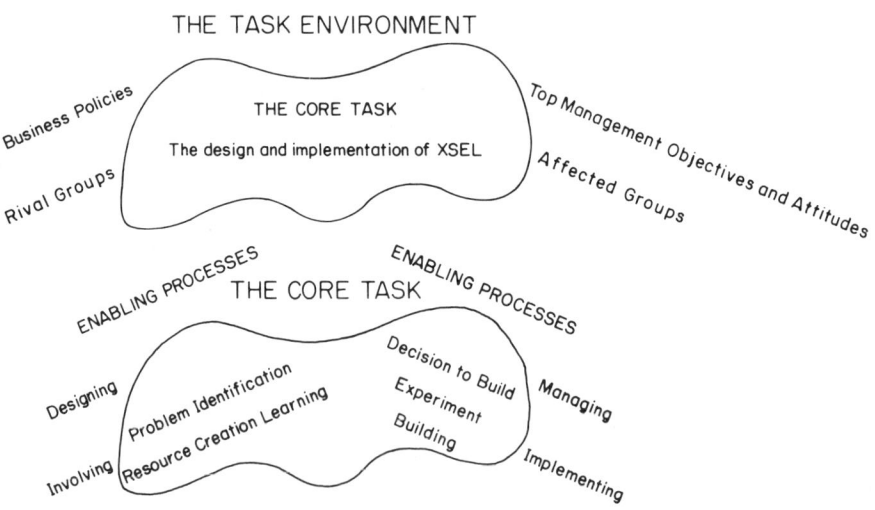

FIGURE 13.1

THE TASK ENVIRONMENT

The Contribution of Company Culture

The decision to build XSEL was taken once management recognized that Digital's first major expert system, XCON, was contributing to the solution of the configuring problem and saving the company a great deal of money. XSEL was a front end to XCON and directed at preventing configuring errors occurring in the sales offices when salespeople gave quotes to customers and prepared orders for transmission to the manufacturing plants.

Both XCON and XSEL were risky ventures in that Digital had no experience of building expert systems at the beginning of the 1980s. Few, if any, commercial companies had this knowledge at the time. Artificial intelligence was still in an embryonic state and largely located in university departments. But the configuring problem was sufficiently costly and difficult to warrant a venture into the unknown.

A first lesson that can be derived from the XSEL experience is the unsurprising one that difficult, innovative endeavours are more likely to be brought to a successful conclusion if the problem which they are addressing is seen as both critical and expensive. Small projects embarked on to gain experience in building expert systems may provide some technical knowledge and learning experience but they are unlikely to produce very useful results. Nor are they likely to generate much enthusiasm and interest.

Many companies would have balked at embarking on a high-risk project such as XSEL. The fact that Digital did not was due to its pioneering culture and to the need to be constantly ahead of the market in a highly competitive industry. Both of these factors meant that the company was very good at producing new technical developments and, perhaps even more significant, at introducing major change into its own organization. It knew how to handle change because change was an essential and continuing part of its successful commercial existence.

Digital's history, culture, knowledge and experience all contributed to the creation of XSEL and assisted its implementation, although implementation was to prove more difficult than design.

Changes in Business Strategy

The development of XSEL was never a smooth and easy path. The route to success was strewn with unexpected hazards and unanticipated events. A number of these arose from new business policies and options. In the early 1980s Digital rethought its business strategy and changed its structure. This caused a period of stress and trauma as departments and functions were altered and roles and responsibilities reformulated. The consequent upheaval pushed

XSEL into the background at a time when Bruce—the project manager, and the User Design Group were actively seeking top management support for the venture.

A potentially more threatening policy change was a move to increased product standardization which occurred in 1984. This could have made XSEL less necessary by simplifying the configuring process through reducing the number of models and options that were available to customers. An increase in standardization did take place but the extent of this was not sufficient to affect configuring in a major way. XSEL was still a required solution.

The impact of organizational change and new business strategy on XSEL had to be recognized and responded to by Bruce, his development team and the User Design Group. Effective reaction required good intelligence so that warnings of impending change were received at an early stage. It also required the ability to respond quickly and effectively to challenging events.

This provides another lesson in the management of change. A recognition that a change programme is never an isolated, protected island, able to exist without external disturbance. It is similar to an island on a lake in the middle of a large town, likely to be visited by people who want to live there, or take it over, or even get rid of it. If it is to continue to preserve itself and its own harmony it must be able to attract and accommodate those visitors who will support it and enable it to prosper. It must also be able to recognize and protect itself from visitors who are undesirable and threatening.

Project steering groups can be very helpful in providing intelligence and protection. Senior managers who are members can provide information on new company strategies, and on events that can significantly affect the project. They can also plead the project's cause with their top management colleagues. XSEL's progress was hindered by the lack of a steering group which included senior sales management and took a proprietary interest in its development.

Top Management Attitudes

Top management attitudes were an environmental factor of great importance to the progress and acceptance of XSEL throughout its design and implementation. Technical and AI management were always supportive and helped ensure that the resources for building XSEL were available. Sales management, seen by Bruce and his group as the eventual owners of XSEL, were ambivalent. Before accepting ownership they wanted definite proof of XSEL's effectiveness, accuracy and ability to save money.

Whereas Manufacturing management recognized that XSEL could help their interests by preventing configuring errors reaching the manufacturing plants, Sales management was less concerned with configuring and much more focused on selling. They wanted evidence that XSEL could help them do this. In the early days of XSEL's design it was not easy to provide this evidence. Bruce secured the cooperation and interest of the sales force by involving them in the design of XSEL. He did not have a comparable strategy that would identify sales management with XSEL.

This securing of support from senior sales management was one of the most difficult aspects of the project in both the United States and Europe. Once US Sales had become committed to XSEL and convinced of its value, Bruce had to start again and try to win the acceptance of a sceptical European sales management.

It is not easy to suggest how this problem could have been avoided. Senior sales management was probably wise to require proof of XSEL's effectiveness before accepting it wholeheartedly. They were going to have to pay for it and their staff would use it. But their coolness slowed down XSEL's implementation in both the US and Europe.

There is an important lesson that can be learnt from these cautious attitudes to XSEL. It is that designing an expert system is one thing, getting users and their managers to accept the system is another and may prove much more difficult. User involvement in design can assist acceptance but it will not be totally effective if important groups do not join in the participation processes. Acceptance will also be hindered if the problem which the expert system addresses is not regarded as highly significant by the user group.

Configuring was seen as a serious problem at the top of Digital where its financial implications were clearly recognized. It was seen as a serious problem by Manufacturing management whose staff lost time and money because of inaccurate orders sent to it through the order process. It was also seen as a personal problem by salespeople who received criticism from customers if systems were delivered with missing parts. But corporate sales management were not as close to the configuring problem and did not experience the same trauma because of it. They were more concerned with meeting sales targets.

These points highlight the difficulties that can be encountered when expert systems are designed by one group for another. Acceptance may be easier to achieve if a group of experts are designing a system for their own use—although experience suggests that this is not always the case.

Interested Groups

The work of a number of groups could be assisted or affected by XSEL and their interests had to be known and kept in mind throughout the design process. Sales were the critical group, but Manufacturing also had a considerable stake in XSEL as orders based on error-free configurations could make life easier for them. Orders would not have to be sent back to the sales offices for correction before they were put through XCON and a diagram of component relationships produced. Digital also had a committee examining the order administration process in sales offices and XSEL would be an important input to this. The field service groups in the sales offices would also be affected by XSEL. They had responsibility for hardware installation and were accustomed to prepare floor layouts for siting machines in customer's premises. XSEL's floor layout function could make some of their activities redundant.

Throughout the design process these different groups had to be recognized, consulted and their different interests taken account of as XSEL progressed. Ideally, they had to be supporters of XSEL, seeing it as helpful rather than threatening. This recognition that others besides the sales force had an interest in XSEL was important. The acceptance of innovation can be inhibited if powerful groups, although not the direct users of a system, see themselves as adversely affected by it.

Rival Systems

Another environmental factor that had an impact on the morale of the User Design Group was the occasional attempt by other groups, inside and outside Digital, to solve the configuring problem in different ways. Rival attempts were to be expected, of course, given the high visibility and cost of the configuring problem for Digital. These initiatives can be thought of as either attempts to solve the problem through simplification, or through different ways of dealing with the existing complexity. The latter covered both rival automation schemes as well as alternatives to automation.

In the simplification category, only one major effort appeared—the standard system approach. Eventually, some systems were indeed sold largely in standard configurations, although these were in the minority. Nevertheless, over a considerable period of time, internal uncertainty about how widespread this approach would become delayed implementation of XSEL. This, in turn, had a negative effect on the User Design Group and the technical team.

In the category of rival schemes which dealt with complexity, a number appeared over the years. These included two early attempts to demonstrate that the implementation of XCON could be done better in traditional technology than in AI. Neither of these were successful, but both caused some uncertainty while they were in progress. They also included at least two attempts to build non-automated check-list schemes that were intended to produce accurate configurations. In both cases these schemes were abandoned, one after XSEL became available in the area, and the other before it even started, as a result of the planners learning about XSEL.

Still another challenge was the CTS role in Europe. Here, a human expert was provided instead of an expert system. As has been described in the book, this rival method caused considerable problems for the acceptance of the automated system. On the positive side, the CTS role provided a context for experimentation.

Such rival schemes have the potential for demoralizing and distracting the design effort, and the manager is called upon both to assess their worth, and to protect his or her own endeavours from undue interference.

These rival efforts annoyed and worried the User Design Group who feared that their own efforts might be put in jeopardy. However, it can be argued that duplication of effort does have some advantages. A number of solutions are directed at a common problem and one may prove to be superior to the others. But competition can be demoralizing if it is threatening rather than cooperative. And effort can be wasteful if development takes place through an absence of knowledge that a good solution is being created elsewhere in the company.

The Impact of the Environment on the Change Process

The design of XSEL was not, therefore, a neat self-contained process. It was constantly influenced by events and attitudes in other parts of the company. These had to be recognized, responded to and managed. Unexpected challenges came because of changes in business policy, top management attitudes, the interests of groups XSEL could assist or affect and attempts to solve the configuring problem with alternative solutions. Designing XSEL required the creation and maintenance of a stable design environment in which thinking, discussing, building and testing could all take place. Bruce tried to provide this by monitoring and responding to events which could disturb or slow up the 'designing' process and lower the morale of the User Design Group and the development team.

Any group embarking on major change of this kind requires a good understanding of the organizational culture in which it is operating (Schein, 1969a). Schein tells us that we cannot understand organizational phenomena without considering culture both as a cause and as a way explaining such phenomena. Understanding also needs a good intelligence system to provide warning of significant events in the design environment. And it requires good management skills to assist a quick and effective response to these challenges. Pettigrew had suggested that successful change is the effective management of the interaction between what is being changed (the change content), how it is being changed (the change process), and what is happening in the change environment (the change context) (Pettigrew, 1985). The XSEL project provides support for this view.

THE CORE TASK AND ITS PROCESSES—DESIGNING

Designing was the core task associated with XSEL—involving and managing were facilitating processes to enable this task to be achieved. A number of general definitions of design were provided in Chapter 1 of this book. A more specific definition that fits well with the technical part of XSEL's design is 'the use of scientific principles, technical information and imagination in the definition of a structure, machine or system to perform pre-specified functions with the maximum efficiency and economy' (Jones, 1981). This was always the intention of XSEL's technical design, although the reality involved searching for relevant principles and information and, on occasion, coming across these through chance.

Intellectual Activities

Freeman differentiates the intellectual activities involved in designing from the managerial and building activities (Freeman, 1983). He calls the former 'construction activities' and the latter 'control activities'. Intellectual construction activities include creation and reflection. Control activities are vertification and validation. He sees creation as a complex process which includes breaking the initial problem down into manageable parts (decomposing); separating the essential from the inessential (abstracting); examining the essential in detail (elaboration); checking that ideas fit design objectives (evaluation); generating alternatives and making choices amongst these (decision taking).

Reflection is the process of looking backwards to ensure that the factors that are influencing the design process at each stage are clear and understood.

Controlling Design

Control is defined by Freeman as methods used to check that the system, as it is developing, will achieve the current goals. Beer makes an important contribution to our thinking on design by arguing that any viable system requires a stable situation if it is to operate successfully. He believes that the control of uncertainty requires the management of variety. Using Ashby's law of 'requisite variety' as his theoretical base, he argues that a system that contains a certain amount of variety, requires an equal amount of variety in the regulatory mechanisms that are used to control it (Ashby, 1956; Beer, 1974). In other words inputs must equal outputs.

This sounds difficult but Beer provides a simple example of a department store to explain what he means. If a department store does not contain enough staff and goods to meet the demands of its customers, they will stay away and the store will no longer be financially viable. It has become an unstable system. Similarly, if the number of staff and the variety of goods are greater than the customers require the store will again be financially non-viable and unstable. What is required is a match between what the store provides and what the customers want. In other words 'variety must equal variety'.

This notion can be applied to the design of XSEL. Designing was a very complex process involving intellectual, building and managing activities. If it was to take place in a stable, stress-free environment the management activities that regulated it had to contain a sufficient amount of variety to maintain the necessary stability. This required not only the coordination of the design effort but also a recognition that this was likely to be affected by events in its environment—the behaviour of other individuals and groups within Digital (Leech and Turner, 1985). The stability of the User Design Group required that it should either assimilate these inputs easily and without major disturbance or avoid them.

The creation of the User Design Group was another means for assisting stability, especially at the implementation stage of XSEL's history. Its existence introduced more variety into the designing activity but also acted as a mechanism for avoiding undesirable and excessive variety at the implementation stage when user resistance could put the successful operation of XSEL into jeopardy.

This leads to a useful cybernetic principle that is supported by the XSEL design experience. Because designing is complex it will not be successfully managed if it is seen as a simple building procedure that can be controlled using management science techniques alone. Its complexity and uncertainty is caused by the interaction of a large number of human, organizational and technical factors. The nature of this variety must be recognized and management techniques and processes used which contain an equivalent amount of variety. Multidisciplinary problems will require multidisciplinary resources and regulators to cope with them. The design of XSEL demonstrated how this could be achieved.

Design Activities

We have described the activities associated with the core task of creating XSEL as problem identification, the decision to build XSEL, resource creation, experiment, and learning and building. Let us briefly consider each of these. The development of XSEL was stimulated by the existence of a major business problem—configuring. The fact that a solution to this problem was desperately needed was a major factor in the success of the project. The expert system had a clear and significant objective. The decision to build XSEL came from the AI group and was supported by top management. The success of XCON meant that this was not a difficult decision to take once the Carnegie–Mellon prototype had demonstrated that the system could be built.

Resource Creation

Obtaining the necessary skill resources to commence the design task was not easy as industry had little experience of building expert systems at the beginning of the 1980s. This absence of expertise enabled Digital to create its own skills and it took the innovative approach of recruiting a new group of staff to develop and build XSEL. These people, including Bruce, were given the necessary training and experience. This approach enabled the company to develop an effective multidisciplinary and participative philosophy for the building of expert systems which it has continued to apply.

Other required resources were money, time, knowledge, interest and commitment, tools and techniques and hardware. The initial funding for XSEL was provided by ISTG and Sales, although once the system was implemented Sales had to bear the full cost. Time was only occasionally a serious problem although the size of XSEL meant it took a number of years to build. Nor was the need to elicit expert knowledge a serious problem. In contrast to XCON, the XSEL effort did not require the direct involvement of human engineering experts. These experts were already providing the input to the XCON process, upon which XSEL was built. So, while XSEL did ultimately require knowledge elicitation, it was acquired indirectly.

XSEL's rules are largely 'abstractions' of the more 'concrete' XCON rules. Therefore hardware engineers did not have to be directly a part of the User Design effort. Also, many of the AI technical group had acquired sufficient knowledge to be regarded as experts on configuration. Therefore, if needed, technical information was readily available to the User Design Group.

Interest and commitment in the project were stimulated and maintained through the User Design Group and the members of this found Enid's ETHICS methodology a useful tool for helping them to analyse their business needs and problems. Perhaps surprisingly in a manufacturer of computers, hardware was not always easily available and XSEL's testing and implementation were often slowed up because of a shortage of VAX machines.

Effective management and facilitation proved as important a resource as any. Social and management skills were required to manage the group processes involved in designing and implementing XSEL. These were vital to the project's successful completion. They were an aspect of the project's complexity that could easily have been neglected.

Experiment and Learning

Experiment proved to be a crucial part of the building of XSEL and was directly associated with learning. Bateson has defined learning as requiring stimulus, response and reinforcement (Bateson, 1980). The iterative design approach of discuss, build, test, evaluate, provided this. Knowledge was acquired in a step-by-step evolutionary manner as new routes and techniques were identified, tried out and used or abandoned, and as XSEL grew in size and sophistication.

Knowledge had to be continually passed from the technical and development teams to the User Design Group and from the User Design Group back to them. High quality decision making depended upon the success of this communication process. Bruce had an important role in ensuring that knowledge was distributed, evaluated, coordinated and effectively used. He required a good personal intelligence system so that he could find out about events in Digital that could affect the progress of XSEL. The User Design Group became increasingly knowledgeable about the mission and work of the sales offices and about how to build and evaluate an expert system. This knowledge was of continuing benefit and enhanced the group's ability to contribute to the company's business objectives once XSEL was operational.

Designing XSEL required original thinking and a great deal of hard work. And it required marketing skill—the ability to make its potential known to other groups.

INVOLVING

A feature of the XSEL project, and a major contributor to its success in the United States, was the involvement of the future user group—the sales force— in the design of the expert system. This involvement required the creation of a new structure that would enable collective discussion and debate to take place. It also required a 'facilitator', someone who would help the user group to examine their needs and problems systematically and take reasoned decisions. The User Design Group became the vehicle for discussion and decision taking while Bruce took on the role of facilitator.

The User Design Group was a mix of salespeople and members of the AI development team who had responsibility for physically building XSEL. Individual experts in the technical aspects of the configuring problem were less important than would be the case with other expert systems, because members of the AI development team became configuration experts in their own right.

Bruce believed strongly that a participative approach would assist XSEL's acceptance by creating a system that really did meet the needs of the sales force. Enid, who had helped other groups to design systems participatively, believed that this approach enabled users to influence the design of the system; assisted learning and the exchange of information; created a strong user identification with the system and a sense of ownership, and ensured that an effective, acceptable system was the eventual outcome. Most groups have difficulty in achieving these things without assistance and the role of the facilitator is to provide this. He or she must help the group learn how to work together, acquire knowledge, solve problems, agree solutions and take decisions.

Early Uncertainties

All new user design groups experience uncertainty at the start of a project. Participants arrive at the first meeting with no clear idea of their roles or of the task ahead, and with little confidence in their ability to complete this task. The facilitator too will have feelings of doubt and confusion and Bruce was no exception. He was new to Digital, to expert systems and to the role of XSEL project manager. He had no experience of participative design or of acting as facilitator to a user design group.

He knew that he had to help the group master the four essential tasks ahead—acquiring knowledge to build the system, building the system and handling the problems associated with this, managing its own group relationships and persuading external groups to support the project. He was unsure how best to do any of these things.

ETHICS enabled him to solve the problem of the first three meetings by providing a structure for collecting information (Mumford, 1986). The User Design Group members were asked to think about their work missions—what they were trying to achieve in their jobs. They were also asked to consider the extent to which the successful management of the configuring task contributed to this mission. They were then requested to describe the problems which hindered efficient configuring and caused them frustration and a reduction in job satisfaction.

Carnegie–Mellon University was building a prototype of XSEL for Digital. Soon after the first User Design Group meeting the members were given access to this in their sales offices. They were asked to try it out and send their comments to ISTG via a comments facility in the system.

Uncertainty was therefore reduced and knowledge building started in two important areas—an intellectual consideration of the salesperson's mission and role and the importance and nature of the configuring task in these; and a practical test of XSEL in its embryonic state. This iterative mix of thinking and practice was to continue throughout the design and building of the system. It proved very successful—the User Design Group saw themselves as both visionaries and entrepreneurs.

Once the prototype was seen to work, responsibility for building XSEL as an operational system was transferred to Digital. The ISTG group did the actual building of the system, responding all the time to the guidance of the User Design Group. The members specified what was required and tried out each version of XSEL as it was developed.

Bruce found that one of the most difficult aspects of using a participative approach was helping the User Design Group to be clear about its role. Prior to XSEL the sales force members had rejected software which they did not find useful. Now they were required to improve it and Bruce had to keep reminding them that they were in a development role. This needed creative thought, good judgement and the careful weighing of alternatives.

Once the User Design Group meetings were established Bruce found that the interest of the sales force in XSEL increased and more people wished to attend. This meant that the meetings became larger and more difficult to manage.

There was also the problem of communicating what was taking place to members of the sales force who were unable to be present. This was solved through the electronic mail system. At the end of each meeting options that had been discussed were relayed to non-attending members of the sales force and their views sought. Account was taken of these when the final decision on how to proceed with a particular aspect of systems design was taken.

Acceptance Problems

But there was a problem. Neither senior sales management nor the regional managers of the sales offices had played any role in the participative processes. Nor did they know much about XSEL and what it had to offer. The task of the User Design Group now had to move beyond systems development to communication and persuasion. These, and implementation, proved to be more difficult tasks than design.

In 1984 XSEL began moving slowly into some of the US sales offices but the task of the User Design Group was by no means over. As the number of users increased so more ideas for improvement flowed in via the system's comments facility. All of these had to be evaluated and suggestions for changes made to the technical team. A further complication was that as XSEL continued to grow in size and to become more versatile, plans had to be made to link it to other automated systems which were being introduced into the sales offices. Systems integration had to replace systems introduction.

Why Did User Involvement Work so Well?

To answer this question we need to consider both company effectiveness and individual needs. The cybernetic theories of Stafford Beer can throw some light on the factors that assist an organization to flourish. He has developed a five tier hierarchic model which he calls 'the viable system' (Beer, 1981). This model is shown in Figure 13.2.

A User Design Group is also a viable system. It requires a system 5 strategic control function to ensure that it is setting the right objectives for its activities and formulating the best policies. It needs to ensure that these are in line with company objectives and policies. It also requires a system 4 intelligence gathering function which enables it to collect relevant information. This information will include task-related inputs such as available methods and options, and also political news about external reaction to the design and building of the system. At the system 3 level it requires an optimizing and monitoring activity to ensure that plans are successfully carried out. At the system 2 level there must be a means for keeping the design process on course by identifying potential problems and avoiding or solving these. Level 1 has the essential task of designing, building and implementing the system.

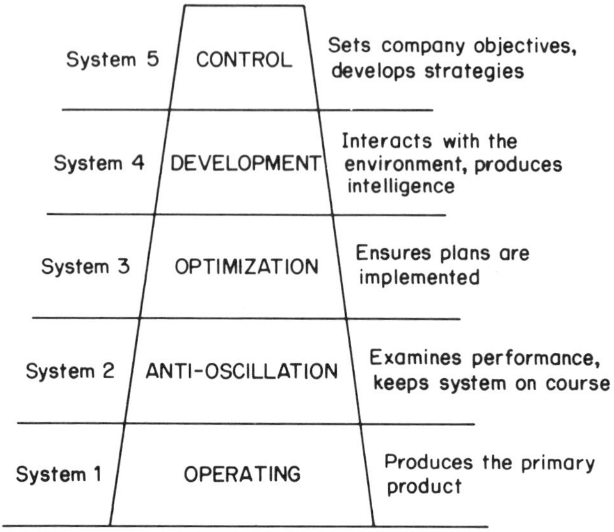

System 5	CONTROL	Sets company objectives, develops strategies
System 4	DEVELOPMENT	Interacts with the environment, produces intelligence
System 3	OPTIMIZATION	Ensures plans are implemented
System 2	ANTI-OSCILLATION	Examines performance, keeps system on course
System 1	OPERATING	Produces the primary product

FIGURE 13.2

Each of these five system levels need to communicate with the others and the activities at all levels must be coordinated. This requires people to work closely together. It can be argued that if one group builds an expert system and another group implements and uses it then the feedback loops between the different levels of the viable system will not work smoothly. There are likely to be both coordination and communication problems.

One way of getting the design task's viable system to work effectively is through bringing the different interests together in a single group. Burnand argues that agreement and shared objectives are assisted by:

> 'finding out other people's views and expectations and conforming or compromising with them, cooperating and coordinating one's activities with others, supporting others views, and by bringing deviants into line with others by discussion and persuasion.' (Burnand, 1982)

He also makes the point that sensitivity to problems arises from an awareness and understanding of other people's difficulties.

The involvement of both technical staff and future users in the design of XSEL made the development of a smoothly functioning viable system more possible. The strong feedback loops between intelligence gathering, design and the testing of XSEL by sales staff reinforced the viability of the system.

From the company's perspective, participation assisted communication and the passing of information from technologists to users and vice versa. It brought groups with different interests together in a situation where they could talk to each other and this greatly helped the solving of problems in a new development activity. It highlighted and reinforced areas where there was identity of interest between technologists and users and enabled conflicts of interest to be brought out into the open and rationally discussed. It also assisted group learning and an understanding of the feelings, interests, needs, anxieties and hopes of the technologists and the sales staff.

Although the dual role of project manager and facilitator was not an easy one to handle, Bruce was able to combine the control functions of a project manager with the teaching and motivating attributes of a facilitator. He had to become a leader. Burnand has defined leadership as having a central, linking role; helping develop and maintain group activity; helping a group to deal with its problems so that it continues and grows in stability, power, rewards for members, unity and performance (Burnand, 1982).

The alternatives to this participative approach might have been either a 'let's guess' or a 'let's try it and see what happens' strategy. The first occurs when a group of technical designers build a system believing that they know what the future users want and that there is no need to involve or consult them. The second is when the technologists, without much prior consultation, produce a prototype of the final system for the users to play with. The first approach can lead to expensive disaster. The second to the acceptance of a system that works adequately but does not really meet complex needs because these have not been identified and carefully thought through.

Participation produced some clear advantages from a company point of view, but it also provided benefits to the individual members of the User Design Group. Two benefits were that participation in group decision taking brought with it feelings of personal freedom and control. Bion, a pioneer in group processes, has described how groups can be helped to move from a state of uncertainty to one of maturity in which they are able to analyse situations, reach agreement and take decisions. The mature group can work on a problem by seeking relevant data, building on experience, developing and applying principles and generating support for their solution. This process gives the group a sense of progress and success. The mature group is also able to handle stress successfully (Bion, 1961).

From the individual User Design Group member's point of view being in control meant that he or she could exert influence. Psychologists tell us that this reduces stress. If we are in control of the roller coaster then we do not want to get off (Miller, 1980). Psychologists also argue that the pleasure of being in control does not come from the knowledge that allows us to hold that position, but from the excitement that comes from making things happen (Chanowitz and Langer, 1960). There is a feedback loop between these two activities—the process of acquiring new knowledge makes it more possible to make things happen. Also, the more we have opportunities for working as a member of a group, the more our involvement with the group activity deepens.

Participation in group activity enabled the User Design Group to have more control over events and a better knowledge of the environment to be controlled. As the group got close to its desired objective of an operational XSEL, enthusiasm, motivation and excitement increased. Individual members felt both competent and confident—they had succeeded in making things happen. There was a great sense of achievement. The opposite to feelings of control is feelings of helplessness. The individual sees himself or herself as a passive victim. Unable to influence events which are going to have a dramatic impact on work and life.

The experience of designing XSEL suggests that participation pays off. A participative approach means that the finished product is likely to be a well designed system that achieves user objectives. The emotional response to the finished product is also likely to be very positive. In both instances the result may be better from the Company perspective than would otherwise have been achieved.

MANAGING

Schein has defined leadership, or what he calls 'managership' as a highly variable kind of behaviour which depends upon the person, his or her subordinates, the nature of the job requirements and the kind of problem solving to be dealt with (Schein, 1969b). The 'managing' task for XSEL, and how it was interpreted by Bruce, was certainly influenced by all these things.

Bruce arrived in Digital understanding the company values of entrepreneurship and open management and supporting these, but not directly influenced by the Digital culture which he had not yet experienced. His early behaviour in the company was greatly affected by his own philosophy and values. These led him to decide at the start of the XSEL project that a participative approach and user involvement in design was the route to take. He was aware that this strategy would fit with the Digital philosophy and he had a pragmatic belief that he could not succeed without it. Unless the sales force were participants in the design of XSEL, they would not accept and use the expert system.

His experience as a school administrator had led him to recognize that management was more than the use of a set of techniques. It required human qualities such as personal sensitivity, human warmth and the ability to understand the interests and attitudes of other individuals and groups. He had already decided to define his project management task as both managing and facilitating. In addition to controlling a project he also had to help a newly created group of people to tackle and succeed with a difficult task.

At the start of the project he was probably not aware that managing XSEL would require him to assume the various roles of evangelist, explorer, motivator, mediator, protector, planner, and problem solver. His responsibility and task was to be the management of a complex organizational sub-culture. He was to become what Schein has called a 'culture manager' (Schein, 1985).

Managing as 'Evangelizing' and 'Exploring'

Bruce was not required to be an evangelist for XSEL in the sense that he had to persuade the AI group that it was a worthwhile project. This case had already been made and accepted. But he did have to convince top sales management that XSEL was worthy of support, and his search for a sponsor was a continuing source of anxiety and effort. To succeed he required emotional strength, the ability to marshal evidence and to argue cogently, and the skill to convince a cautious top management group of the soundness of the XSEL project.

He also had to be an evengelist as new members joined the User Design Group. He had to articulate and explain the group's participative philosophy and ensure that they accepted this. Many of the User Design Group meetings began with Bruce making a statement of mission and values. This helped to clarify a number of issues. It demonstrated that the project manager was not deviating from a participative strategy; it reinforced the group's belief in this approach and it ensured that new members were aware of, and accepted, the group's cooperative method of working.

Bruce's 'explorer' role was even more demanding than his role as 'evangelist'. In the course of creating XSEL he and his group had to cope with a great deal of uncertainty and stress. There was no expert to guide them and no set of well-tried techniques to assist them in their task. Managing in this unclear environment was very much an art. It required what Schon has described as 'reflection-in-action'. The ability to use intuitive judgement, to criticize one's own actions, to change direction, to restructure an activity (Schon, 1983).

Confidence was needed to do this. Also relevant organizational experience which could provide some guidelines. At the start of the XSEL project Bruce had to rely on his previous life and work history to provide this. But the project provided its own learning environment. He not only had to internalize the lessons himself, he had to help his group learn as well. Schon suggests that one of a manager's most important functions is the education of his or her subordinates. Helping others to learn the required interpersonal skills of self-awareness, communication, tolerance for ambiguity and the ability to manage conflict.

XSEL's journey, from start to finish, involved discovery and learning. New knowledge was acquired and new problems were successfully tackled. Bruce had to encourage the User Design Group to participate in difficult collective tasks where success was uncertain. Like other explorers they came to accept unexpected events as normal (Znaniecki, 1940). This not only helped Bruce and his group to learn new things, it brought new knowledge into Digital that would spin-off on many other projects.

Managing as 'Motivating', 'Mediating' and 'Protecting'

Bruce had three motivational tasks throughout the project. He had to motivate himself and ensure that his energy, drive and enjoyment of the task did not flag; he had to motivate the User Design Group and maintain their interest and enthusiasm, and he had to motivate the development team who were building XSEL according to the directions of the User Design Group. Motivating oneself is not easy, motivating others is even more difficult although a great deal of advice is now available on how to do this. Once again interpersonal skills, rather than formal techniques, are the critical factors.

Carl Rogers, one of the pioneers of psychotherapy, has provided three principles for influencing other people. He calls the first of these 'congruence'. Congruence is the ability to have honest, open relations with others without interposing a 'front' or façade that conceals true feelings. The second is that of showing 'unconditional positive regard' to others—showing that one likes and values them. The third is what he calls 'empathic' understanding—relations characterized by genuineness and by a warm acceptance of the other person as a unique individual (Rogers, 1957, 1961). These ideas have influenced a great deal of thinking on the successful management of change and undoubtedly influence the Digital open management philosophy.

Despite the length and complexity of the XSEL project, motivation was never a difficult problem. Bruce tried to manage in a style similar to the Rogers' principles, and the excitement of the design task kept the User Design Group interested until XSEL was built. The continuing large attendance at User Design Group meetings in 1987 shows that motivation is still high even though discussion now focuses on how XSEL can be developed in the future.

One of Bruce's managerial roles that assisted group motivation was that of mediator. All major change involves the collaboration of a number of different groups, and XSEL was no exception. Inevitably, these groups will have different objectives and perhaps some conflicting objectives. These can sour relationships and prevent active cooperation. It is important to recognize that this conflict exists and to have mechanisms for bringing it out into the open so that it can be discussed and worked through.

The User Design Group was an important vehicle for doing this. It helped overcome difficulties that sometimes arose between the sales force representatives and the members of the development team. These could be discussed in a positive and friendly atmosphere.

Bruce also had to try and mediate between the interests of the US group and those of groups in other countries. In Europe there were two groups with an interest in XSEL within the sales offices—the salespeople and the Customer Administration Services Group. In addition, the manufacturing plants had a keen interest in how the sales offices used XSEL, as did senior sales management in Geneva. This was a much more difficult situation for Bruce to handle as it was largely outside his control. He organized meetings at which issues would be aired and problems discussed but generally Europe went its own way.

Another challenge for Bruce was to keep the morale of the User Design Group and the development team high by protecting them from outside threat and interference. In effect, he was trying to reduce stress and keep their anxiety level low. He had to create a fast response system to handle unexpected, threatening events—which could cause the project to halt, slow down, or change course. Quinn has described this as protecting against invaders, generating support and getting and giving information (Quinn, 1980a). In this important role the manager is acting like a defence force—the soldier ant protecting the queen bee, the secret service around the President.

Bruce had a number of potentially threatening situations to handle. These included the request by the Vice-President Sales for XSEL to be ready by Christmas, 1982; the rise of various rival programmes and methods; Digital's move to product standardization, and the difficulty of securing European acceptance of XSEL.

Managing as 'Planning' and 'Problem Solving'

Planning and problem solving are two of the tasks of managers which are most discussed in the textbooks. This may be because they are viewed as rational activities which require logical thinking and action. The other aspects of managing which have been discussed in this chapter are often perceived as ambiguous and unclear—relying on intuition and interpersonal skills as much as on rational thought. Nevertheless the XSEL experience shows that these process-related skills are equally, if not more, important in determining the outcome of a project than those that are seen as more amenable to 'scientific' thinking.

XSEL required a great deal of planning although not all of the plans which Bruce made were used. He constructed careful plans for the business of the User Design Group meetings, for the building of XSEL and for XSEL's implementation. This was a valuable activity. Beckhard and Harris have described plans as the 'roadmaps for the change efforts' (Beckhard and Harris, 1977). They can provide a timetable of events, a list of activities that need to take place and a strategy for communication. Plans should be 'purposeful', with activities closely linked to change goals. They must be 'task-specific', with activities clearly identified. They must also be 'integrated'—so that discrete activities are linked together. And they must be adaptable, agreed by top management and cost-effective in time and people.

Beer stresses the importance of adaptability, arguing that if a plan conceived at time A is implemented at time B, then there is a strong likelihood that it will be the wrong plan. The situation will have changed in the intervening period (Beer, 1969). Beckhard and Harris also argue for a commitment plan. A clear identification of who in the organization must be committed to the change if it is to be successfully implemented. They recognize that this is a political activity but regard it as one that requires systematic analysis (Beckhard and Harris, 1977).

Planning and plans are, of course, two very different products. Planning is a process which requires problem solving, the generation of resources and support, and strategies for implementation. Plans are usually documents which are the outcome of planning. They may bear little relation to what happens in the real situation, but they can act as very useful communication aids, setting out clearly what is intended and how it is to be achieved. They can also be useful as historical documents—showing ideas and intentions which were strong enough to be formalized but never happened because they were overtaken by real world events.

Planning and problem solving are two activities which are usually highly visible and therefore subject to evaluation. Schon suggests that they affect a manager's credibility like stock in a stock market. His or her credibility goes up or down with the external world's perception of success or failure. He claims that 'there is a corporate market for credibility. Each person strives to maintain this at all costs' (Schon, 1983).

Bruce found that planning and the production of plans helped him to think clearly about needs and outcomes. They helped ensure that the User Design Group meetings covered all important issues and enabled him to identify necessary strategies and resources for XSEL's implementation. Plans also acted as excellent communicators of the User Design Group's intentions and ideas to top management. Few of his plans were implemented precisely as he intended. Planning was often followed by a need for rapid rethinking as unanticipated events changed the situation.

We have categorized the principal 'managing' activities into a set of processes called 'evangelizing', 'exploring', 'motivating', 'mediating', 'protecting', 'planning' and 'problem solving'. They could have been categorized in many different ways. These particular 'action' verbs were chosen as the emphasis in this book has been on the processes associated with the development and implementation of XSEL.

The management task appeared very similar to what Schon has described as management artistry. It involved dealing with unique and changing situations; designing and executing on-the-spot experiments, and constantly examining the meaning of old and new situations. It required what he calls a 'reflective' manager to create XSEL. It also required an 'influential' manager. One who could generate support and stimulate others to work productively and enthusiastically. This required considerable political knowledge and skill. And it required a 'confident' manager. Schon suggests that credibility, commitment, confidence and competence are all interdependent (Schon, 1983). The XSEL experience suggests he is correct.

This book will make a traveller of thee, if by its counsel thou wilt ruled be.

John Bunyan

Chapter 14

IMPLEMENTING XSEL IN EUROPE

INTRODUCING INNOVATION

The introduction of major change is never easy. It involves the guidance of complex systems in difficult environments (Gross, 1967). Implementation is often its most difficult aspect. The fact that a new system exists, meets a need and works well is no guarantee that it will be accepted and used. Those responsible—the change agents—have to understand clearly what they are trying to achieve. They have to have organizational strategies and skills in order to shift the change area from an old to a new state. New technology and work practice will have to be integrated with existing norms and culture, and the change situation restored to a state of organizational equilibrium so that the system performs more effectively than before. All this requires considerable social skill—the ability to generate interest, manage conflict, assist learning and remove anxiety.

If coercion is not an option, and this undesirable approach will only work if there is some punishment for non-compliance, careful thought must be given to those factors in the situation that will assist the change and the obstacles that will prevent or slow it down. Most social situations are only partially controllable and unforeseen reactions and complications are always likely to affect results (Gross, 1967).

Implementation requires changing attitudes, behaviour and structures in a volatile environment. Ashby's Law applies here (Ashby, 1956). Implementation strategies, if they are to succeed, must contain an amount of variety equivalent to the variety in the change situation. They must be directed at changing the social situation as well as the technical.

Although the American implementation of XSEL had been achieved without too much difficulty, there had been problems in acquiring the hardware necessary to run XSEL in the sales offices. Also, in 1988 when this book was completed, despite all the US sales offices having access to XSEL and a potential user group of 4000 salespeople, many did not use it. Those that did used it in a more restricted way than had been intended by its designers. Few configured systems with it. Most used it to check configurations that they had done manually. ISTG believed that the reasons for this restricted use were insufficient training, and continuing uncertainty over whether salespeople directly, or sales support people were responsible for clean configurations.

This limited acceptance of innovation can be viewed as resistance to change and therefore undesirable. This may be true but there can be positive effects. First, the user is accommodating the new system to his or her needs and achieving a good 'fit' between the two. Second, in its early days the over-enthusiastic use of a new system may disturb other activities and impair the overall efficiency of the work situation. It is often wise to phase innovation in gradually. There is also a danger that developers are over-committed to their particular solution and have too high expectations of what can be achieved. The recipients of change may well be the best judges of what is possible and desirable. They should, however, ensure that the reason their systems are partly used is not inadequate training. Learning to use XSEL required several training sessions. The first to familiarize new users with what XSEL had to offer. Later ones to teach them how to use XSEL effectively.

Serious resistance to change usually occurs because of conflicts of interest. The future users see the new system as threatening their jobs or skills, or wasting their time, or increasing their vulnerability to criticism. One of the advantages of a participative design approach is that these reactions can be identified at an early stage in the project. The system can then either be rethought or abandoned. The participation of users in planning for implementation also helps avoid the splitting of planners and users into two camps, with each misunderstanding the views and needs of the other.

Implementation, like design, is helped through the mobilization of supporters. These can take three forms: key activators who play a major role in getting the change introduced, active allies who give positive support and passive collaborators who go along with the change but play little part in facilitating it (Gross, 1967). In the United States, as implementation approached, Bruce spent a great deal of his time finding sales offices with managers who fitted the first two categories.

One way of generating support for innovation is through good communication. Here again user participation in implementation strategy formulation can pay dividends by providing a forum for the discussion of major issues. But participation will not be enough. There will be a need for continual, ongoing information, explanation and demonstration of the new system. There must also be opportunities for questions and feedback from those who will use or be affected by it.

Lastly, it is critically important that first attempts at implementation are reasonably successful. Nothing attracts rumour, the most powerful communicator, more than stories of mishaps, disappointed expectations and failure.

IMPLEMENTING XSEL IN EUROPE

When XSEL was implemented in Europe the sales offices were extremely busy and experiencing a great deal of innovation and change. There was frequent restructuring of functions and activities as Digital's markets expanded. At the same time other automated tools were being introduced to assist the selling and order administration processes. The reception of each innovation was affected by attitudes to those which had preceded it. Earlier technology that had worked well produced positive attitudes, poor systems created negative attitudes. Further pressures arose because, while accommodating and responding to multiple change, the sales offices were having to carry out their normal activities. This combination of factors had the potential to cause stress and anxiety and lead to resistance to further change.

In the United States there were positive factors in the sales offices that assisted the implementation of XSEL. Change is most likely to be acceptable and effective in those groups which are successful in their tasks but experiencing tension, difficulty or failure in some part of their work (Vickers, 1981). This was exactly the situation in the US sales offices where the salespeople were solely responsible for configuring and sometimes found it a difficult and onerous task. Their membership of the User Design Group meant that they understood XSEL and had confidence in its ability to provide accurate configuring assistance.

The European situation was very different. The European sales offices knew little about XSEL and had not been involved in its development. Also, the Configuring Technical Specialist (CTS) role that had been introduced by Geneva prior to XSEL's arrival in Europe, meant that a partial solution to the configuring problem had already been found. Because of these factors implementation in Europe was more difficult than in the United States. Care had to be taken to ensure that XSEL was not seen as an unhelpful disturbance by sales offices grappling with increased business and new automated tools.

Implementation in Europe, particularly the UK—Digital's largest European sales area—required very careful handling. Sales offices needed help in understanding XSEL and what it could offer; they had to have confidence in its accuracy and, most important, they had to decide how best to use it. Despite the Geneva decision that XSEL should initially be used only by the CTS, the response of many CTSs was that XSEL was of limited value to them. They were already expert configurers. They would value XSEL's help with old systems and with very complex systems but had the knowledge to configure other systems without automated assistance. Many saw XSEL as a rival rather than as a helpmate.

These attitudes made XSEL's acceptance more problematic in Europe. The US wanted XSEL to be introduced into Digital sales offices world-wide and had evidence that very considerable financial benefits would result from its use.

Geneva, after carefully examining the evidence and much discussion, had accepted this. But would the European sales offices be able to implement XSEL successfully given their heavy work-loads, the amount of innovation they were experiencing and the apparent absence of a serious configuring problem? Very carefully thoughtout implementation strategies were required to ensure that XSEL was accepted and used effectively. There was a danger that the sales offices would give XSEL a token acceptance and then hardly use it.

IMPLEMENTATION STRATEGIES

Given the existing situation, what form did change strategies for the European sales offices need to take? Systems theory suggests that, first, the sales offices must be structured in a way that enabled them to accommodate a great deal of internal change without excessive stress. This required them to be flexible, which they already were. It would help if the impact of change was distributed around the sales office, rather than directed at a single area or function. This would make it organizationally easier to accept.

Second, following Ashby's law of 'requisite variety', the amount of change coming into the sales offices should not be more than they were able to assimilate comfortably at any one time (Ashby, 1956). If it was more, then, if possible, it should be phased in over a period of time. This required the effective management of the organizational boundary between a sales office and the external world.

Third, success in creating this environment for change required information, communication, planning, participation and a mixture of institutional, technical, administrative and social resources. Institutional resources were change agents, training programmes and support groups. Technical resources were the physical requirements of the new system—networks, hardware and software. Administrative resources were new work procedures and controls. Social resources were positive attitudes—the interest and enthusiasm of staff in the sales offices; knowledge—the willingness to lean and apply a new technique and the skill and motivation to use this effectively; supportive management, and the reinforcement provided by the successful introduction of previous systems.

IMPLEMENTATION STRUCTURES AND DECISIONS

The case for XSEL's implementation in Europe was made by a Geneva Headquarters Proposal Team chaired by a senior European sales executive. This group contained representatives from Management Science in Geneva, from FMIC in Ayr and from Customer Administration Services (CAS), the function in which XSEL was to be located. But an important group was missing—the sales force. Yet it could be argued that even if the sales force were not going to use XSEL, and their views on this matter were never sought, their input was essential. The CAS function existed solely to service the sales force and enable them to sell more effectively. The participative philosophy was not as strong in European Headquarters as it had been in the United States.

Once senior European management had agreed to XSEL's introduction detailed plans for implementation had to be made. In 1986 an XSEL implementation manager, based in Valbonne—Digital's European Research Centre, was appointed to oversee the systems introduction into Europe. In addition, planning teams were created for each of the larger countries and the FMIC group in Ayr were given responsibility for all XSEL training. The new European implementation manager believed that he had four immediate and critical tasks. These were (1) The communication to all sales offices that XSEL existed, was to be introduced, and could help them in a number of ways. (2) The restarting in Europe of the participative design approach that had been an integral part of XSEL's US development. Like Bruce he believed that participation would assist XSEL's acceptance. (3) The creation of a first appreciation and training programme to demonstrate what XSEL could do and how it could be used. (4) The selection of one or more sales offices in each country to act as pilot sites for XSEL's general introduction. These offices must provide a situation where XSEL could be implemented easily and successfully. This meant that they must have the hardware necessary to run XSEL available.

In February, 1987, the implementation manager organized a meeting in Utrecht to explain and demonstrate XSEL to the CTS in the European sales offices. CTSs from sixteen countries attended—those from the larger countries representing a number of sales offices, while many of the smaller countries had only a single office. At the end of the meeting the CTSs were asked to return to their offices, spread the word about XSEL and develop a plan for its introduction into their country. In September the first XSEL training sessions for CTS were held in Valbonne. The intention was to hold the first formal meeting of a European User Design Group in December, although this was seen as consisting solely of CTS initially. This had to be cancelled as Digital had an economy drive at that time, part of which was a reduction in staff travelling costs.

The UK had the largest number of sales offices in Europe and was likely to be the slowest in adopting XSEL. There were resource problems. First, there was a machine problem. No UK sales office yet had the spare computer capacity necessary to run XSEL. Second, there was a personnel problem. The staff in the UK sales offices were very overworked. They had to be convinced that the additional effort of introducing XSEL was worth while. Ideally, for XSEL to be accepted by staff in a sales office a comprehensive communication programme was required. XSEL needed to be explained and demonstrated to all staff in each sales office.

It was particularly crucial that the district sales managers understood what XSEL had to offer as they were accountable for the performance of the sales offices. The enthusiastic acceptance of XSEL required that the District Sales Manager and the CAS group were positively interested in acquiring it. They must be the 'product champions' (McLeish, 1969).

It was also important that the salespeople and their secretaries know what XSEL could do, even though they were not involved in its initial use.

In the UK the offices which had tested XSEL out in the first pilot— Basingstoke and Leeds—were, with Warrington, chosen to be the implementation pioneers. Their experience and response would greatly influence the attitudes of the other sales offices. In these pilot offices the CAS manager and the CTSs had to be 'credible activists'—individuals able to generate enthusiasm in other staff and competent to introduce XSEL quickly and flexibly (Quinn,' 1980b). Although the UK sales force had had no say in the decision to use XSEL, the UK sales manager had become aware of XSEL's existence and was favourably disposed to its implementation. He believed that sales were increasing so rapidly that if it was not used he would have to double the number of CTSs in the sales offices.

Warrington received XSEL in February, 1988, and was the first to use it operationally. The CTS there found it useful for checking configurations for large and difficult systems. But he did not use it for anything else. He was a technical expert and could configure and check most configurations faster manually than with XSEL. He believed that it would be more useful when linked to the Automated Quotes System (AQS). This would take place at the end of 1988 and would enable a single input of data specifying the components for a new system to be checked by XSEL and given a price by AQS. While XSEL was being tested the sales people continued to configure manually and pass their configurations to the CTS for checking.

An important early decision that had to be taken was the nature of the hardware to support XSEL. This choice would determine who could use the system. If each sales office ran XSEL on a microVAX-II, a small machine, only two people could use it simultaneously. Its use would then be restricted to the CTS and an assistant. If, however, a number of large machines were networked together to support all the sales offices, there need be no restriction on the number of users. The sales force could then have the operation to use XSEL for configuring.

The UK now had its own implementation manager. His role was to help the sales offices assimilate and use XSEL in a way that increased overall effectiveness. He recognized that this required an 'integrated' solution—a strategy that was broad enough to ensure that all interested groups in a sales office felt they had gained from the arrival of XSEL (Follett, 1941). This strategy had to be clearly formulated and flexible enough to contribute to the different needs and problems of these groups. Each group has to be assisted to acquire confidence in XSEL (Sayles and Chandler, 1971).

To assist XSEL's successful introduction the UK implementation manager had to have a really good understanding of the organizational issues and pressures that were present in each sales office situation. The change process had to move forward in a planned and systematic manner. There had to be good two-way communication lines to Geneva, Valbonne and Ayr so that general problems could be discussed and new knowledge and learning passed on to help others.

The participation of the sales office staff in local planning and implementation also had to be facilitated. XSEL was unfamiliar, not clearly understood and could have considerable organizational consequences. Formal presentations and demonstrations would show what XSEL had to offer but these methods had to be accompanied by informal discussion so that short- and long-term questions could be raised and answered.

Ideally, XSEL's introduction needed to be managed in a way that can be described as both 'top down' and 'bottom up'. Organizational issues and problems must be identified and tackled at all levels in the sales offices and each needed to develop its own organizational strategy. The following questions needed to be asked and answered. How could XSEL be fitted into existing sales office structures most effectively? To what extent was change required? Would XSEL and the other automated systems alter job content? Would the introduction of new tasks disrupt established ways of working? Would they disturb existing group relationships? The answers to many of these questions were likely to be 'yes'.

The first meeting of the European User Design Group was held in May, 1988. The aim of the meeting was to produce a charter statement describing the Group's mission and role and to decide what issues concerning XSEL needed to be discussed. The European implementation manager organized the meeting and the participants were the European CTSs. There were no representatives from the sales force. At the meeting each CTS described how he was using XSEL. Most used it to check configurations but not to configure, and they did not use it a great deal. Each was seeking to identify its most effective use for his sales office, and all were agreed that it should not yet be made available to the European sales staff. The CTS view was that it was too slow and too difficult for salespeople to use. It needed further development to make it right for Europe.

But the CTSs did recognize that in the future more people would want to use XSEL, and to use it in different ways. They were uncertain how to fit it into the organization of the sales offices and it was agreed that a number of the salespeople should be invited to the next meeting, to help address this problem. XSEL was already being used in different ways around the world. In Canada, for example, each salesperson had a terminal on his or her desk and could access XSEL through this.

The User Design Group discussed the technical and organizational support that such a large system needed. Running XSEL required comprehensive technical services to ensure that the system worked efficiently and did not break down. Hardware had to be acquired and networks maintained. Introductory and advanced training courses had to be provided for all CTS so that they could use XSEL effectively and teach other XSEL users. European product naming and pricing conventions had to be standardized so that XSEL could handle the information. All of this required excellent planning which, while providing general guidance, could also accommodate the preferences of the individual sales offices. Control was required but also flexibility. Integration had to be accompanied by differentiation.

The User Design Group recognized that this was a complex and difficult task. A bureaucratic 'it shall be done this way' approach would be unacceptable to the sales offices and they would not want to change existing efficient ways of working simply to accommodate a new technique. Also, once XSEL was operational each sales office would want to use it in the way that best fitted its particular selling situation. There was a great deal of work to be done.

The implementation of XSEL in Europe was still underway when this book was written, and moving through the three stages of dependence, interdependence and independence. Initially, the sales offices were dependent on the implementation team for guidance on how to use XSEL and for training. In the second stage XSEL was introduced into all the sales offices with the CTS seen as the principal user and given responsibility for its management. The European User Design Group provided a means for assessing this strategy and deciding the route for further development. Once XSEL was fully operational and resourced, the sales offices would be encouraged to develop their own independent solutions on how best to use it. This is now happening.

CONCLUSION

XSEL's journey demonstrates that the route to successful change in a new area of innovation is not an easy one. It requires knowledge, skill, endurance and motivation. There must be a good understanding of the difficulty of the task that is being undertaken and an excellent knowledge of the environment where the innovation will be located. Clear human and organizational objectives are required from the start of the design process together with effective plans to ensure these objectives are achieved. Plans will need to be constantly reviewed and revised as circumstances alter and unexpected problems affect the development route.

Managing this kind of complexity requires political and social skills of the highest order and a recognition that social processes are crucial to success. Groups with very different interests and objectives must be involved, motivated and held together in a common task.

XSEL's successful introduction into the US sales offices was greatly helped by the strategy of participative design that involved the future sales office users from the start of the development process. This legitimized XSEL in their eyes, persuaded them to accept ownership and gave them a vested interest in its successful introduction. The sharing of knowledge that was an important part of participation assisted the management of a complex and uncertain task by bringing developers and users together as joint problem solvers. Participation occurred late in Europe and was concerned with implementation not design. In its initial stage User Design Group membership was restricted to the CTS and did not represent all the interested parties in the sales offices. Despite these problems it got off to a good start, recognized its deficiencies and took steps to correct them.

XSEL's journey has included both the Slough of Despond and the Delectable Mountains with their vision of achievement. It has not been easy and much can be learnt from it. Change is never a simple, straightforward road. Like Pilgrim's Progress it involves unexpected obstacles and disasters and new visions and opportunities. Plans and techniques are helpful but they cannot solve all problems. The real challenge is the successful management of the social processes that are an integral part of innovation and progress. XSEL demonstrated that the involvement of people in the design and implementation of innovation that will affect them is an excellent strategy for success. It is hoped this book will provide some guidelines for others who tread the same route to successful innovation.

References

Ashby, W. Ross (1956) *An Introduction to Cybernetics*. Chapman & Hall.

Bateson, G. (1980) *Mind and Nature*. Fontana.

Beckhard, R. (1969) *Organization Development: Strategies and Models*. Addison-Wesley.

Beckhard, R., and Harris, R.T. (1977) *Organizational Transactions: Managing Complex Change*. Addison-Wesley.

Beer, S. (1969) The aborting corporate plan. In E. Jantsch (ed.), *Perspectives of Planning*. OECD.

Beer, S. (1974) *Designing Freedom*. Wiley.

Beer, S. (1981) *The Brain of the Firm*. Wiley.

Bion, W.R. (1961) *Experiences in Groups*. Tavistock.

Booker, P.J. (1964) *Proceedings of the Conference on the Teaching of Engineering Design*. Institution of Engineering Designers, London.

Burnand, G. (1982) *Via Focal Problems*. Leadership Ltd.

Carroll, J. (1974) *Breakout from the Crystal Palace*. Routledge & Kegan Paul.

Chanowitz, B., and Langer, E. (1960) Knowing more (or less) than you can show. In J. Garber and E. Seligman (eds), *Human Helplessness*. Academic Press.

Checkland, P. (1981) *Systems Thinking, Systems Practice*. Wiley.

Dewey, J., and Bentley, A.F. (1949) *Knowing and the Known*. Beacon Press.

Emery, F.E., and Trist, E.L. (1960) Socio-technical Systems. In C.W. Churchman and M Verhulst (eds), *Management Science Models and Techniques*, Vol 2. Pergamon.

Follett, M.P. (1941) Business as an integrative unity. In H.C. Metcalf and L. Urwick (eds), *Dynamic Administration*. Management Publications Trust.

Freeman, P.J. (1983) Fundamentals of design. In P. Freeman and A.I. Wasserman (eds), *Software Design Techniques*. IEEE Computer Society Press.

French, J., Israel, J., and Aas, D. (1960) An experiment in participation in a Norwegian factory. *Human Relations*, **13**, 3–19.

Gross, B.M. (1967) Activating national plans. In B.M. Gross (ed.), *Action Under Planning*. McGraw-Hill.

Jones, J.C. (1981) *Design Methods: Seeds of Human Futures*. Wiley.

Lammers, C.J. (1967) Power and participation in decision making in formal organizations. *American Journal of Sociology*, **73**, 201–216.

Leech, D.J., and Turner, B.T. (1985) *Engineering Design for Profit*. Ellis Horwood.

Likert, R. (1961) New Patterns of Management, McGraw-Hill.

Mayo, E. (1949) *The Social Problems of an Industrial Civilization*. Routledge & Kegan Paul.

McDermott, J. (1982) XSEL a computer salesperson's assistant. In J.E. Hayes, D. Michie and Y-H. Pao (eds), *Machine Intelligence*. Wiley.

McDermott. J. (1984) Building expert systems. In W. Reitman (ed.), *Artificial Intelligence Applications for Business*. Ablex.

McGregor, D. (1960) *The Human Side of Enterprise*. McGraw-Hill.

McLeish, J. (1969) *The Theory of Social Change*. Routledge & Kegan Paul.

Miller, S. (1980) Why having control reduces stress. In J. Garber and E. Seligman (eds), *Human Helplessness*. Academic Press.

Mumford, E. (1983) *Designing Human Systems*. Manchester Business School.

Mumford, E., Bancroft, N., and Sontag, B. (1983) Participative design. successes and problems. *Systems, Objectives Solutions*, **3**, 133–142.

Mumford, E. (1986) *Using Computers for Business Success: The ETHICS Method*. Manchester Business School.

Nelson, W.N. (1980) *On Justifying Democracy*. Routledge & Kegan Paul.

O'Connor, D. (1984) Using expert systems to manage change and complexity in manufacturing. In W. Reitman (ed.), *Artificial Intelligence Applications for Business*. Ablex.

Olsen, K. (1986) Digital Equipment Corporation: the first twenty-five years. Address to a 1982 Massachusetts Meeting of the Newcomen Society in North America.

Pateman, C. (1970) *Participation and Democratic Theory*. Cambridge University Press.

Peters, T.J., and Waterman, R.H. (1982) *In Search of Excellence*. Harper & Row.

Petre, P. (1986) America's most successful entrepreneur *Fortune*. October 27th.

Pettigrew, A. (1985) *The Awakening Giant*. Blackwell.

Polit, S. (1985) R1 and beyond: AI technology transfer at DEC. *AI Magazine*, Winter edition.

Poole, M. (1982) Theories of industrial democracy. *The Sociological Review*, **30**, 182–207.

Quinn, J.B. (1980a) *Strategies for Change: Logical Incrementalism*. Irwin.

Quinn, J.B. (1980b) Managing strategic change. *Sloan Management Review*, **21**, 3–20.

Rifkin, G. (1986) A whole new DEC. *Computerworld*, **20**, 38A.

Rogers, C. (1957) The necessary and sufficient conditions of therapeutic personality change. *Journal of Consulting Psychology*, **21**, 95–103.

Rogers, C. (1961) *On Becoming a Person*. Houghton Mifflin.

Sawtell, R. (1968) *Sharing Our Industrial Future*. The Industrial Society, London.

Sayles, L.R., and Chandler, M.K. (1971) *Managing Large Systems*. Harper & Row.

Schein, E.H. (1985) *Organizational Culture and Leadership*. Jossey-Bass.

Schein, E.H. (1969a) *Organizational Psychology*. Prentice-Hall.

Schein, E.H. (1969b) *Process Consultation: its Role in Organizational Development*. Addison-Wesley.

Schon, D.A. (1983) *The Reflective Practitioner*. Temple-Smith.

Schumacher, E.F. (1974) *Small is Beautiful*. Abacus.

Sell, P. (1985) *Expert Systems: a Practical Introduction*. Macmillan.

Selznick, P. (1948) Foundations of the theory of organizations. *American Sociological Review*, **13**, 24–35.

Simon, H. (1981) *The Science of the Artificial*. MIT Press.

Sommerhoff, G. (1969) The abstract characteristics of living systems. In F. Emery (ed.), *System Thinking*. Penguin.

Trist, E. (1981) *The Evolution of Socio-technical Systems*. The Ontario Ministry of Labor.

Vickers, G. (1981) The poverty of problem solving. *Journal of Applied Systems Analysis*, **8**, 15–21.

Wasserman, A.I., Freeman, P., and Porcella, M. (1983) Characteristics of software development methodologies. In T.W. Olle, H.G. Sol, and C.J. Tully (eds), *Information Systems Design Methodologies: a Feature Analysis*. North-Holland.

Waterman, D.A. (1985) *A Guide to Expert Systems*. Addison-Wesley.

Ways, M. (1967) The road to 1977. *Fortune*, January.

Znaniecki, F. (1940) *The Social Role of the Man of Knowledge*. Columbia Press.

Index